'Compassionately but without se... lands victimised in the recent past by militarism at its wor... and now assaulted by consumerism at its most ... also pr... ...any entertaining v... ...TAE LUIMNI route, ... ERICK CITY ...ded ...NTY LIBRA... kind peop... ...ons of ...

'Antonia Bolin... ...e-Kent's new ... is a gripping travelogue which is at o... e both intimate and worldly-wise. Honest in her bravery (and brave in her honesty), she recounts a thrilling journey...'   Charlie Carroll, author of *No Fixed Abode*

'An epic book about an epic trail. Bolingbroke-Kent captures the sights, sounds and colour of the legendary Ho Chi Minh Trail in all its surviving glory.'
                          Kit Gillet, freelance journalist and videographer

'Ants has pulled off not only a demanding and original adventure but a great read too. *A Short Ride in the Jungle* informs and entertains in just the right measures...'
                          Lois Pryce, motorcycle adventurer and author

'A beautifully written tale teeming with descriptive gems and wickedly funny anecdotes, all delivered in an earthy, self-effacing style that has the words spilling off the page... A traveller's delight and classic-to-be!'
                          Jason Lewis, author and the first person to
                          circumnavigate the world by human power alone

A SHORT RIDE IN THE JUNGLE

THE HO CHI MINH TRAIL BY MOTORCYCLE

ANTONIA BOLINGBROKE-KENT

summersdale

A SHORT RIDE IN THE JUNGLE

Copyright © Antonia Bolingbroke-Kent, 2014

Maps by Bee Hayes

All rights reserved.

Antonia Bolingbroke-Kent has asserted her right to be identified as the author of this work in accordance with sections 77 and 78 of the Copyright, Designs and Patents Act 1988.

Summersdale Publishers Ltd
46 West Street
Chichester
West Sussex
PO19 1RP
UK

www.summersdale.com

Printed and bound by CPI Group (UK) Ltd, Croydon, CR0 4YY

ISBN: 978-1-84953-543-4

Substantial discounts on bulk quantities of Summersdale books are available to corporations, professional associations and other organisations. For details contact Nicky Douglas by telephone: +44 (0) 1243 756902, fax: +44 (0) 1243 786300 or email: nicky@summersdale.com.

'Yet we were wrong, terribly wrong.
We owe it to future generations to explain why.'

Robert S. McNamara, US Secretary of Defence 1961–1968

AUTHOR'S NOTE

In western cultures the Truong Son Mountains are known as the Annamites, but throughout this book I refer to them by their Vietnamese name, the Truong Son, meaning 'Long Mountain'. The Vietnamese called the Ho Chi Minh Trail the Truong Son Strategic Supply Route, hence to refer to them as Truong Son is more apt in this context.

In 1975 the southern city of Saigon was renamed Ho Chi Minh City by the North Vietnamese victors. Today, in spite of this change, the city is still largely known as Saigon, except by some northerners, and for official purposes. I refer to it by its pre-1975 name, Saigon.

Although the war that took place in Southeast Asia in the sixties and seventies is generally called the Vietnam War, the broad term that refers to the war in Vietnam, Laos and Cambodia is the Second Indochina War. This book is a journey through these three countries, hence I refer to the conflict as the Second Indochina War, as opposed to the Vietnam War. Often I just call it 'the War'.

American intelligence and Vietnamese military cartographers used a different numbering system for the Trail on maps of the time. For example, the main north–south road through Laos was called 911 by the US and 128 by the North Vietnamese. Since I have been working from old North Vietnamese maps, I use their numbering system, as opposed to the US one.

There is some disagreement as to whether the Honda Cub is a motorcycle or a moped. It has an automatic clutch and is rather smaller than your average motorcycle, but on the other hand has three gears, no running board and bigger wheels than most mopeds. Most Cub fans will insist their steed is a motorcycle and within this book I refer to it variously as a motorcycle, moped, bike, Cub and C90.

THE (MOSTLY) MIGHTY PINK PANTHER

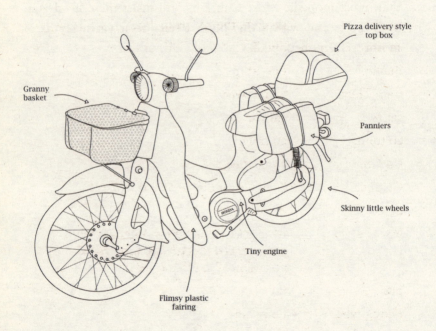

Pizza delivery style
top box

Granny
basket

Panniers

Skinny little wheels

Tiny engine

Flimsy plastic
fairing

BRIEF PRONUNCIATION GUIDE

ăn chay	an chai, the 'ay' as in 'bye'
ao dai	ow die
Bualapha	Boolafar
Cẩm Thủy	Cum Twee
cắt tóc'	cat toc
co tuong	co tung
Cu Chi	Koo Chee
Cuong	Kung, as in the 'u' sound in 'cook'
đi đi	dee dee
Mu Gia	Moo Zaa (In northern Vietnam 'gi' is pronounced 'z'. A Saigonese would pronounce it as 'Moo Jeeya')
pho	fur
Phong Nha	Fong Nar
Tân Kỳ	Tan Kee
Truong Son	Trung Son, the 'son' as in 'con'
Vo Nguyen Giap	Vo Nwin Zaap
xin chào	sin chow
xin lỗi	sin loy

CONTENTS

CHAPTER 1

THE WORLD'S DEADLIEST ROAD

It was early March and a thick grey pall hung over Hanoi. Standing on the first floor balcony of my hotel in the capital's Old Quarter, I hunched my shoulders against the chill morning air. Still on British time, I took a beer from the minibar, lit a cigarette and leant over the concrete balustrade. Below, a buzzing, beeping river of mopeds and taxis flowed down narrow Nguyen Van To Street. Women squatted on the pavement hacking the heads off fish, their hands glistening with silver scales. Others sawed at slabs of raw meat, trickles of crimson blood running into the gutter. On the balcony opposite, two yellow songbirds chirruped in an ornate wooden cage. And in every direction stained buildings leant on each other like a crowd of drunkards, clothed in an unkempt mass of tangled wires, crooked balconies, grimy air conditioning units and half-open shutters. The drab, colourless order of London couldn't have felt further away.

Excitement and anxiety about what lay ahead had kept sleep at bay for the entirety of the flight from England. Now in Hanoi, I was eager to get on with the task at hand. Sleep could wait. In a couple of days' time I would be loading my panniers and setting off down the Ho Chi Minh Trail. For the next seven weeks it would just be me and my two-wheeled partner, a twenty-five-year-old Honda C90. No back up, no mechanics - just the hum of my tiny 90-cc engine.

Impatient to meet my bike, I dialled Digby's number.

'Ants-oi!' said Digby as he answered, suffixing my name with a Vietnamese colloquialism. 'Welcome to Hanoi. Are you ready to meet your wheels?'

'Absolutely, I can't wait. How is she?'

'She's very pretty actually – shockingly pink. The boys have done a great job. I'll pick you up in half an hour and you can come and meet her yourself.'

It had all started almost exactly a year previously. I was supposed to be going to Siberia. Flights had been reserved, drivers booked, permits applied for. But a week before I was due to fly, Fate stuck her oar in. Turning around with a guilty smile on his face, my boss said to me, 'How do you feel about a little trip to Vietnam and Laos instead?'

'Err, great,' I replied hesitantly.

'Wonderful, we'll book you a flight for the end of the week.'

As a freelance television producer I was used to being thrown into things at the last minute, dropping everything to fly to Alaska, Argentina or Aberdeen with barely a moment to pack my toothbrush. It was exciting, unpredictable and at times infuriating. This time though, I could never have foreseen how this abrupt change of plan would affect the next few years of my life.

A month earlier I'd accepted a job producing the popular BBC television series *World's Most Dangerous Roads*. Since then I'd been having crackly Skype conversations with fixers in Magadan and watching grainy films of hollow-cheeked prisoners digging Siberia's 'Road of Bones' out of the ice. But unexpected changes in the filming schedule meant I needed to get on a plane to Hanoi and recce the Ho Chi Minh Trail instead. Someone else would go to Russia in my place. It was January, half of Britain was snivelling with flu and in Siberia temperatures were plummeting towards minus fifty. I'd be less likely to get frostbite in Southeast Asia, or be forced to eat reindeer's testicles; neither of which was on my bucket list. A trip to the tropics sounded like an extremely good idea.

I'd heard of the Ho Chi Minh Trail and knew it was something to do with the Vietnam War, but beyond that I was ignorant. With only four days until my flight I had to find a local fixer, wade through a pile of research, get a Vietnamese visa (I'd have to get my Lao one in Hanoi), pack my bags and go.

My boyfriend Marley was less than delighted about my latest task.

'So, let me get this straight, you're going to be spending a week riding a motorbike through the jungle with your thighs wrapped around another man? I'm not the jealous type, but…'

'Well, it *is* my job,' I replied weakly before heading East.

The 'other man' was our programme consultant Digby, the Australian head honcho of a Hanoi-based motorbike tour company, Explore Indochina. Digby was obsessed with both bikes and the Ho Chi Minh Trail, and had been riding all over Vietnam and Laos for the best part of two decades. I'd been told about him by a television acquaintance of mine who had described him as 'aloof... but one of the few people alive today who really knows about the remaining whereabouts of the Trail.' Thirty-eight years on from the war in Southeast Asia only a handful of devotees knew the routes of this once gargantuan transport network. Digby was one of them.

Since we were making a primetime BBC series with two well-known presenters, every inch of the route had to be scrutinised in advance. The BBC had to know it was dangerous enough to make good television, but not so dangerous that we'd kill off the talent. The presenters' agent needed reassurance that the amenities along the route provided a whiff of the luxury her charges were accustomed to.

As Digby was a biker we opted to do the recce on a single Kawasaki 250-cc dirt bike with me riding pillion. I'd never ridden off-road, and now wasn't the time to start.

'I've never ridden the Trail two-up,' Digby had admitted on the phone the day before I left. 'I'm not even sure it's possible. But we'll give it a go. Just be prepared to get a very sore backside.'

The next thing I knew I was pouring myself into the tiny space between Digby and our bundle of luggage, barely room for a Higgs boson between us. For six exhilarating, bottom-numbing days we rode through south-eastern Laos, mapping a route for the programme. Charismatic, mercurial and possessing eagle-like acuity, Digby's knowledge of the Trail was impressive. After almost two decades of studying it, it seemed there was nothing he didn't know.

A week later I flew home to deliver my findings. The BBC was satisfied that we'd ticked all the boxes. The danger element was provided by the remote terrain, the unexploded bombs that littered the jungle, and some hefty rivers to negotiate. Unsurprisingly the presenter's agent was jittery about the luxury quotient – Egyptian cotton, fluffy white towels and daily massages were not going to be in abundance. She wasn't sure how the celebs would cope.

The following month the television circus returned to film the two celebrities bumping down a one-thousand-mile section of the Trail. This time we had four jeeps, two medics, four drivers, two Laotian government officials, a translator, the two presenters and the camera crew – sixteen in total. It was a bumpy ride in more ways than one.

In my two encounters with the Ho Chi Minh Trail, I'd been astounded by how fast such an important piece of history was being swallowed by development. Even in the six weeks between the recce and the filming, new roads had been started and new patches of jungle stripped of their valuable wood. Like a poor man who had just found the key to the treasure chest he was sitting on, Laos was damming its rivers, selling its precious forests and handing out mining licences like raffle tickets. Gold, copper, zinc, bauxite, coal, gypsum, tin, hydropower, teak, yellow balau, keruing, rosewood – the mountains of Laos hid an inestimable wealth. People with first-hand knowledge of the Trail were getting old and dying, and the new generation were more interested in western fashion and smartphones. In a decade all traces of the original Trail could be gone, buried under tarmac and dug up by mining companies.

I wanted to return to the Trail, to explore some of the remaining sections of what was once the world's deadliest road; to know more about the lands it cut through, the people who built it, walked it, bombed it and died on it, before it was lost forever.

This time I wanted to do it without medics, translators, jeeps and drivers. This time I wanted to do it alone.

The Truong Son Strategic Supply Route, better known by its American moniker, the Ho Chi Minh Trail, was one of the greatest feats of military engineering in history. A paragon of ingenuity and bloody determination, at its peak this twelve-thousand-mile transport network spread like a spider's web through Vietnam, Laos and Cambodia; an ever-mutating labyrinth of roads, tracks, communication lines, fuel pipelines, command centres, supply bases and waterways. Constructed in the face of an unprecedented onslaught of modern warfare, forged through inhospitable mountainous terrain, and subjected to the biggest bombing campaign in history, the Trail was the fulcrum of the Second Indochina War.

The Trail was the bastard child of the 1954 Geneva Accords, an international agreement which divided Vietnam into two separate states: the North to Ho Chi Minh's Communist Party, the South to the US backed president, Ngo Dinh Diem. The aim was to turn the South into a model capitalist, non-colonial Southeast Asian country – a buffer against the disturbing swell of Asian communism. Unification elections were set to occur in 1956, but when they never happened Ho resolved to 'liberate' the South and unify the country under a single communist flag. In May 1959 secret instructions were given to Colonel Vo Bam of North Vietnam's Ministry of Defence to organise 'a special military communication line to send supplies to the revolution in the South.' Three weeks later he and 308 *boi dois*, North Vietnamese soldiers, set off from a village just north of the seventeenth parallel, the dividing line between North and South Vietnam. Carrying bundles of rifles and ammunition and dressed in simple pyjamas and palm leaf hats, they spent more than two months walking south, living by the motto: 'To walk without footprints, to cook without smoke, to speak without sound.' Tracks were crossed using plastic sheets and leaves placed over any incriminating footprints. On 20 August the men and goods arrived at the A Shau valley in South Vietnam. Little did these pioneers know that their two-month mission was the seed of the legendary Ho Chi Minh Trail.

From the beginning life on the Trail was harsh. The *boi dois* lived on a meagre diet of rice, salt and wild roots. Foot soldiers carried up to their own weight in supplies – military equipment, medicine, a rifle, ammunition, rice, salt and sugar. Sunburnt peasants pushed bicycles loaded with 300 kg of supplies, and horses and elephants lumbered south with rice, big guns and boxes of ammunition.

In 1961 an agreement was made with the Laotian communists to extend the Trail over the Truong Son Mountains into Laos. These high peaks and virgin forests – the natural barrier between Vietnam and Laos – would provide perfect cover for Trail activity. But this wild landscape, as well as being an ally, was also a formidable adversary and the *boi dois* had to claw and grope their way through the jungle. Later on, once the War was underway, one North Vietnamese soldier counted twenty-four ways in which you could die on the Trail – bombs could vaporise you, tigers and bears attack you, mud, rivers and landslides wash you away, and malaria and dysentery suck the very life from your veins. Hunger, thirst, fear and loneliness were omnipresent.

US intervention in 1965 called for an escalation of the war effort. The following year motorised transport joined the march southwards. Driving at night with little or no lights, bombed relentlessly, hunted by AC-130 Spectre gunships and deprived of food and sleep, life for truck drivers, the 'pilots of the ground,' wasn't that much easier.

The Trail embodied Vietnam's struggle for a unified, independent nation. Without it, there could have been no war against the South, a fact America knew only too well. For eight years they subjected the Trail to a scale of warfare that still seems inconceivable. Vast swathes of Indochina were reduced to a burning, blistered mass of bomb craters, charred corpses, rubble and blackened tree stumps. Steeped in Cold War neuroses, desperate to stop Hanoi feeding the communist insurgency in the South, the US dropped more bombs on neutral Laos than were dropped by *all* parties in the *whole* of World War Two. They seeded rain to produce landslides, stripped the jungles with toxic chemicals and wired the forests with electronic listening devices.

But even the might of the most powerful nation on earth could not cut the Trail or weaken Hanoi's resolve. With limitless guile and resilience, the communists fought back. The Vietnamese had been one of the few races to defeat the marauding Mongols on the battlefield. They had broken the French; they weren't going to be beaten by America and the South.

Despite its significance, few westerners have taken a serious interest in the Ho Chi Minh Trail since the war ended, or made more than cursory efforts to explore what is left of this

THE WORLD'S DEADLIEST ROAD

once mighty web. Scores of backpackers ride a tourist-friendly version of the Trail in Vietnam, replete with guides and a T-shirt, but only a smattering of devotees have followed the guts of the Trail into Laos and Cambodia.

Digby started his explorations in 2003, first crossing the border into Laos in late 2004. Riding a Minsk, he was only able to get as far as Sepon, slowly pushing farther south each year. Since then he has returned to the Laotian side of the Trail sixteen times, finding, among other things, a US spy camera, a pilot's radio rescue beacon, the dashboard from a Chinese tank and two AK47s. The only other person to have travelled the Trail as extensively is Don Duvall, an eccentric American biker based in Vientiane who has spent more than a decade exploring the Trail in Laos from the back of his Honda XR400. I'd met Don the previous year when he joined Digby and me for a section of our BBC recce ride.

As far as I knew I would be the first female to travel the Trail solo, and certainly the first person to attempt it on an antiquated pink Cub. My seven-week journey was going to take me several thousand miles through some of the most remote and difficult terrain in Southeast Asia. From Hanoi I would follow the recently constructed Ho Chi Minh Highway south, cross into Laos, clunk on to Cambodia and finally end in Vietnam's southern metropolis of Saigon. Unlike the hundreds of thousands who walked, drove and worked on the Trail in the sixties and seventies, I wouldn't have to deal with a daily deluge of bombs. Neither would I have to push a bicycle loaded with 300 kg of ammunition or survive on roots and 150 g of plain rice a day. But to some degree, many of the other dangers were still very much present. UXO, unexploded

LIMERICK CITY AND COUNTY LIBRARY

ordnance, littered my route south. Cerebral malaria, dengue fever and dysentery were still prevalent. The trees slithered and crawled with deadly vipers, venomous scorpions and spiders bigger than my hand. And although tigers, bears, panthers and clouded leopards were sadly now extremely rare, an attack by one wasn't inconceivable.

All of these things were unlikely, but they were by no means impossible, and thinking about them opened a mental Pandora's box of potential catastrophes. During braver moments I told myself that I was just going for a short ride in the jungle. At other times fear of the impending trip stalked my consciousness. Whatever happened, it was unlikely to be an easy trip.

Exactly on time, Digby's motorbike pulled up outside my hotel. In the intensity of television shoots you get to know people pretty well, and it was good to see him again. Small and dark, his mischievous face was creased from two decades of Asian sun, tens of thousands of miles on motorbikes and a surfeit of booze and laughter. Brought up in Canberra – much to his dismay – and trained as a lawyer, he had fled the constraints of Australian society aged twenty-six and never gone home. Rebellious by nature, Digby never seemed to care what other people thought of him, and had the sort of uproarious laugh which could infect a roomful of curmudgeons. Occasionally, his garrulousness was replaced by unpredictable silences, the source of his supposedly aloof reputation. But his generosity, humour, razor-sharp intellect and passion for bikes and the Trail far outweighed the occasionally taciturn aspects of his personality.

As soon as I had decided to tackle the Trail solo, I'd contacted Digby. Doing it by bike was the only logical solution, and although I'd be travelling alone I wanted someone in Hanoi to source and pimp my wheels for me. Digby's knowledge of the Trail would be vital, and his Vietnamese business partner, Cuong, was the best motorbike mechanic in Vietnam.

In the last decade riding a motorbike in Vietnam has gained cult status on the Southeast Asian traveller circuit. Not content with dancing till dawn at Full Moon Parties in Koh Pha Ngan and tubing in Vang Vieng, travellers seeking the ultimate thrill now head for Hanoi, saddle up and explore the country on two wheels. Biking has become as synonymous with Vietnam as partying is with Thailand. Almost entirely responsible for this burst in biker tourism are Digby and Cuong. Cuong famously built the three bikes for *Top Gear's* iconic Vietnam special, which culminated in the Unholy Trinity floating across Halong Bay on a pink Minsk, a Honda C90 and a Vespa. If he could construct three semi-amphibious motorbikes, there was no doubt Cuong could dig up a C90 capable of taking on the Trail. Fortunately for me, they agreed to help.

Explore Indochina's Hanoi warehouse is a biker's fantasy. Lines of beautifully restored vintage Urals and Minsks stretch from wall to wall, serried ranks of the finest Soviet steel. Rarely seen in western Europe, these machines were the work horses of the former USSR, their popularity and usage spreading to Vietnam on the tide of communism. The larger 650-cc Urals, based on a stolen 1940s BMW R71 design, took Stalin's troops to the battlegrounds of the Eastern Front, and have carried Russian farmers ever since. Leviathans among motorcycles, they still roll off the production line of their original factory in Irbit, Siberia.

The Belarusian Minsks, smaller 125-cc beasts, are equally robust. Their service manual states: 'These motorcycles are especially suitable for use in the countryside where there are bad or no roads.' Both are the sort of bikes that conjure visions of speeding across snowy wastes, tweed scarf flying in the Arctic wind. While they are eschewed by most Vietnamese as outdated, unreliable technology, Digby and Cuong have created a cult around them. To see so many of these rare and handsome machines under one roof was quite a sight.

Eager to see my bike, I scanned the warehouse looking for a glint of pink among the rows of gunmetal grey and army green.

'There she is,' said Digby, pointing to the gloom at the back of the building.

Dwarfed between two muscular Urals, a gamine blonde in a sea of burly weightlifters, was a small, perfectly pink Honda Cub. With the classic curved lines of the older models, spotless pink paintwork and a sparkling steel exhaust, she was a truly beautiful specimen.

'Take her for a ride,' suggested Digby. 'She goes like the clappers.'

As I wheeled her out, two of the mechanics stood up from the Ural they were working on to watch. For a nanosecond, as I sat on her and fumbled with the key, I felt like I'd never ridden a bike before.

This could be embarrassing, I thought, trying not to look flustered.

But as her engine purred to life everything felt normal again. Compared to my old C90 at home she sounded like a well-serviced Bugatti, and we flew around the block without incident.

Minutes later Cuong arrived at the warehouse on a beaten-up red Honda moped. Dressed in an immaculate white silk shirt and pressed black trousers, he looked far too dapper to be a motorbike mechanic, albeit the best in the country. Thin and boyish looking, with close cut hair, he appeared younger than his forty-three years. The self-confessed 'country boy' had been the black sheep of his village when he was a teenager, so naughty that none of the families in the area would allow their daughters to marry him. Mad about motorbikes, he and his friends would cut the brakes on their 100-cc Honda Wins and race them to Hanoi and back. Even his eventual wife's parents – 'peasants' as he called them in his accented English – took more than a year of persuasion before they would hand over their daughter. The man in front of me now had come a long way since then.

The master mechanic soon got down to the nitty-gritty.

'Do you know how to change wheels?' he asked.

'No, I'm afraid not,' I replied, slightly sheepishly.

'We had five punctures in a single day on one of our rides, you got to know how to do this,' he said, getting out his tools.

Without tarnishing his shirt, Cuong squatted on the ground and deftly showed me how to take off a wheel and repair a puncture. The whole process took him no more than four minutes. I suspected it might take me a little longer.

Near where we squatted lay the battered, rusted remnants of James May's green Honda C90 from *Top Gear*. It was a sorrowful sight, never having recovered from its dunking in the salty waters of Halong Bay.

'Why don't you take a part from it for good luck?' suggested Digby.

I was already carrying a small arsenal of lucky talismans: a Buddha icon from Nepal, a piece of Mexican lapis lazuli given to me by a friend, a Bolivian offering to Pachamama, an evil eye and my well-travelled teddy, Wirral. Adding a piece of James May's bike to my collection was an excellent idea. Taking the seat, fairing or major engine parts was impractical so I settled on the key, tying it around my bike's handlebars.

Before leaving the warehouse I asked the boys what they had done to the bike – apart from spraying it pink as I'd requested – which had started life as a 1989 green Honda C50.

'I buy from someone in my village for $350. It look like total crap when we got it,' laughed Cuong. 'I wish I take pictures of it then, you wouldn't believe how much it change. Since then it's had new *everything* – piston, valves, spokes, chain, cam chain, exhaust, suspension – everything.'

'What about the tyres?' I asked, looking at her smooth city slicks. 'They're not going to be much good on the dirt, is there any way of getting off-road ones to fit her?'

'I look everywhere in Hanoi to find off-road tyres for Honda Cub, but no find,' replied Cuong.

Much of my journey was going to be through mud, sand and mountains; having off-road tyres would be a huge advantage. But if Cuong said he couldn't find any to fit, I believed him.

'During the rainy season the tribal people tie rubber straps around their wheels for extra traction. You could try that if you get really stuck' suggested Digby, noticing my furrowed brow.

I turned to one of the mechanics who had worked on her with Cuong.

'Do you think the Ho Chi Minh Trail is possible on a C90?'

'Yeah, easy,' he replied, looking proudly at his handiwork. 'As long as you remember to put oil in.'

'Look, it's the best bloody Honda C90 on the planet,' added Digby. 'You won't even need a toolkit. Nothing's going to go wrong with this bike. It'll be a breeze.'

I hoped he was right.

CHAPTER 2

THE CITY OF THE ASCENDING DRAGON

Now that the bike was mine, there was nothing else to do but take the bull by the balls and start riding. The pathetic notion of blaming jet lag and saying I'd pick her up tomorrow prodded my tired brain, then was rapidly admonished by my braver self. I had to start somewhere. Tucking my bike in behind Digby's, we dived into the mass of vehicles, the buzz of my little Cub's engine swallowed by the throaty chug of his single-cylinder Minsk.

Cast aside those western notions of traffic, where cars queue with bovine patience and bicycles glide down neatly painted lanes. The chaotic, raging torrent that barges its way through Hanoi's narrow streets is a wholly different beast. This is traffic red in tooth and claw; a seething, surging, clamorous cavalcade of man and metal. Lissom girls weave through the melee on Honda mopeds, their faces and arms covered from the sun, high heels teetering on running boards. Taxis career in all directions, horns blasting. Girls riding large old-fashioned bicycles wobble insouciantly between the lanes, pedalling gracefully at the same unhurried speed. With their conical hats and flowing black hair, they seem to float rather than pedal, oblivious to the hooting machines that flow around them. Women in their traditional *non la,* palm leaf, hats stagger under back-breaking yokes of fruit and vegetables. Mopeds loaded with whole families, pigs, cupboards, washing machines and beds squeeze through non-existent gaps. And through the middle of it all pedestrians dash hopefully. It makes Pall Mall in rush hour look like a Cotswold backwater.

Scanning the road in eight directions at once I gripped the handlebars, left thumb hovering over the horn, right foot poised above the back brake. In the middle of a busy any-way-you-fancy junction I swerved to avoid a family of four, who stopped their moped to disgorge two children into the fray. Apparently, looking in the wing mirror or pulling over to the side of the road before doing so was unnecessary. In England such driving would have people taking your number plate and dialling 999. Here it was perfectly normal.

Despite the insanity of it all, I felt a smile spreading across my face. Fingers of excitement crept up my spine, throwing aside lingering nerves. I was here, in Hanoi, united at last with my bike; my Ho Chi Mission finally in the starting blocks.

Chickenchaser, Clunk, Super Clunk, Cub, Super Cub, step through – mention these words to bikers of a certain age and they'll go misty-eyed, as though remembering a first date. They might ride BMWs and Ducatis now, but once upon a time they learnt to do wheelies and strip an engine on a humble Honda Cub.

With just three gears, an automatic clutch and an engine the size of a watermelon, Cubs are (almost) idiot proof and (supposedly) indestructible. Designed by Soichiro Honda as the answer to post-war Japan's need for an inexpensive mode of transport, the Cub was an instant success. Since production started in 1958, over sixty million have been sold in fifteen different countries. James May, writing about the experience of riding his in Vietnam, described them as 'a best-seller to make other best-sellers look like mere fads... the greatest machine of all time; nay, the single most influential product of humankind's creativity.'

OK, so he might have been a little hyperbole-happy there, but there's no getting away from the fact that the Honda Cub is the single most produced machine ever made. Yes, you read right, the single most produced machine ever made. Immortalised as a 'groovy little motorbike' by California rockers The Beach Boys in their 1964 song *Little Honda*, in 2006 the Discovery Channel voted it the Greatest Motorcycle Ever Made. To prove the point, the programme's presenter Charley Boorman attempted to batter a Cub to death. The poor little beast was thrown from the roof of a building, loaded with 200 kg of pizzas and filled with cooking oil, but it refused to die.

Their brilliance wasn't new to me. A few years previously Marley and I had bought two Cubs on eBay for £300 each, painted them in animal print livery and ridden three thousand miles around the Black Sea. In three punishing, stormy weeks neither bike had put a piston wrong. Even when I'd omitted to put oil in my engine, Soichiro's marvellous machine had clunked on, drier than the Skeleton Coast. It wasn't until Trabzon, in the far east of Turkey, that Marley noticed my error. If it had been any other bike, I'd have been getting the train back to Istanbul.

There were other reasons behind my choice of vehicle. Firstly, I was a novice when it came to mechanics. It wasn't that I *couldn't* do it, it was just that I'd never applied myself to learning about the inner workings of an engine. In all my previous travels there had always been someone else to do that bit. My role had been filming, passing the odd spanner or sitting on the kerb smoking and offering verbal support. Marley had taught me some basics before I left home, such as how to tighten the brakes and chain, but – despite Digby's confidence and my desire to learn – there might be times when I needed help. Cubs are simple machines to fix and, where I was going, most boys over the age of ten knew how to bash one back into shape. The same couldn't be said for a new-fangled BMW tourer.

Secondly, my route would pass through some of the poorest parts of Southeast Asia; mountainous tribal lands where the sight of a foreigner was still an extreme rarity. Some of the people still lived in near Stone Age conditions; in bamboo villages absent of schools, sanitation, electricity or material wealth. Me with my white face and motorbike gear were going to be enough of a shock. I hoped that riding a cheap, familiar bike might fractionally lessen the cultural chasm between us.

And finally, doing it on a proper dirt bike seemed too easy. There was infinitely more comedy value in attempting to trundle up and over the Truong Son range on a twenty-five-year-old pink Honda Cub.

More than any other Southeast Asian capital city, Hanoi exudes an antiquated charm; its streets oozing with a thousand years of history and conquest. A hotchpotch of architectural styles lean crookedly together: crumbling neo-classical façades, shuttered shopfronts, dragon-filled pagodas. Narrow frontages mask a labyrinthine world of passageways and multi-generational family life. Several Hanoians told me that the maze of ancient streets around Hoan Kiem Lake is the most densely populated place in the world, home to more than 100,000 people per square mile. How you prove this is impossible to know, but the traffic and sheer volume of humans makes it highly believable. While the roads are bursting with traffic, the pavements are cluttered with parked mopeds, men playing *co tuong* – Chinese chess – and huddles of people sitting on small plastic stools eating *pho*, the ubiquitous noodle soup. Privacy is not part of the fabric of Vietnamese society and the streets are an extension of people's homes – conservatory, dining room, living room and kitchen combined.

United with my wheels, my first appointment in the capital was tea with the British Ambassador. Navigating the maze of streets and avoiding collisions was so far proving a challenge. Craning my neck to read a street number, I lost concentration for a vital second and *bang*! My front wheel and mudguard collided with the car in front, leaving a guilty smear of pink paint clinging to its new black bumper. The front doors of the car opened and two men got out angrily. A passing old woman clucked at me in disgust.

'*Xin lỗi! Xin lỗi!*' I squeaked, rubbing at the pink splodge apologetically, thankful that 'sorry' was one of the few Vietnamese words I could remember. Fortunately, their initial anger dissipated. Shrugging their shoulders and laughing, the men returned to their seats and drove away. It was a good lesson for me – concentration was going to be key to my survival on this trip.

Dr Antony Stokes, British Ambassador to the Socialist Republic of Vietnam, is typical of many diplomats who fly the Union Jack in distant corners of the globe. Charming, modest and intelligent, he has been instrumental in furthering British-South Asian relations for over a decade. As a matter of courtesy I had emailed the Embassy to let them know of my plans and Dr Stokes had invited me in for a chat. Over a very English pot of Earl Grey we talked about his time in Vietnam and my impending journey, and he wished me luck on the road ahead.

'Now don't be a distressed British citizen – and always wear a helmet,' he advised, handing me his card as I left.

The next morning, two days before I was due to leave, I woke up feeling awful. My jawline had disappeared into swollen glands, my eyes ached and my back muscles had tied themselves in knots. I didn't feel stressed, but weeks of latent anxiety and anticipation must have crept up on me. Two evenings spent with Digby's hard-drinking friends might not have helped. I was sure I'd feel better once I was on the road, and with lots still to do before I left on Sunday morning there was no time to dwell on feeling ill.

My biggest issue at this point was deciding how and where I was going to cross the border into Laos. Although there are six legal overland crossings between Vietnam and Laos, rules regarding foreigners riding motorbikes are notoriously murky and there was no guarantee I'd be able to cross at any of them. There was no simple stated rule on this matter; it was just an infuriating bureaucratic glitch. As Digby succinctly put it, 'It's down to the ***** on the border that day.'

The border post I had the best chance of getting through was Na Meo, one hundred and fifty miles west of Hanoi. The crossing was on the well-trampled tourist trail between Hanoi and the Plain of Jars, a famous archaeological landscape in Laos, and the guards were used to a daily flow of foreigners. But the whole point of my journey was to follow the Ho Chi Minh Trail, and none of its main arteries had passed this way. Na Meo was my safest option, but it would be a disappointing compromise.

The crossing I wanted to take was much further south, at the Mu Gia pass. This narrow passage through the mountains had been North Vietnam's main route to the West Truong Son road, the Trail in Laos. The Truong Son may not be the highest mountains in the world but they have to be among the most impassable, and the Mu Gia pass is one of the few conduits through this formidable natural barricade. For a decade an indefatigable swarm of trucks carrying men and munitions had plied this route, feeding the war in the South. Desperate to stem the flow, the Americans hurled tens of thousands of tonnes of bombs, napalm and defoliants at the pass. US president Nixon even mooted the use of nuclear weapons here. But try as they might, America's efforts never closed the pass for more than a few hours, the CIA noting that 'The communists will spare no effort to keep it open.'

But the small border post was little used by foreigners and Digby and Cuong had been turned back from there a few months before. A travel company I knew in Vientiane told me there 'was no amount of money in the world' that would get me across at Mu Gia.

Nevertheless, I stubbornly refused to drop the idea.

Digby, Cuong and I discussed my options. It turned out they were going to be driving a pair of restored US army jeeps across Mu Gia with two American veterans at the end of the following week. The four of them were doing an exploratory two-week trip down the Trail to see if future jeep tours were viable. I'd met the veterans – a fighter pilot and an intelligence officer – the previous year with the BBC, and wanted to see them again. As members of an elite US fighter squadron they had been tasked with disrupting North Vietnamese activity on the Trail in the late sixties. Meeting up with them was sure to provide some interesting stories.

We made a plan to meet on the Vietnamese side of the border in five days' time and attempt it together, Digby half-jokingly proposing we dismantle my bike and smuggle it across as 'spares'. The worst that could happen was that I'd be turned back and have to drive five hundred miles north to Na Meo. It would be an inconvenience, but at least I'd know I had tried.

My last day in Hanoi was spent dashing around the streets of the Old Quarter, gathering together final bits of equipment and paperwork. It was International Women's Day - a day which passes with barely a mention in England, but remains hugely popular in countries such as Russia, Bulgaria and Vietnam - and the city was fragrant with the scent of flowers. Started as a socialist political event in 1911, it evokes the Soviet era when women were awarded medals for multiple births and longevity. In Vietnam, one of the last bastions of communism, woe betides the man who omits to buy flowers for his wife or girlfriend on 8 March. Women crouched at the roadside selling piles of fresh daffodils. Others pushed bicycles across the roads, bunches of lilies, carnations and roses spilling out of baskets. The streets were full of happy couples on mopeds, the women clutching beautifully wrapped bouquets.

We humans are adaptable creatures and after three days in the city I was beginning to drive like a local, edging down one-way streets the wrong way and beeping liberally. I passed whole streets selling the same goods, be it haberdashery, motorbike accessories or silk, many still bearing the names of the trade guilds that were established here a millennium ago. One of these, Ngo Hàng Cỏ – Grass Alley – was named after the tall grass that once grew here, used by the state to feed the several hundred elephants that lived in the city. Early travellers to the citadel of Thăng Long, The City of the Ascending Dragon – Hanoi's name from 1010 until 1831 – often mention these pachyderms, used for firefighting, war, transport and even capital punishment. French traveller Jean-Baptiste Tavernier, who lived in the city from 1639 to 1645, observed how adulterers were executed by being impaled on an elephant's tusks, ripped limb from limb and trampled upon. Today no trace of the fields that once filled this area remains and, luckily for adulterers, the elephants are long gone.

At lunch I stopped at one of the multitude of *pho* stalls on Hàng Trống. Sitting on a plastic stool, I watched as the *pho* mistress whipped up my steaming bowl of noodle soup with well-practised dexterity. Operating from a single seat, a conductress amidst her orchestra of food, she moved continuously; swivelling, plucking, pouring, ladling and stirring. The bottom half of her body remained rooted to the same point, while her upper torso and arms were in constant motion. With an octopus-like movement, one rubber-gloved hand dived into the gelatinous white noodles, the other swiftly plucked a handful of chopped spring onions. A scattering of tofu and a ladle of steaming broth finished the process. Immediately she started again: noodles, swivel, meat, reach, spring onions, scatter, tofu, swivel, ladle, broth. It was a mesmerising sight. I felt sure she could have fed the Truong Son army without moving from that stool.

That evening I went to Colonel Quy's cafe on the shores of West Lake, the largest of the capital's seventeen lakes. The café, owned by an English painter and a glamorous former Vietnamese army actress, had become my favourite spot to drink the local brew, *Bia Hanoi,* and watch the sun slide into the mist. Over the course of an evening Digby's expat friends drifted in and out, a motley collection of drinkers, artists, rebels and drifters. Hanoi seems to attract a particular type of expat – renegades who revel in the freedom, exoticism and old world charm of the city. If you're male, a plentiful supply of cheap beer and beautiful women also help. As author and former Hanoi resident Phil Karber wrote, 'If you arrive in Hanoi with bad habits, they aren't going to get any better.'

On the eve of my departure our group consisted of Australian, Bulgarian and Vietnamese painters, a red-faced cockney, a long-haired American, Digby and myself. On the next table a famous Vietnamese film star was drinking champagne with three friends. One of our group, a man introduced to me as George, spoke with a clipped accent which could have originated from anywhere between Paris and Vladivostok. It transpired that he was the son of maverick Australian war correspondent, Wilfred Burchett. Burchett was a brave, enlightened man who counted among his close friends and acquaintances Ho Chi

Minh and Cambodia's King Norodom Sihanouk. He wrote one of the most famous books about the Trail, *Inside Story of the Guerilla War* which, bizarrely, I was currently reading. Feeling this was a good omen I pulled the tattered hardback copy out of my bag and asked George to sign it.

Burchett Snr walked the Trail in 1963, two years before the first American combat troops had landed in Vietnam. Vietnam had been divided into North and South nine years previously, and Ho Chi Minh's North were fighting a guerrilla war against the American-backed South. A communist sympathiser, Wilfred later spent much of the war embedded with North Vietnamese and Viet Cong soldiers, dodging US attacks. Incredibly, he was in his sixties at the time. Two decades earlier, he had been the first journalist to enter Hiroshima after the bomb. George's accent was the result of his father's itinerant career, which took the family variously to Vietnam, Cambodia and Bulgaria.

The conversation soon turned to my trip.

'So what are you most worried about?' queried George.

I reeled off a selection of the things that had kept me awake at night during the past few months. 'Spiders, snakes, ghosts…'

Thousands of people had died horrible deaths on the Trail and the jungle was bound to be infested with restless spirits. The only time he'd camped out on the Trail in Laos, Digby had had vivid nightmares about ghouls trying to get into his hammock, and sworn he would never do it again.

'… loneliness, having an accident, tigers… '

At the mention of tigers, everyone laughed. With so few left I had as much chance of seeing one as I did of encountering a Great White in a public swimming pool.

'How do you think you'd feel if you came face to face with one of Southeast Asia's last remaining tigers?' asked Digby. 'Do you think you'd ask it to pose for a photo before it ate you?'

Titillated by his own humour he continued. 'You know tigers always attack from behind, so you should wear a mask on the back of your head to fool them.'

'Don't worry,' I assured him. 'If I sleep in the jungle, I'm not taking my motorbike helmet off.'

'Well, I think you can assume that if you do have a close encounter with a tiger you're pretty fucked, whatever. Even Mace spray will be useless. By the time the tiger's close enough for you to use it, you're Kitekat.'

'But you're not going to meet any tigers, you'll be fine. Your greatest enemy is yourself,' summed up George wisely.

Ilza, his bird-like Bulgarian wife, sucked on a Marlboro Light and peered over her glasses at me. 'Yes, exactly. You've got nothing to fear except yourself.'

They were probably right. I was far more likely to encounter mental demons than I was any man-eating big cats.

As I stood up to leave at the end of the evening, George walked over to the bike to wish me goodbye. 'You're a brave girl,' he said. 'Good luck.'

'I'm not brave!' I retorted. 'I haven't done it yet. Tell me that when I've finished.'

And with that I kick-started my bike and rode off into the Hanoi night.

CHAPTER 3

GOING SOLO

I awoke as the first glimmer of dawn broke through the hotel curtains. Vietnam rises early and already the street outside was humming with the noise of mopeds and the clatter of opening shutters. It was almost too much to comprehend that in a few hours I'd be zipping up my panniers, turning into the traffic and heading south. But here I was, the swirling depths of the unknown beckoning me forward. There was no going back now.

Despite my fears about the journey, I'd been determined to do it alone. Bar a stint backpacking around India in my early twenties, all my travels had been with other people. In 2006 my dear friend Jo and I drove a bright pink Thai tuk tuk a record-breaking 12,561 miles from Bangkok to Brighton. Aside from an altercation in Yekaterinburg over Jo's snoring we got on brilliantly, splitting the driving and responsibilities, making each other laugh and mopping up the odd tears. Then there was my Black Sea trip with Marley, where I'd too easily fallen into the dependent female role, never so much as picking up a spanner as we trundled through six countries. The following year, in a shivering attempt to cajole an old Ural to the Russian Arctic Circle, I'd been with two fearless male friends, one a tap-dancing comedian, the other a consummate mechanic. On every other expedition I had organised, or television programme I had worked on, there had been translators, drivers, medics and crew. It doesn't mean that each and every mission wasn't difficult in some way, but having other people around greatly mitigated the risk and adversity.

As my insurance company had nervously pointed out, it would be 'a lot easier if you modified your plans and went with a travel companion.' Travelling alone on a motorbike was a travel insurance nightmare. Not only had I opted for a vehicle with a high accident rate, but what would happen if I had a serious mishap miles from anywhere? If I was with another person, at least they would be able to ride or call for help. But alone, with a broken leg, bashed head or worse, there would be no one.

But the dangers weren't enough to put me off. Company makes us idle, gives us masks to hide behind, allows us to avoid our weaknesses and cushion our fears. By peeling away these protective layers I wanted to see how I would cope, find out what I was really made of, physically and emotionally. Would I be able to fix my bike if it ground to a halt in the middle of a river? How would I handle nights spent in a hammock in the depths of the jungle? What would it feel like to ride into a remote tribal village alone? How would I react in times of real adversity? And could I outstrip Usain Bolt if confronted by a many-banded krait?

A month before, I'd been relaxing with a cup of tea during a television shoot in Tanzania when I spied something red and black crawling across my shoulder. I screamed and leapt a foot in the air, sending tea and filming equipment flying into the dust. After several hysterical seconds on my part, the camera assistant confirmed it was no more than a harmless beetle.

'Jesus – and you're going to Vietnam in a few weeks?' he laughed.

And on another occasion, driving into Bristol not long before I left, Marley had asked me what I was going to do about fixing the bike.

'I'll get a book called *The Complete Idiot's Guide to Motorcycles*.'

'I think that might be a bit advanced for you,' he jibed.

At that point I'd driven across a roundabout and failed to see a car coming out of a small road to the right. There was a sharp intake of breath from my left.

'God, the thought of you driving a motorbike in Vietnam is terrifying.'

I couldn't go through life acting like a character from *The Only Way is Essex* every time I encountered something with more than four legs. Nor did I want to turn into one of those women who relies on their other half so much they end up unable to change a light bulb. If I always travelled with other people, I would never have to confront my weaknesses. There would be times when I'd want to share a laugh or a moment with Marley or have a stiff gin with friends. But hopefully there would also be moments of simple achievement. It was times like these that going solo were all about.

I breakfasted in a daze, my back still knotted, a ball of anxiety lurking in the pit of my stomach. For the first of many times,

I packed up my hotel room and loaded the bike. I'd wanted to keep my luggage as simple and light as possible. I would be loading and unloading the bike every day, so it would be foolish to travel with any more than the bare minimum. Plus, in the same way that I'd wanted a simple bike, I didn't want to be riding through poor villages clanking with showy, expensive equipment. My kit consisted of two small textile panniers – bought on eBay for £20 – which slung over the seat behind me cowboy-style, a pizza delivery-style top box and a ladylike wire front basket. The top box carried essentials such as my laptop, compact toolkit, camera and paperwork: International Driving Permit, driving licence, bike registration papers, photocopies of passport and visas. The front basket – added in Hanoi at the last minute – held bike spares Cuong had given me, plus my daily water supply. One side pannier fitted my limited wardrobe: a fleece, a single pair of jeans and one long skirt, a handful of tops, a floral shirt, a sarong, waterproof trousers, a bikini, three pairs of knickers, two pairs of socks, one decent set of matching underwear and flip flops. Shoe-horned into the other side pannier, along with a basic medical kit, balloons to give to children, solar charger and jungle hammock, was a precious bottle of Boxer Gin. Embarking on a solo expedition into the jungle was unquestionable without an emergency supply of the juniper nectar.

Round my waist I strapped a concealed money belt containing a debit card and a small supply of cash. And over my top I wore a nerdy but incredibly useful bumbag with: an iPhone, a small amount of dollars and local currency, a handheld GPS unit, a local phrasebook and my coterie of lucky talismans. Other stashes of currency were hidden in my backpack and in a secret sealed compartment on the bike. Designed to hold a few tools, it was the perfect size for a small waterproof bag containing a spare credit card and an emergency supply of dollars. With money hidden in four different places, I'd be unlucky to be cleaned out entirely.

Without much ado I said goodbye to the hotel staff, pulled on my Weise helmet, jacket and gloves and set sail. No big rush of nerves, no big fanfare, just a quiet 'Right, let's go!' to the bike, a slight wobble, and off we were.

I was thankful I hadn't asked anyone to come and see me off. I didn't need the added pressure of people or photographs this morning. Digby had come to bid me goodbye the night before.

'Don't forget to go to lots of *cắt tóc*,' he advised, pointing to the hairdresser next to the hotel where a woman was having her head massaged. 'They're fabulous; you can get your hair washed all the way down the Ho Chi Minh Trail. You don't even need to take shampoo with you.'

Given the dangers and challenges I'd be facing on the road, hair washes and head massages weren't something I had envisioned.

'Is that your parting advice? I asked, probing for something more applicable.

'Yes. It's about the little things in life. Now goodbye and good luck.'

Then I'd watched him turn right and vanish into the darkness, the last familiar face I would see before my journey began.

It was a Sunday morning and the pavements were splashed with colour: piles of fuchsia dragon fruit, ripe green mangoes, scented white lilies, juicy yellow pineapples. Women strolling in floral pyjamas added to the kaleidoscopic effect. Amidst it all people slurped their morning bowls of *pho* and drank gritty black coffee. No one took the slightest bit of notice of a foreigner on a pink moped, driving up busy Điện Biên Phủ Street and stopping opposite the Ho Chi Minh Mausoleum.

Passionate idealist, founder of Vietnamese communism, Stalinist dictator, revolutionary, visionary, charmer, saint, demi-god, hero, bringer of light – Uncle Ho was the founder of modern Vietnam. President of North Vietnam from 1954 until his death in 1969, Ho was driven by a single belief, 'The Vietnamese country is one, the Vietnamese people are one. Rivers may run dry, mountains may erode, but the truth is unshakeable.' It was this conviction that led him to risk everything in a war against the South.

Ho died six years before his lifelong dream of an independent, unified Vietnam was realised. Upon his death, contrary to his final wishes for a simple cremation, his body was embalmed and later placed in the specially built mausoleum. Forty-four years on, more than fifteen thousand people still file past Ho's waxy body every week. The image of his long, ascetic face with its Confucian beard and sunken cheeks is on every note of currency and in every public building. Opinions, broadcasts and publications criticising Ho are ruthlessly suppressed. Although the outdated Party is losing its grip on the hearts and minds of the people, Uncle Ho – a sobriquet he gave himself – is the glue that still holds the communist ideal together.

Across an immaculate green park, obedient crowds filtered into the darkness of the solemn grey monument to pay their respects. Watching them, I asked Ho to look after us on the Trail ahead, promising to come back and see him after our safe passage to Saigon. I then sprinkled a small pot of glitter over my handlebars and proclaimed, 'I christen you the Pink Panther. May you be strong, brave, pink and never let me down.'

My route out of Hanoi took me south west through the heart of the city. In an effort to calm my nerves and focus my mind I talked out loud, commentating on the road ahead like a demented racing pundit.

'Woman crossing the road... bicycle... oh God! Bus!... car turning without indicating... family having a conversation in the middle of the road... crumpets, lady with a baby!... man on mobile phone driving on the wrong side of the road – bloody hell, why can't he drive on the right side?... old woman in pyjamas... durian fruit seller on bicycle parked in slow lane...'

And so on. As I edged slowly out of the maelstrom my observations of the road around me poured out in a staccato stream of consciousness. At times my situation made me laugh hysterically, as if possessed. Minutes later I would feel momentarily close to tears, or engulfed by a surge of elation. It was exhausting.

Hanoi is now the most polluted city in Southeast Asia, and a soupy veil of mist and filth clung to the skeletal new developments and cranes of the capital's western suburbs. Beyond these, at Hà Đông, a satellite town to the west of Hanoi, I pulled into a roadside stall, switched off the engine and breathed a sigh of relief. This was going to be a journey of small victories, and getting out of Hanoi was my first significant achievement.

Ordering a coffee, I sat down on a rickety wooden bench next to three men, one of whom, I realised too late, was a policeman. Before leaving, Cuong had rung to say the registration and ownership papers for the bike weren't going to be ready until the following week. Anxious to start the journey, I'd opted to take the risk and head off anyway: I could get them from Cuong when we met up before the border. It meant I would be travelling with no insurance and nothing to prove I hadn't stolen the bike, but with only seven weeks until my return flight to England I couldn't afford to wait any longer.

'It should be fine,' Cuong had said. 'Just try not to get stopped by any policemen.'

With this in mind I smiled, hoping my neighbour wasn't going to ask me any inconvenient questions.

The policeman's face creased into a laugh and he leant over to shake my hand, the smell of alcohol on his breath enough to power a small engine. The two other men followed suit, revealing mouths full of tar-stained teeth and equally noisome breath. Immediately came a volley of friendly questions, none of them involving my absent paperwork, each one answered with the help of a Vietnamese phrasebook. I was definitely the best entertainment the inebriates had had so far this morning, and our encounter was punctuated with laughter and much thigh-slapping. One of the men jokingly swapped his insubstantial Burberry-check bike helmet with my rather more robust carbon-fibre motocross model. Motorbike helmets may now be a legal requirement in Vietnam but the majority were, like his, about as useful as wrapping a banana skin around one's head. No wonder he was eying mine covetously.

The only serious moment came when I explained where I was going. At the mention of 'Laos and Cambodia' there was a general sucking of teeth. 'On that bike?' they queried.

Although Honda mopeds are ubiquitous in Vietnam, the classic older Honda Cubs – C50s, C70s and C90s – are seen as the preserve of the poor. Anyone who can afford to rides a new *Honda Dream*, *Honda Wave* or the dreadfully named *Yamaha Smash*. In the developing world, new is everything; the notion of vintage or retro has yet to catch on.

And with that, the policeman prodded me on the knee and told me to be careful, before insisting on a photograph.

Vietnam curves around the edge of the Indochinese landmass, scooping up her inland neighbours like the long middle finger of an aye-aye. Four hundred miles wide at its northern border with China, the bony finger prods south between Laos and Cambodia to the west and the South China Sea to the east. At its narrowest point, in Quang Binh province, it's a mere thirty miles wide. I would follow this finger south from Hanoi, riding four hundred miles through the northern provinces of Hoa Binh, Than Hoa, Nghe An, Ha Tinh and Quang Binh. From there I would turn west over the mountains into Laos.

In many ways, this was the easy bit. There would be no mud or mountains, and Vietnam is more populous and developed than its inland neighbour. Food and shelter would be in abundance and Panther could glide along the new tarmac of the Ho Chi Minh Highway. Constructed at huge cost to the nation's purse and fast-disappearing forests, the Highway stretches for two thousand miles down the entire length of Vietnam, roughly following parts of the original Trail. Capitalising on the nation's reverence for Uncle Ho and the Trail, Prime Minister Vo Van Viet announced the ten-year project in the year 2000 with a propagandist flourish, 'We cut through the Truong Son jungles for national salvation. Now we cut through the Truong Son jungles for national industrialisation and modernisation.'

Five years after the country's opening of trade with America and the West, the national road was a symbol of Vietnam's new wealth. But it was a massive undertaking. Over three hundred bridges were built, hills were flattened, tunnels excavated and thousands of unexploded bombs defused. Not everyone was happy about it and environmental groups labelled it a major threat to Vietnam's fragile biodiversity. Over a decade later, their voices had been drowned by the din of development and the road was complete. For most of the way to Mu Gia, I would be following this Highway.

As I continued to drive west the suburbs petered out into a scrappy chain of continuous settlement, neither town nor countryside. Rice paddies filled the spaces between the concrete, their green muted by the persistent mist. Lorries hurtled along the dual-track road, sending me swerving onto the dirt verge on several occasions to avoid being run over. Looking out for these lethal loads in the wing mirrors was as important as looking at the road ahead, and my eyes constantly switched between the two. It made me think of something a former Battle of Britain Spitfire pilot had once said to me, 'It's always the ones you don't see that get you.'

At Xuan Mai I stopped for lunch at a roadside shack. I'm a vegetarian, and in a carnivorous society like Vietnam, this can make the simple act of feeding oneself surprisingly difficult. Walking between the low plastic tables to where a plump lady was dishing out bowls of *pho*, I used my best Vietnamese to ask for one with no meat. To clarify, I pointed at a stinking bowl of tripe and shook my head. If you're an English speaker, the

Vietnamese language is a mine of amusing linguistic innuendos; the phrase for 'no meat' is a prime example, sounding exactly like 'cum tit'. It's also a complex tonal language, imperceptible variations completely changing the definition of a word - one slip and your sentence takes on an entirely new meaning. Laotian is the same; a Lao-speaking friend of mine had warned me that the words for 'I' and 'penis' were almost identical, as were the words for 'near' and 'chicken'.

In this case, my version of 'cum tit' was apparently coming out as something very different. The *pho* arrived, floating with grey chunks of 'tit'. This being Vietnam, it could have been frog, pork, beef or the dog I'd just seen two boys dragging into the restaurant on a chain. I took it back, but the woman looked at me blankly and carried on serving her other customers. When she finally understood, thanks to a passing lady who spoke a few words of English, she burst out laughing. I'd had the same response a few times in Hanoi; vegetarianism was seen as a sort of insanity. When my second bowl of noodles arrived, two women pulled up their stools and watched me closely, as if studying a rare animal. Trying not to feel self-conscious, I pulled out my map to study the afternoon's route as I ate.

On International Women's Day, instead of flowers from Marley, I'd received a few torn-out pages of a map of Vietnam from Digby.

'I'm not giving you too much information, just the basics,' he told me. 'It's a road trip after all, your adventure; you need to find things out for yourself.'

He was right, of course. Embracing the unknown and discovering things for myself were the essence of this journey. Navigation was not my strong point though, and the temptation had been to extract as much information as I could from him before I left. The human mind fears the unknown, and every square mile of those torn-out pages was unfamiliar territory. Just as medieval cartographers painted uncharted waters with nefarious nymphs and wild-eyed monsters, so I was filling the road ahead with wrong turns and loneliness.

Now, as I left Hanoi's suburbs behind me and rode across the first torn-out page of the map, my mind continued to see-saw with emotions: fear, excitement, uncertainty, elation. I analysed my fear as I drove, questioning what I was afraid of and why. Was I afraid of injuring myself, of dying, of not living up to expectations, of discovering things about myself that I would rather not? The first day Marley and I had left Bourgas in Bulgaria to drive around the Black Sea, my brain had been awash with dreadful visions of lost limbs, death and mutilation. I had imagined being squashed under the wheels of a Russian truck and having to spend the rest of my life in a wheelchair. Or worse, Marley having to go home and tell my parents about my unfortunate demise. I even wondered how I would cope if I was disabled. Would I be brave or would I sink into a sedentary existence of *EastEnders* and self-pity? After a night of drinking whisky under a harvest moon my fears had subsided, and three weeks later we still had our life and limbs intact.

A motorbike is the most dangerous mode of transport in the world. Fear of being killed or injured while riding one is entirely rational. In Vietnam, where ninety million people crowd the roads and around forty people die in traffic accidents every day, the risk is far higher than in England. Drink driving is *de rigueur* and traffic rules are routinely ignored. Yet bizarrely,

I wasn't afraid of this. Not a single thought regarding death or mutilation on the road crossed my mind. I realised that what I was afraid of was *myself*; of letting myself down, of my reactions to obstacles and solitude.

A few months earlier I'd read Christopher Hunt's book *Sparring With Charlie* about his one-man Minsk ride through Vietnam in the mid-nineties. Several times in the book, Hunt refers to the aching loneliness of the jungle. Would I feel the same? For almost two months I would be travelling alone. In Laos I might go for several days without seeing anyone. Lots of people had told me I was brave, but would I prove myself worthy of such a compliment? I wasn't feeling brave today. To be afraid of my own mind as opposed to the very real fire and metal of an accident was ridiculous. George and Ilza were right – the greatest danger was indeed myself.

Cement factories, brick works, flat agricultural land – this wasn't Vietnam's prettiest face. Its brown fields and grey pallor reminded me of the Fens, the sort of place where whole villages have the same surname. It would never make it into any glossy tourism brochures. Driving steadily, my eyes flicking between the road in front and my wing mirrors, we purred along at around twenty miles per hour. Not only did this speed suit my little engine, but it was slow enough to stop or swerve in the likely event of an unexpected dog, human, buffalo, truck or moped in my path. My odometer had stopped working that morning but by 4 p.m. I estimated we'd covered around a hundred miles, quite enough for Day One. My neck, shoulders and arms were aching, my backside was numb and I was tired. It was time to find somewhere to stop for the night.

The next town on the map was Cẩm Thủy. Miles off the Birkenstock-beaten backpacker trail and too near Hanoi to be a stopover on 'Ho Chi Minh Trail' biker tours, it wasn't a town that saw many tourists.

Riding slowly along the main drag – past *pho* stalls; past two men cutting steel cables, the sparks flying towards their unprotected eyes; past shops selling motorbike parts; past clutters of signs I didn't understand; past people turning to look and point – I saw no sign of a hotel. Stopping to ask a group of teenage girls, they giggled nervously, shaking their heads and putting their hands to their mouths in embarrassment. Several more people reacted in a similar manner, their eyes widening in panic at being approached by a foreigner. Suspecting my beginner's Vietnamese might be betraying me, I pointed to 'Where can I find a hotel?' in my phrasebook. No, that didn't help either. Finally, a pretty young girl sweeping outside a restaurant smiled and said in English, 'Yes, I know hotel, follow me.'

She led me to an unmarked green house down a dusty alleyway, at the end of which was a river where the flags of a pagoda fluttered in a fluvial breeze. A cluster of children flew kites at the water's edge.

My arrival sent the matronly proprietress into a hand-wringing fluster, scurrying between doors with sheets and detergent. She was so surprised to have a guest I wondered if it really was a hotel. Handing over my passport and 150,000 dong – £5 – I unloaded Panther and sunk onto the granite-hard bed in a fog of exhaustion and happiness. The elation at having made it through the first day! The relief of being on the road!

Wanting to repay the kindness of the girl who had led me to the hotel, I walked the 500 metres or so back to her family's restaurant for supper. A group of women and children trailed me up the alley, firing me with questions. Halfway there a toothless crone joined the fray, getting up from her stool to peer at me myopically. Pressing her face towards mine, she shouted in Vietnamese, very slowly to make sure I could understand, 'Where are you from?' before returning to her regular perch.

Before I left Hanoi I had given myself three simple rules: be safe, have fun and say 'Yes' – within reason. Sitting down to a quiet dinner of rice, omelette and vegetables, I felt the eyes of a rowdy, drunk group of men on the next table watching me. It wasn't long before they insisted I join them. I hesitated, a little wary of getting into a drinking session with so many men. But saying 'No' was against my rules of the road. Saying 'No' was the boring option. I pulled my chair over and eight red faces looked at me expectantly, hands enthusiastically pushing dishes and vodka my way.

Not wanting to let the side down, I said 'Cheers' and threw a shot of the firewater down my throat. They clapped and shouted in appreciation, immediately thrusting the bottle at me again. It was only 7 p.m. and their table was a blitzkrieg of half-eaten dishes and discarded vodka bottles. Stray dogs licked at the scraps that splattered the floor. One of the men grabbed a chunk of meat with his chopsticks, helicoptering it towards my plate with a 'dog, dog, woof, woof'.

'No!' I said, recoiling.

Their faces split into laughter.

Questions, more shots, a few suggestive winks – then they all staggered into two black Land Cruisers to drive back to

Hanoi. It was a pertinent reminder of why I should never drive after dark.

Sleep was fitful that night. Fuelled by the unexpected vodka, thoughts and images of the day catapulted around my head. Outside my window a dog barked until kicked into silence. Around midnight I heard raised voices outside, a man and woman engaged in an escalating row, followed by a loud hammering. I soon realised it was the man's fists beating on my door and stumbled out of bed to unlock the chain. A flushed young policeman stood before me. Accompanied by the furious proprietress, he waved a photocopy of my Vietnamese visa at me, indicating that it was out of date. In Vietnamese law every hotel in the country has to register every single foreign guest with the local police. It's a pernickety, form-filling process; a remnant of the xenophobia of communist ideology. Unused to foreigners, the proprietress had accidentally photocopied the previous year's outdated visa, sending the local police into paroxysms of illegal alien hunting. Disappointingly for the policeman, I showed him the correct visa in my passport and the matter was closed. How very different my two encounters with the police had been that day. Closing the door on the disgruntled duo, I fell back into bed.

CHAPTER 4

THE LITTLE THINGS

'We do not want an expanding struggle with consequences that no one can foresee, nor will we bluster or bully or flaunt our power. But we will not surrender and we will not retreat.'
Lyndon B. Johnson, US President, 28 July 1965

At 7 a.m. a small man pushed a trolley loaded with speakers down the alley, howling into a hand-held microphone. Nothing about it was pleasant – the speakers were blown and the man's voice sounded like a pig being butchered. Karaoke struck me as an odd profession to choose for someone who was evidently tone deaf. I half expected people to pelt him with rotten eggs, or at least yell at him to desist his wailings. But no one seemed to notice. There's no such thing as 'noise pollution' in Vietnam; silence and space are there to be filled. If it's not dogs, pigs or chickens, it's government tannoys, twittering women or awful karaoke.

We associate Southeast Asia with scorching temperatures and violent monsoons, but in the winter months temperatures in northern Vietnam can be surprisingly British. Mist and drizzle can last for days and temperatures average around fourteen degrees. Many a backpacker has found themselves in Sapa or Halong Bay at *Tet* – Vietnamese New Year – shivering miserably in their Thai trousers and flip flops. In comparison, the south enjoys a year-round tropical climate. Even during the monsoon rains, which douse the whole of Indochina between May and October, the mercury rarely dips below the high twenties.

During the war, Dong Sy Nguyen, Commander of the Truong Son Strategic Supply Route from December 1966 onwards, wrote, 'We have two opponents: One, the enemy; Two, the harsh weather conditions.' The monsoons created havoc; storms destroyed bridges and buried miles of roads under landslides. Such extremes meant that motorised traffic could only move south between October and April. The summer months were limited to rest, resupply and repairs. Determined to overcome this, in May 1968 Dong Sy conducted an experiment to see if it was possible to open the Trail to trucks during the rainy season. In his memoir he recalls, 'The sky was like a huge black lid covering the vast mountains and forests. Water from mountain slopes ran onto the roadways… rivers and streams became violent torrents… within ten days we had tried everything… but to no avail. All kinds of vehicles were stuck in the mud.' The experiment was abandoned after less than two weeks.

The mist and rain affected the Americans too. In a war that hugely relied on air power, bad weather grounded their planes for days, leaving the Vietnamese essential breathing space.

Work commitments meant I had been unable to leave England any earlier than March, but with the monsoon approaching, I was cutting it very fine. If I was unlucky and the rains came early, Panther and I would be in for a very sticky mud bath.

Winter was still clinging to the north, and I shivered under my fleece and waterproofs as I rode south from Cẩm Thủy. Rain made wearing goggles impossible and water lashed my face, stinging my eyes and clogging my lashes. Soon my gloves were soaked through, and my hands froze around the handlebars. Travelling alone makes you acutely aware of the fluctuations of your emotions, intensified by the purity of solitude. This morning – cold, wet and homesick – my mood sank. Chastising myself, I remembered a Tim Cahill quote a friend had told me before I left, 'An adventure is never an adventure when it's happening. An adventure is physical and emotional discomfort recollected in tranquillity.'

If I'd wanted a nice, easy holiday I should have gone to Tenerife and lain on the beach. The point of this adventure was to take away the cocoon of everyday life, to see how I would react when the journey threw me the odd curveball. Inevitably there would be moments of physical and mental discomfort, and while I couldn't control when and how these might afflict me, I could control my reaction to them. Feeling sorry for myself was not an option. It was the attitude of explorers like Scott and Livingstone that made them so admirable, as well as their physical accomplishments. Beaten to the South Pole by Amundsen and facing imminent death, Robert Falcon Scott's stiff upper lip never so much as quivered. Instead he wrote his infamous diary to the very end, simply saying that that his demise was 'a pity'. It would be absurd to suggest riding a motorcycle in Vietnam was in any way comparable to struggling to the South Pole in

1912. But at times like this when I felt my mood darkening, it was helpful to recall their fortitude.

The smooth tarmac of the Ho Chi Minh Highway carried me south through Thanh Hoa province. Yesterday's pallid scenery had given way to gently undulating hills, waterfalls of rice paddies, banana plantations, sugar cane fields and patches of verdant forest. Even here, in the countryside, there were people everywhere. Phalanxes of children pedalled slowly to school in their blue and white uniforms, fanned out in gossiping lines across the road. Men in pith helmets – a hangover from years of war – led sullen water buffaloes along the verge, muddy and mooching like grumpy teenagers. Farmers tended to their paddies, hinged at the waist like compasses, plucking at the green shoots. Men and women everywhere chopped, sorted and loaded newly harvested sugar cane, piling it onto waiting buffalo carts. Once they were satisfied that not a cane more could be loaded onto the straining contraption, the buffaloes lurched forward, hooves splayed under the weight, leaving in their wake a greasy slick of ochreous mud and filthy mulch.

There were few cars on the road, save the occasional red-plated Party vehicles that careered past – because of hefty import taxes, few people in rural Vietnam can afford the luxury of four wheels. Aside from ponderous bicycles and the slow-moving buffalo carts, the majority of the traffic was made up of mopeds. No other country in the world relies on the might of the moped as much as Vietnam. These two-wheeled beasts of burden are as much a part of the Vietnamese scenery as rice paddies, *pho* and *non las*. Yet the most surprising thing isn't the volume of mopeds, it's the unfeasibly large loads you see them trundling along with. In a society where few people can afford vans, the moped is an admirable substitute. Whereas we might move house using a Mercedes Sprinter, the Vietnamese will think nothing of lashing three cupboards, a pig, a television and four small children to the back of their antique moped. In the middle of it all is usually a tiny woman, her face covered by a mask, an old pair of flip flops hanging off her feet. Out here in the countryside, riders would rarely be wearing a helmet. My armoured jacket and expensive helmet made me feel rather overdressed.

At a roadside shack a few hours south of Cẩm Thủy I stopped for tea and water. A dusty glass cabinet displayed a few packets of Vintaba cigarettes, a bar of soap and three cans of Red Bull. A man swung idly in a rope hammock, his wife dandled their baby on her knee and two grandparents sat on white plastic chairs, staring at the road. Shy at first, soon two young girls were clambering on my lap, insisting on having their photographs taken, then leaping up to look at the results on the screen. The parents and grandparents crowded around me, flicking through my phrasebook, stutteringly trying to pronounce English phrases.

The Vietnamese are as curious as ferrets and such interactions came to typify my experience of the country. Everywhere I stopped people approached, smiling, wanting to know more about the foreigner in their midst. Seldom would I be alone for more than a few minutes. Where was I from? Where was I going? Was I married? Did I have children? What was my job? Did I like Vietnam? Why was I travelling alone? Explaining I wasn't married but lived with my boyfriend was too complicated, so I usually just said yes to this question and showed them a photo of Marley. This led to more confusion, as the only photo I had with me was one of him wearing a pink tutu at a fancy dress New Year's Eve party.

As for travelling solo, this vexed the Vietnamese, to whom the idea of doing anything alone was anathema. Occasionally they would deviate to more personal queries such as how much I weighed, but normally the questions were as predictable as the passage of day and night. Their curiosity was never aggressive, rarely intrusive and nearly always delivered with a snaggle-toothed smile. Even buying phone credit would attract a small crowd, passers-by straining to see how much credit I was buying and what sort of phone I had. It was like travelling in a petri dish. This daily barrage of curiosity meant my Vietnamese improved rapidly. With no one else to rely on and no translators to hide behind, the linguistic learning process was greatly accelerated. Within a week of being in Vietnam, I could give cursory answers to the standard round of questions, count to ten, decipher basic directions and ask for a hotel. I had also mastered the pronunciation of ăn chay – vegetarian – which seemed to produce more reliable results than my version of 'cum tit'. My accent probably sounded akin to Cilla Black trying to speak French, and my tonal slip ups meant I was replacing 'where is' with 'island' – and goodness knows what else – but it was progress. The previous year, in a total of three weeks in Vietnam with the BBC, I'd never advanced beyond 'thank you'.

Having covered another hundred miles on my second day on the road, I drove into the town of Tân Kỳ in the late afternoon. In Uncle Ho's native province of Nghe An, Tân Kỳ had been an important staging post on the Trail. Panther had gone splendidly again, purring and spinning through the mud and wetness all day without the slightest hesitation. I was already developing great affection for the old girl. Another day under my belt, another small victory – it felt good. Drenched and in need of a treat, I unloaded my soaking panniers into a grotty £5 hotel and went in search of a hairdresser. You can't walk more than a few hundred metres in a Vietnamese town without seeing a sign for 'photocopy,' a laundry, a moped mechanic, a *pho* stall and a hairdresser. Tân Kỳ conformed to this rule and after a few minutes of dodging holes in the pavement a *cắt tóc'* came into view.

Lying back on a bed as deft fingers washed my hair and massaged my scalp and face, I realised that Digby's advice hadn't been so bad after all. So often in life we focus on the big things – the destination, the career, the house, finding true love – that we neglect the little details of our lives. But as Iris Murdoch once said, 'One of the secrets of a happy life is continuous small treats.' It's the simple, achievable things that can create moments of real happiness: a proper gin and tonic at the end of a long day, walking through a bluebell wood, making a lovely pot of Darjeeling, having a bubble bath, stopping to admire a beautiful view, having your head massaged after seven hours of riding in the rain. Such basic pleasures, yet so utterly delightful. Nurturing myself with little treats like this over the next few months was going to be vital. Not knowing how much to pay the smiling woman, I dreamily held out a handful of notes, from which she took 20,000 dong – 80 pence. It would be the first of numerous visits to Vietnamese hairdressers.

Most of us know about the Second Indochina War through films such as *Apocalypse Now* and *Full Metal Jacket*. Muddy, bloody jungles populated by spliff-smoking, trigger-happy GIs and vengeful Viet Cong. We might have an idea that it was something to do with fighting communism, stopping the Red Terror in its detestable tracks. But the seeds of America's disastrous dalliance in Southeast Asia were scattered two decades previously.

In August 1945, as World War Two ground to an end, Ho Chi Minh stood on a platform in a Hanoi park and declared himself President of an independent Vietnam. His rousing speech – ironically inspired by the American Declaration of Independence of 1776 – contained the immortal words, 'All men are created equal. They are endowed by their Creator with certain inalienable rights, among them are Life, Liberty, and the pursuit of Happiness.'

His declaration infuriated Vietnam's French colonisers and an eight-year conflict ensued. Known as the First Indochina War, it culminated in France's catastrophic defeat at Dien Bien Phu in 1954. An impossible battle fought in remote jungle, the French grossly underestimated the ingenuity and tenacity of the Vietnamese. They may have had tanks and aeroplanes, but the Vietnamese had nationalism – something France's largely Algerian and Moroccan troops were short on. Led by the diminutive General Vo Nguyen Giap, barefoot peasants hauled howitzers up muddy mountainsides and supplied the front lines by pack bicycle. Ho Chi Minh described it as a war between an elephant and a tiger, the lumbering elephant defeated by the stealth and cunning of the jungle-dwelling cat.

Ho watched from a nearby jungle hideout accompanied by his friend, the journalist Wilfred Burchett, whose son George I'd met in Hanoi. When Wilfred asked the communist leader what he thought the outcome would be, Ho took off his pith helmet and turned it upside down. He ran his finger round the rim and said, 'The Vietnamese are all around here.' Then pointing to the bottom of the helmet, 'And the French are down here. They'll never escape.'

On 7 May 1954, 10,000 French troops surrendered. France had lost the war, and with it Vietnam, Laos and Cambodia. In the process, 100,000 French and 300,000 Vietnamese had died, indicating quite how far Ho's revolutionaries were prepared to go in order to free their homeland from foreign powers. Responding to French criticisms about his apparent disregard for his soldiers' lives, Giap responded, 'the life or death of a hundred, a thousand, tens of thousands of human beings, even our compatriots, means little.' America would have done well to take note.

It was following this war that Vietnam was divided in two at the Geneva Accords.

With Hitler dead and Japan long defeated by the atom bomb, communism was the West's new bogeyman. France had been booted out of Indochina, China and North Korea had fallen to the Reds and the British were battling communist insurgents in Malaya. In Laos civil war had broken out between the North Vietnamese-backed Pathet Lao and the US-funded Royal Lao Government. Communism had to be stopped, and Southeast Asia was the key. Eisenhower famously summed this up in 1954 with his 'domino theory' speech, where he stated, 'You have a row of dominoes set up, you knock over the first one, and what will happen to the last one is the certainty that it will go over very quickly. So you could have a beginning of a disintegration that would have the most profound influences.'

If China, North Korea and North Vietnam were the first dominoes, Laos and Cambodia and South Vietnam were next in line. Vietnam's seventeenth parallel was the frontline, Marx's ideology could be allowed no further.

During the course of the next ten years America crept deeper and deeper into the quagmire of Indochina. By 1960 the US was funding the South Vietnamese army, the ARVN, to the tune of one million dollars *a day*. And by the time JFK had been assassinated in November 1963, there were sixteen thousand US 'military advisors' in Vietnam. JFK may have balked at an all-out war but his successor, Lyndon B. Johnson, inherited a poisoned chalice from which there was no turning back.

March 1965 and 3,500 US Marines stepped onto the sand at Da Nang greeted by a brass band playing rock and roll and girls with flower garlands. They were the first US ground troops in Vietnam.

America was at war.

Riding out of Tân Kỳ the following morning I was swamped by a thunderous cavalcade of mopeds. The air vibrated with the sound of a thousand engines and men, women and children of all ages rode past me, jubilantly waving yellow and white flags. There were only two things that could generate such fervour at 8 a.m. on a Tuesday morning: religion or politics. Curious, I joined the throng and followed them out of town. A few miles south the horde turned down a rutted track and bumped through villages and rice paddies. People ran out of their houses to see what all the commotion was about, holding up their mobile phones to capture the scene. Minutes later we swarmed around a corner and a church came into view;

not the modest country church you might expect in such a place, but a gargantuan pastel blancmange of a building. Pink turrets soared incongruously out of the rice paddies and gaudy roundels of the Virgin Mary dotted the exterior. It was straight out of the pages of Disney. I imagined the architects fussing over dog-eared copies of *Cinderella*, picking their favourite shades of pink and width of crenellation, and the priest swaggering down the aisle dressed as Prince Charming.

Adding Panther to the ranks of parked mopeds, I followed the chattering crowds up the steps. Inside, hundreds of people milled around a sickly pastel interior, chivvied by a young man bleating down a microphone. Stunned by the scale and weirdness of the place, I simply stood and gawped, wishing someone could explain the mystery of the gathering. Sure enough, as I stood there a voice piped up, 'Hello, my name's Van. I'm an English teacher.' A bespectacled young woman held out a hand and smiled.

Van's introduction drew an instant audience, and soon thirty people hemmed us in, filming our conversation on their phones. Asking her what all the fuss was about, she explained that the church was welcoming a new priest into the fold. She went on to tell me that the church was five years old and had been built with money sent back by overseas Vietnamese, known as *Viet Kieu*. Since 1975 millions of Vietnamese have fled to other countries, escaping war, communism and retribution. Around 1.8 million live in the United States alone, many of these being southerners who fought alongside America against the communist North. Squirrelling away hard-earned funds in Los Angeles, Sydney, Frankfurt and London, the *Viet Kieu* send home an estimated $8 billion a year – a significant chunk of Vietnam's annual GDP. By the look of things, quite a few of these dollars are being spent on the bricks and mortar of a new breed of Catholicism.

As we talked on the steps, a procession started and at least forty po-faced priests filed past, their white robes edged in gold. Behind them walked more than a hundred women wearing matching red and white *ao dais*, the traditional Vietnamese dress. Drummers, confetti throwers and eager members of the crowd brought up the rear. What a contrast to the dwindling congregations and locked churches of the English countryside.

Communists have never been fond of religion. The Big Daddy of communism, Marx, famously wrote, 'Religion is the sigh of the oppressed creature, the heart of a heartless world, and the soul of soulless conditions. It is the opium of the people.'

Since that utterance, every communist autocrat worth his salt has wheeled out this quote, the worst of them using it as an excuse to murder tens of thousands of monks and lamas. Vietnam's current communist rulers have never mirrored the worst excesses of Chairman Mao or Stalin, but they definitely don't like Catholics. In January 2013 thirteen Catholics were jailed for between three and thirteen years for the 'crime of aiming to overthrow the people's administration.' Mainly bloggers and students, the group's crimes were no more than publicly criticising the one-party state.

In a country where the ruling party forbids all political debate and controls all media, such opposition is forbidden. So much so that saying you would prefer a multi-party state can earn you a prison sentence. In August 2013 the government took this further and passed Decree 72, which outlawed the sharing of news articles and comment pieces on social media sites.

Backed by foreign money and growing in popularity, Vietnam's eight million Catholics are seen as a threat and hundreds have been hauled before courts in the last five years. Despite ardent criticism by human rights groups and western governments, it doesn't look like things are going to get easier for Vietnam's Catholics in the immediate future. Still, the religion continues to grow.

That morning, among the pomp and thrill of religious fervour, my anxiety about the journey fell away. This was what it was all about, being immersed in the unpredictable ebb and flow of life on the other side of the world. Every day was going to be a dive into the unknown; every moment unpredictable.

How glorious.

Riding away from the church, I felt my shoulders drop and my face split into a smile. It was the kind of elation you only get from the freedom of the open road, meditation or drugs; a certain liberation of the mind. The kind of elation that makes you want to do a wheelie, whoop excitedly and wave at everyone you pass. I couldn't wait for whatever the Trail was going to throw at me. As if echoing my happiness, the first bit of sunshine I had seen all week elbowed its way through the clouds.

CHAPTER 5

THE SORROW OF WAR

Unkempt and daubed in graffiti, a single slab of concrete sat at the edge of an unmarked roundabout. Skinny mongrels sniffed at plastic bags that clogged the grass at its base. The faded inscription explained that this was the 'Pho Chau Intersection of the Ho Chi Minh Trail,' marking the path of an east–west road to Laos 'used as a truck transport route across the Truong Son from 1968–69.' A spider wove its web over the lettering, its bloated abdomen suspended over a 'Minh'. Five miles on, a second even less notable stone sat crookedly at the edge of the road. This one simply stated 'Km 0 Ho Chi Minh Trail 1970'.

Stopping to look at both memorials, I wondered as to their point. The second was the most puzzling; not only did the Trail begin in 1959, but it certainly didn't start here, in a rice paddy three hundred miles south of Hanoi. A constantly evolving, highly complex land and water network which spanned much of the Asian continent, its roots lay thousands of miles away in the factories of the Urals and the industrial centres of northern China. It was from these production lines that Gaz and Zil trucks, MiG fighter planes, Chinese tanks, Kalashnikovs and SAM missiles flowed into Vietnam. Without this military support from their powerful Red allies, the communists would not have been able to sustain the War.

In Hanoi the previous year I had met Bao Ninh, author of *The Sorrow of War*, Vietnam's most well-known book on the conflict. A thinly veiled memoir of Bao's own experiences during more than a decade of fighting, the novel speaks of the brutality and misery a generation of young men and women endured. At odds with the Party's version of the war, where young volunteers skipped merrily to noble deaths, joyously sacrificing themselves for the good of the nation, its publication was banned for many years. When I asked the old man where he thought the Trail had begun, he picked up a pencil and scrawled arrows on my map of Asia, across the expanses of Siberia and China and south into Vietnam. Bao should know, he was one of the million North Vietnamese soldiers who 'đi B' – went south – down the Trail. Unlike thousands of his comrades, he was one of the lucky ones who survived.

At a restaurant in Dong Loc, ten miles on from the second monument, a sea of empty plastic chairs waited expectantly for lunchtime customers. In the kitchen a woman poked a brace of plucked chicken's legs into a metal pot, betel juice staining the corners of her mouth. After pointing to eggs, rice and some unidentifiable greenery, I sat down to eat, watched closely by the woman and her husband.

Minutes later five men walked in and were soon noisily gnawing chicken thighs and clinking glasses of rice wine, beckoning me over with greasy hands. When I declined, the drunkest of the five took to blowing kisses and leering at me with broken brown teeth.

Interrupting the cook from her open-mouthed gawping of the scene, I paid for my food and walked outside to where Panther was parked. As I shrugged on my jacket, the Chief Letch came over, grinning and wiping oil and bits of chicken off his face with the back of his sleeve. He took out a 500,000 dong note – about £16 – waved it in my face and pointed to me, his trouser zip and the back of the building. His companions laughed encouragingly. His intentions were clear as gin.

Amused and revolted in equal measure, I looked him in the eye and said in my clearest English, 'Look mate! Firstly I have a boyfriend, secondly I'm not that cheap and thirdly you are *definitely* not my type.'

I'm sure he got the gist. Without hesitation I stamped the kick-start, gave him a wave and wheeled off leaving him standing there, still waving the crisp 500,000 dong note. Agreeing to lunchtime offers of a quickie from a stranger wasn't part of my 'Yes' rule.

At Dong Loc, Vietnam is almost at its thinnest. Fifteen miles to the east is the ocean, forty miles westwards the impenetrable jungles of Laos. A vital intersection on the Trail, Dong Loc was pummelled by the Americans, whose objective was never to topple or destroy North Vietnam, but to force Hanoi to stop its infiltration and activities in the South. Between April and October 1968 alone they dropped 50,000 tonnes of bombs here, pulverising the earth into a featureless morass of mud and craters.

Communism loves a martyr, and today Dong Loc is a shrine of remembrance to the heroic deaths of ten young girls who breathed their last here while working to keep the Trail open. Of the thousands of Vietnamese who were killed at this intersection, many were young female volunteers like these, killed by a single bomb on 24 July 1968. The oldest was twenty-four, the youngest only seventeen.

Pulling Panther over to a pagoda-like complex, I bought a wad of incense from a one-eyed man and walked up the wide steps to the graves of the girls. Visited by thousands of Vietnamese each year, the ten white marble tombs lie in a row, adorned with photos of the dead, flowers, smouldering incense and offerings to the spirits of the girls. The Vietnamese have a modern take on what spirits from the sixties might require and combs, lipstick, fruit, money and mirrors were piled next to paper mobile phones. Not wanting to offend the spirits, I placed a few sticks of incense on each tomb, leaning over the offerings to look at the faces in each photo. They looked so tragically young; children in plaits and pith helmets. A man next to me bowed at each grave, placing a single white chrysanthemum on every one.

There can't have been much left of the girls to put in a tomb; bombs have a nasty habit of vaporising blood and bone. Thousands of American GIs went home to their parents in coffins marked 'This Way Up: Unviewable'.

It was a dismal grey day and I sat on the steps of the pagoda, contemplating the human tragedy of war. Across the road a group of teenagers smoked, flirted and giggled – just as English teenagers would on a Saturday afternoon – under a statue of square-jawed victors. After a few exploratory 'Hellos' three of the girls sidled over to talk to me, cracking sunflower seeds with bright pink fingernails. Between their nervous titters I learnt that they were seventeen, the same age as the youngest martyrs. It was hard to imagine girls so young coping with the noise and terror of war. When I asked to take a picture of them and counted to three – *một, hai, ba* – they pouted and flicked their limbs into Victoria Beckham style poses. Forty-five years on from the deaths of the ten martyrs, these teenagers were a very different breed; the product of nearly two decades of Free Enterprise. Facebook and celebrity gossip websites were much higher on their agenda than Party loyalty.

In a four-wheel drive, the thirty miles from Dong Loc to Huong Khe would take less than an hour. It wouldn't matter that there were a few roadworks or that your tyres bounced through potholes and over rocks. You would barely notice the drizzle, or the few times you splashed through a puddle and soaked a passing moped, and you would relish the chance to put your new car to the test on some proper mud after the tarmac of the Ho Chi Minh Highway. Neither would you notice the pungent musky smell emanating from a thicket of trees and wonder what size of animal it came from.

How different it was to be driving a moped along the same stretch of road – sliding, bouncing, tensing, sniffing. How I cursed the red-plated Party cars that sped past me, spraying me with orange mud.

At one point I passed a rail crossing where a group of men stood by the side of the road, calmly surveying a truck which had fallen foul to the mud, sliding down a bank into the field below. It was unclear whether it had happened a few minutes ago or a week before, and no one seemed to be doing anything about it. They simply stood there, smoking, hands clasped behind their backs. Stopping, I asked if anyone had been killed, using the universal symbol of a finger across the throat. Cackles of laughter and shaking heads ensued. Taking out my iPhone for a photograph, one of them grabbed for it, suggesting the others take a picture of us together. Ah, they were drunk. What a surprise!

Two and a half hours after leaving Dong Loc I parked Panther outside the Duc To Hotel in Huong Khe, left my muddy boots by the glass doors and asked the yawning receptionist for a room. Desirous of a hot shower after 150 miles on the road, I pointed to the word 'Hot' in my phrasebook noticing, as I did so, the word 'Women' directly under it. The receptionist gave me an odd look, nodded and handed me a key.

The Duc To was one of those inexplicably large hotels which must never be fully occupied. The stairs led up to long corridors of musty rooms, dust gathered in the cavernous dining room and heavy carved wooden chairs lined the empty lobby. Whatever the receptionist had understood, for 150,000 dong – £5 – I had Wi-Fi, an empty fridge, two clean single beds and a deliciously hot shower. Later, during dinner, I was approached by a beautiful teenage girl who took it upon herself to keep me company as I ate. She spoke not a single word of English, so we communicated via the stilted, silent medium of Google Translate, passing my iPhone to each other to tap in questions and answers.

Our BBC crew had stayed at this hotel the previous year. On that occasion one of the presenters had come down to supper looking disgusted, complaining of crumpled, stained sheets. Under duress from Digby, the receptionist had admitted that yes, a prostitute had used the room earlier that day, and they might have omitted to change the sheets since. But, the receptionist had added defensively, there *had* only been one prostitute, which hardly counted did it?

'That's the problem with booking the VIP rooms,' warned Digby. 'They're always the ones the businessmen use when they hire hookers.'

It was possible my dinner companion was the cause of those stained sheets and, although fairly sure of the answer, I asked her what her job was. Her typed reply confusingly came out as 'I am heard joking in the garden.' I couldn't imagine what she had really meant to say; was it a Vietnamese euphemism for prostitute? Google Translate was apt to come out with indecipherable answers. That morning a waiter had asked me, 'Do you want my balls for breakfast?' I'd looked at him, searching his face for a hint of perversion, but finding not a trace, laughed and ordered noodle soup instead.

Pulling her chair towards me, the girl persisted. Typing a question into the phone she handed it back, brushing her arm against mine and lowering her eyes suggestively. 'Are you sleeping alone? Do you want company?' the screen read.

My English reserve bristled.

'No thank you, I'm very happy sleeping alone,' I typed, passing the phone back with an apologetic smile.

'But it's my birthday today, and I've got no money for party,' she wrote, playing the emotional card.

Being the only guest at the hotel tonight, I was her only chance of business, and perhaps my sex was of no consequence. But lovely as she was, I wasn't about to have my first lesbian experience. Saying goodnight, I walked up the stairs, my socked feet slipping on the polished stone.

Breakfast was accompanied by a decibel-busting version of 'Gangnam Style' booming out of the karaoke machine in the empty dining room. I later heard that the owner of the hotel had made his fortune from logging, and that his wedding at the hotel the previous year was one of the most expensive ever held in Vietnam. All the same, it wasn't a place I would come rushing back to.

From Huong Khe the tarmac road wound southwards through gently rolling hills of tea and coffee plantations and perfectly flat plains of neon-green rice. In October 1969 thirty thousand soldiers had gathered in Huong Khe, waiting for the rains to end so they could *đi* B, marching down this very road. To the west I could just make out the spine of the Truong Son Mountains, striding southwards along the border with Laos. At a crossroads a boy sat on his haunches, smoking and watching me silently as I paused to look at the map.

Then came the most beautiful stretch of road through the Ka Geo Nature Reserve, my first real jungle. Jagged pinnacles of grey limestone karst rose up on either side of me, draped in thick curtains of foliage, flecked with red hibiscus and an unknown white flower. Kaleidoscopes of butterflies fluttered and danced around me as I rode, the sunlight catching spots of iridescent blue on their wings.

One hundred per cent concentration on the road was hard when there was so much beauty to digest. But beauty can be a dangerous thing on a motorbike, especially in Vietnam where obstacles are apt to appear without warning. Buffalo carts, tractors, bicycles and mopeds burst blindly onto the road from fields and houses when you least expect it. Losing concentration for a second could mean a messy collision. Near one village an old man and I both missed a heartbeat when a handcart he was pulling, piled high with sugar cane, hurtled down a slope and onto the road in front of me. Swerving violently, I saw the whites of his eyes widen in fear as I missed him by a whisker.

At Ba Don the road joined the screaming flood of trucks and buses of Highway One and turned south down the coast. Glimpses of yellow dunes flashed between the traffic and the reek of fish hung on a salty breeze. Pulling over at a roadside stall for lunch, I took off my helmet and jacket and ordered my usual eggs, rice and vegetables. Before I'd even taken a mouthful, I looked up to see an inebriated man walking unsteadily over to where I sat. Pulling out a fistful of dong, he leered revoltingly and thrust the notes towards me, gesturing the two of us go behind the shack for a lunchtime reviver.

Ignoring him didn't work, nor did sternly telling him to *đi đi* – 'Go away!' Pulled away by an apologetic friend and the shooing cook, he retreated to a nearby stool and continued to stare at me as I ate lunch. I glared back, flummoxed by this second lunchtime proposition.

The two incidents hadn't in any way scared me, but it was odd. It was as if I was walking around with 'It's lunchtime and I'm after a dirty shag' written across my head. I couldn't work out if it was the pink bike, the fact that I was a lone western female or the irresistible cocktail of the two. Sweaty, devoid of make-up and dressed in butch biker gear, I really couldn't see the appeal.

In Dong Hoi, a fishing port just north of the former seventeenth parallel, I had arranged to meet up with the two US veterans, Roger van Dyken and George Buchkowski. In a few days' time the three of us would meet Digby and Cuong and attempt the crossing into Laos, where Roger and George were reliving old memories. Both had served with the Misty Fighter Squadron, anelite group of combat-experienced volunteers with one mission: to stem the flow of enemy activity down the accursed Ho Chi Minh Trail. As Forward Air Controllers (FACs), their Top Secret mission was to fly their F-100 jet fighters fast and low over enemy territory, seeking out irregularities and targets. Once they had spotted something, they would mark the position with a 'Willy Pete' smoke rocket and call in the fighter bombers to drop their payloads.

It was a dangerous job. Straining to see telltale dust eddies or glints of metal through the jungle canopy, Mistys often flew as low as 500 metres, well within reach of the Vietnamese anti-aircraft gunners. To evade fire the young pilots had to constantly jink and dive, subjecting their bodies to massive G-force, regularly flying for four or five hours at a time. Of the 157 pilots who flew for Misty, thirty-four were shot down.

When I arrived Roger was standing on the steps of the Nam Long Hotel, where we had arranged to meet.

'Is that your bike – that little pink thing? I knew you were crazy to even attempt this journey, but now I think you're totally crackers. You must be made of titanium.'

'No, more like marshmallows and idiocy,' I replied, kissing him hello.

Roger was a tall, avuncular man, his square face framed by a neatly clipped grey beard. Although drafted into the military against his wishes, he had volunteered to go to Vietnam. In the eyes of the patriotic young Californian, the conflict was part of the 'battle for a free world' and he was eager to save the planet from communist domination. But two and a half years after President Johnson had sent the first US ground troops to Vietnam, things were not looking good. Fifteen-thousand Americans were already dead and 864,000 tonnes of bombs hadn't persuaded the North Vietnamese to 'draw in their horns' as the USAF had hoped. The North Vietnamese were continuing to expand the Trail and push more and more men and supplies south.

The situation on the Home Front wasn't much better. Detroit had recently been rocked by violent race riots, and in October 1967 a hundred thousand anti-war protesters had marched on Washington DC. Roger had spent a year in Vietnam, returning to Washington State unscathed to marry his girlfriend Marlene and father four children.

Suddenly there was a flash of tanned skin, hot pants and bouncing bosoms as George, a slim seventy-two-year-old, tripped in to the hotel lobby with a buxom Brazilian backpacker on each arm. The three of them had been on a day trip to the nearby UNESCO caves at Phong Nha. In the absence of his wife, who had stayed at home in Georgia, George looked delighted with his arm candy. The Brazilians were equally happy to have spent the day with the Real McCoy, a former Vietnam fighter pilot. With his ice-blue eyes, buzz cut and mid-west drawl, he still cut a dashing figure.

George had arrived in Vietnam in October 1968 as a twenty-eight-year-old pilot from Detroit. By now America was floundering even more in the mess of Indochina. A further 16,000 soldiers had died that year alone, and the ranks of the anti-war movement were swelling daily. After the failures and lies of the Tet Offensive, the government was rapidly losing credibility and returning Vietnam veterans were being taunted as 'baby killers'.

In an effort to lure Ho Chi Minh to the negotiating table, President Johnson had halted his bombing of North Vietnam, focusing instead on the back-door war in Laos. Bored of flying regular missions, George transferred to Misty halfway through his tour, preferring the excitement of flinging his plane around the sky, dodging NVA bullets. George flew fifty-three missions for Misty, navigating with simple maps and scouring the ocean of trees below with his naked eye. Although hit five times, he was never shot down and went on to spend thirty years as a pilot for Delta Airlines.

Roger had first returned to the country in 2007. A religious man, he was deeply affected by the wartime plight of the Vietnamese, and had a strong feeling that, all these years later, he had a role to play here. In 2009 he came again, and fate, or God, brought him to the Nam Long Hotel in Dong Hoi. The chain of events that brought him here, and into contact with the owners, Sy and his wife Nga, were so odd that even his travelling companion, an atheist Jew, was forced to admit to the possibility of Divine Intervention. Returning every year since, he now splits his life between running a successful boat charter business in Washington State, and numerous charity projects in Dong Hoi.

Dong Hoi had been a vital trans-shipment point on the Trail, thousands of tonnes of war material arriving here by sea before continuing south and west overland. American intelligence was aware that supplies were creeping down the coast of North Vietnam hidden in ordinary fishing boats, so for almost a decade the town was pounded from air and sea. You don't have to look far to see reminders of the destruction. On the quayside outside the hotel, where the red and gold flags of the fishing boats fluttered like battle standards in the wind, were the charred remains of the Tam Toa Catholic Church. An alleged storage place for guns and ammunition, the church was bombed in 1968, never to be rebuilt.

Sy, the owner of the Nam Long Hotel, was a child at the time and experienced first-hand the destruction wrought by Roger and George's USAF. One night in 1968 his whole family were sheltering from an aerial bombardment, listening to the shells howling down, praying they wouldn't be next. Sickening explosions and screams pierced the night air around them. Then, in a heart-stopping instant, a shell tore through the roof above them, their lives only spared thanks to a faulty fuse.

Once the planes had gone, Sy's father ran from the shelter to assess the damage. Outside, a bloodied body lay in the dust, one arm ripped off by the force of the blast, the lifeless features of his sister illuminated in the bright moonlight. Next door, where her house once stood, a burning bomb crater was all that remained – all six members of the family obliterated. Even today, Sy says he will never forget the smell of explosives and burning flesh.

Sy's immediate family survived the rest of the war, but incidents like these made him grow up eager to be old enough to hold a gun and kill Americans.

How different the situation was in February 2011, when Roger was again staying at the Nam Long Hotel with his wife Marlene. Waking up at 4 a.m. with serious chest pain Roger suspected the worst. Although the Cuban-built hospital in

Dong Hoi was only a ten-minute drive, Sy insisted they get in his car and drive four hours south, over the old seventeenth parallel, to Huế.

'Hospital in Dong Hoi very bad, people go there to die. Equipment not good, no good doctors. We go direct to Huế.'

It was risky, Roger's pain was intensifying and four hours was a long time. He might not make it. In the shadowy dawn they raced south in an old ambulance, dodging cows, mopeds and the odd truck. Roger lapsed in an out of consciousness, dosed up on morphine and oxygen. He later wrote in his diary, 'I grimace a smile at the irony of the situation: here I am above the old DMZ being driven by a North Vietnamese into the former South Vietnam as my former enemy tries to save my life, bouncing over the same roads of the Ho Chi Minh Trail network that my outfit tried to destroy during the War. Same people, same route, different time, different cargo. Now I'm the one being infiltrated into the South.'

They made it to Huế, where an Australian-trained Vietnamese doctor informed him that they had recently been donated a one-million-dollar machine to do angiograms; that this machine was Roger's only chance of life. Later that day he had the operation and a new stent was fitted. He was out of the darkness.

Sy's actions undoubtedly saved the sexagenarian's life.

Sy's eighty-two-year-old father, the man who had found his sister's body lying in the dust all those years ago, had died three days before I arrived. Already over a thousand people had come to their house to pay their respects to a man who had once led the community war effort. Now the family were starting a forty-nine-day vigil at his grave in the belief that their presence would prevent his spirit being lonely as it wandered between worlds. Sy kindly asked Roger, George and me to go with them, so as darkness fell we all climbed into his car and headed out of town.

The graveyard was a few miles out of Dong Hoi, near where the family had fled to during the War. Pylons marched through the darkness, their red lights winking like tracers in the night sky, the sound of bullfrogs and crickets echoing around the graves. The freshly dug grave was submerged under flower wreaths and flickered with a hundred candles. A small crowd of people stoked a fire and prepared what looked like a picnic, their heads wrapped in white material to denote mourning.

Imitating Sy, we made an offering of incense and walked anti-clockwise around the grave before sitting down on a plastic rug. Sy told us it wasn't meant to be a sombre occasion, the point of the fire and our presence was to keep the spirit happy. Crates of beer and platefuls of barbecued pork and beef, sweet potatoes and maize were piled in the middle, around a solar hurricane lamp fluttering with moths. Everyone tucked in with gusto; talking, laughing, eating, drinking, licking sticky fingers, sucking on fat. Faces hovered in the darkness, Caravaggio-like, illuminated by fire and light.

Between mouthfuls of burning-hot sweet potato I turned to Sy and asked him what religion he and his family were.

'No religion, we just worship our ancestors,' he answered simply.

For the Vietnamese, the filial responsibilities of life continue in death. Making sure the old man's spirit made a happy transition to the afterlife was just as important as respecting him during his lifetime.

For much of the gathering, Roger remained quiet, pensively nursing a beer at the edge of the circle. Sy asked him how he was feeling.

'I'm just thinking of your father, and past history, and where we are now; how much you and your father have welcomed me into your family.'

Everyone stopped talking to listen. Roger and Sy's father had shared an intense bond, a mutual comprehension of what the other had been through.

Roger went on, tears filling his eyes. 'How many people get to count their former enemies as close friends, to walk on soil where they once made war? I'm very lucky. I just hope people can live in peace and friendship for ever more.'

During a decade of war fifteen million tonnes of ordnance were dropped on the Vietnamese countryside. Between ten and thirty per cent of these didn't explode, leaving the country with a deadly legacy. Forty years after the last American bomb was dropped up to 800,000 tonnes of UXO – unexploded ordnance – still remains, polluting a staggering fifteen per cent of Vietnam's land surface. Quang Binh, the province just north of the former North–South divide where Dong Hoi is located, was one of the most heavily hit. Today one hundred per cent of communities here are still contaminated with UXO.

Bombs don't just kill during wartime, they remain live for decades. Since 1975 more than 100,000 Vietnamese have been killed or injured by UXO and people are still dying every week. At present the Vietnamese government spends $100 million a year on UXO clearance hoping, rather optimistically, to solve the problem within a hundred years. In comparison, while their annual federal defence budget hovers around the $618 billion mark, the US government has donated a mere $65.5 million since 1993. They are helping, but it's nowhere near enough.

The morning after the grave vigil four members of the English NGO Mines Advisory Group (MAG) picked me up from the hotel. I was raising funds and awareness for them through my trip and they had kindly agreed to show me some of their field operations. Our first stop was the nearby village of Vin Thuy, which had once stood on the Trail – the death knell for any settlement. MAG was conducting a Community Liaison project in the village, a house to house survey to find out the locations and identity of UXO. At the first house we went to, an old lady in rice waders and a *non la* came out and greeted us. Within seconds she was pointing to the end of her garden, the word 'bombie' (cluster bomb) clearly decipherable. As she talked, two young men hovered in the shadows behind her, muttering to themselves, one of them absentmindedly playing with his penis.

The translator turned to me and whispered, 'Her husband fought in the South during the war and was sprayed with Agent Orange. Perhaps that's why her two sons are like this.'

On the way to another house, MAG stopped a man walking past and asked him the same question, 'Do you know the locations of any UXO in the village?'

'Yes,' he said, 'right here in this bamboo bush.' He gestured to a clump of bamboo a foot from where we stood. 'This is where we used to throw any bombies we found. There must be quite a few under there.'

We sprayed the bush red to indicate UXO, and moved on. Less than 10 metres along the path the translator pointed out another red clump of leaves. Underneath it, looking dangerously innocuous, lay a heavily rusted 2.75-inch rocket– a forty-year-old, foot long bit of rusted metal with a deadly blast radius of 500 metres.

At a third village we parked outside a half-built house and a thin, beautiful woman came out and shook our hands, inviting us in for tea. At her side was a young boy, a red scar running underneath his left eye. We sat on the floor below a shrine with burning candles and photos of a serious-looking man and a young boy. Lom, the woman, poured us tea and told us the whole tragic story.

Last August her two sons had gone out to look for scrap metal. Her youngest, the eight-year-old sitting beside her now, was hoping to buy a new kite with the profits of any scrap metal he found. In the nearby forest the boys found half a bombie. Not knowing what it was, the eldest started to hit it with a hammer.

The explosion didn't kill him instantly; he bled to death on the way to hospital.

His younger brother survived; his body filled with tiny pieces of shrapnel. As Lom told us this she pulled down the boy's trousers, showing us skeletal, heavily scarred legs.

'He's already had several operations, and he's waiting for one more. I need to borrow 5,500,000 dong – about £180 – before he can have it though.'

For someone earning around £150 per year farming rice, raising this amount of money meant borrowing from neighbours and loan sharks, and years of debt.

'What about your husband?' I asked, dreading the answer.

As she replied, tears slid over her cheekbones and she struggled to get out the words. The MAG translator started to cry too.

'Her husband died two years ago. He fell off the roof when he was building this house.'

Oh goodness, it was too much to bear. Next I was crying, and we all sat on the mat, tears rolling down our faces. How could one woman possibly be so dreadfully and cruelly unlucky?

I asked the boy what he wanted to be when he grew up.

'I want to be a soldier so I can fight the Americans who killed my brother.'

For him, it didn't matter that the war had ended four decades ago. In their house, it was still happening.

Saying our goodbyes, I shook Lom's hand and gave her a handful of dong, asking the translator to explain it was to help with the costs of the operation. It was only later I realised I'd miscalculated; I thought I'd given her £50 but in fact it was less than £20. How stupid of me. Filming in Botswana a month earlier I'd given a driver a £200 tip by accident, thinking it was £20. Maths never was my strong point.

Our final location of the day was a large site in Phong Nha Ke Ban National Park which MAG had been clearing for three months. On the way in we walked past an ageing Frankfurt Zoological Society and Kolner Zoo sign advertising this as a semi-wild area for primates. A second one had pictures of some of the rare species that lived here: the Indochinese tiger, gibbons, civets, Asiatic brown bears. The sign looked old and was, I suspected, outdated.

'Do you want to see a demolition?' asked the translator, as we puffed up a steep track through the trees.

I nodded vigorously.

She went on. 'At the end of every day, we destroy any UXO we've found. Today there's a Blu 26, a mortar and a projectile. If we wait twenty minutes we can watch the detonation.'

The translator explained that the bombs were put in a pit, surrounded by sandbags and detonated using a donor charge.

'You can press the detonation button if you want,' suggested another of the team.

More vigorous nodding.

With three minutes to go until The Big Bang, loudspeakers warned everyone in the area to scarper. Although we were standing in a cleared patch of jungle and there was no one else visible apart from our team, they couldn't take any chances.

'Even the monkeys know to run away,' smiled the translator.

One of the technical boys knelt down and connected a long cable to the detonation box. Taking my hands, he placed my right forefinger on a red button and my left forefinger on a green button.

'I'm going to say Three, Two, One. On One – press both buttons at once,' he instructed.

I wasn't sure what to expect; I'd never heard a bomb explode before.

'Three! Two! One! Go!'

I pressed hard on the buttons and BOOM! a terrifyingly large explosion thundered through the trees, throwing a plume of black smoke and debris high above the canopy. Letting out an involuntary expletive I leapt up, shocked at the noise. This was only three relatively small bombs, yet the sound and reverberation was astonishing. War must be a deafening place.

CHAPTER 6

INTO THE LONG MOUNTAINS

The roof of the Phong Nha Farmstay is the quintessential spot for a sundowner. Technicolour green paddies fan out in all directions and in the distance the burning red orb of the sun sinks to a new horizon through mist-shrouded pinnacles of karst. *Non las* and water buffaloes dot the paddies as farmers eke out the last of the evening light. As dusk falls, a million cicadas and frogs resume their umbral duty, beating the air with legs, wings and throats.

In a celebratory mood Digby, Cuong, George, Roger and I stood on the roof drinking in the beauty of the scene. Digby and Cuong had spent two days driving from Hanoi in their restored US army jeeps, two of the thousands abandoned when the Americans pulled out in 1973. George, Roger and I had just arrived from Dong Hoi, twenty miles to the east. It was five days since I had left Hanoi and already the nerves and traffic of the capital seemed to belong to another era. I was elated to be here; to have covered four hundred miles; to be riding the Trail with my now beloved Panther. Behind us I could hear the melodious tinkle of fine gin being poured over ice and lemons, the fizz of tonic water. We clinked glasses and said 'Cheers,' our eyes returning to watch the last of the sun. An hour later the bottle of gin was empty and the party was in full flow; the night air noisy with our laughter and conversation. George was swaying slightly in his chair. Next to him, Roger was looking at the gin bottle in disbelief. A pushy English backpacker had muscled in on the action and was hounding us for more gin; there was none.

The Phong Nha Farmstay was the launch pad for my border assault and tomorrow morning I would set off at dawn and attempt to cross the mountains into Laos. Over supper and several bottles of red wine Digby, Cuong and I talked about the border. Cuong, who was terrified of dying young like a lot of the men in his family, hardly ever drank, sipped a Coke as we glugged back the grog. George and Roger retired early, murmuring something about too much gin and having to get up early.

The idea of trying to smuggle my bike over as spare parts had been abandoned and Digby and Cuong both advised me to try the border solo.

'Your trump card is the fact you're a girl on your own on a pink moped,' said Digby. 'Go ahead of us in the morning and if we see each other at the border, pretend you don't know us.

Cuong, if you see Ants at the border you have to ignore her, OK?' He took another slug of wine and laughed.

It went against my instinctive desire for safety in numbers, but I trusted their advice. To give me an even better chance of making it, we decided that I would pretend I was a regular backpacker. It was the bike that was the problem more than the fact that I was foreign.

'Listen, when you get to the Lao side of the border, drive the bike past all the trucks, as far as you can towards the exit,' suggested Digby, slightly slurring his words. The strains of Bob Marley's 'Buffalo Soldier' drifted in from outside, where a group of backpackers were finding themselves around a bonfire.

'Hide the bike behind a truck and just go into the police hut with your passport and smile sweetly. If you get through that OK, just leg it. Forget about getting your bike paperwork stamped by customs, just get into Laos and deal with that issue later.'

Ben and Bich, the owners of the Farmstay, were less hopeful and asked what my Plan B was.

'I don't have a Plan B. I'm going to get across.'

Plans B, C and D all involved driving hundreds of miles extra, as well as not seeing any more of the boys. I was hell-bent on making it.

Leaving Digby opening another bottle of wine, I bid him goodnight with a hopeful 'See you in Laos.' If I made it, we would meet in the village of Ban Langkhang tomorrow afternoon, ten miles the other side of the pass.

Dreams of hatchet-faced policemen and closing barriers invaded my sleep and at 5.45 a.m. a trio of loud clicks jolted me awake, like light switches being turned on in quick succession. For a split second I was back at boarding school, being woken up by a bossy, bustling matron, but instead I opened my eyes to see a gecko's tail slithering past my head.

Dressing in my floral shirt and best underwear for luck, I crept down the dark stairs. No one else was up and I quietly packed Panther and rode through the gates into the bracing dawn air. I'm not a morning person, but there's something magical about riding a motorbike at dawn as the world is just waking; the ghostly grey light suggestive of Other Worlds and Unseen Beings. Heading north west through the fairy tale landscape of Phong Nha Khe Ban National Park, I barely saw another human – unusual for Vietnam. High peaks of limestone karst rose imperiously out of the paddies, floating above a sea of mist, and to my far left were the sheer ramparts of the mountainous border.

At 7 a.m. I stopped to buy some bread – *bánh mì*, pronounced bang me – from two women. They held up one finger, asking if I was alone; laughing when I said yes. Urging Panther on, I reached a record speed of 35 miles per hour along the stretch of an old MiG runway before starting the slow climb into the mountains. A silvery vapour hung in the valleys and swirled around the jungle-clad slopes, occasional rays of sun flooding the scene with an ethereal light. It was breathtakingly beautiful, and again I felt that rush of exhilaration, that purity of solitude. I wouldn't have wanted to be anywhere else.

Gripped by the mission, hunched over the bike like a jockey, I sped – well, as much as a C90 can 'speed' – onwards. I talked to Panther out loud, as if teeing up a boxer before a fight. 'Where are we going to be tonight, Panther?' I'd ask. 'Laos, yes Laos. We're going to be in Laos tonight...' My blood was up. All I could think about was getting over those mountains. There was no way I was coming back down this road later today. We had to make it.

Twenty miles before the border, I turned south west towards the 418-metre pass, overtaking a caravanserai of Vietnamese, Laos and Thai trucks. They crawled up the incline of the old

French road in first gear, just as the Trail trucks would have done. Dropping Panther into second I clunked past, holding my breath against the fug of black exhaust smoke.

The road climbed relentlessly upwards and there was hardly any settlement now, just the odd bamboo hut. A few miles from the border a long line of stationary trucks appeared ahead and my stomach began to churn with nerves. What was the problem? Should I queue too? Taking the risk I drove into the melee, steering between oily drivers squatting in the shade of their trucks. They looked up as I rode past, disturbed momentarily from their games of cards or the flayed tyre they were fixing. None of them seemed bothered by the hold-up.

The queue ended at the entrance to the Vietnamese compound, an empty concrete space the size of several football pitches. On the far side a single policeman sat in a wooden box, eyeing me as I parked Panther inches in front of a small, officious STOP sign and walked towards him. The first layer of the border matrix, he glanced at my passport and waved me through. Beyond was the main compound, a series of new concrete buildings of uncertain function. In the cool, tiled interior of the nearest one a dozen truck drivers were pressed against glass windows, watching two surly female officials as they signed and shuffled paperwork. One of the women looked up and ordered me towards her with a flick of a manicured hand. *This is the easy bit* I tried to tell myself, sliding my passport under the window, my heart thundering against my ribcage.

Stamp! Stamp! went the pleasing sound of bureaucracy in action, and minutes later I was riding through No Man's Land towards Laos, my helmet slung over my handlebars.

Beyond, the Lao side of the border was a far cry from the glass and concrete efficiency of its Vietnamese counterpart. Dusty buses and trucks were parked in higgledy-piggledy rows and battered shacks leant haphazardly against each other. To the left a group of guards were absorbed in a game of *boules*. Heeding Digby's advice I drove past the trucks, the *boules*, the loitering groups of women, and hid Panther behind a large lorry. Taking off all my bike gear and smoothing down my shirt, I took a deep breath and walked up a slope to the wooden police hut.

Step one was to buy my Lao visa. Step two was to get stamped into the country by the border police. Step three was to hoof it before anyone noticed the bike.

Step one went smoothly, and with my heart pounding I handed over the $35 (£23) fee for my visa. In a spartan hut next door, two indifferent looking policewomen sat under a single poster of a red Ferrari counting the minutes until the start of their two-hour lunch break. One of them filed her nails, that common habit of bored women the world over. No flicker of interest registered on either of their faces as I passed my passport through the small window, or as the stamp came down with a thump.

'I can go?' I asked tentatively.

They nodded in unison. I hardly believed it. Step two was complete. Now for Step three – hoofing it.

I hadn't changed any of my US dollars to Laotian kip, none of Panther's paperwork was stamped by customs and I had no Lao insurance for the bike. All of them were important, but not as important as getting the hell out of there. I could deal with the rest later.

Suppressing the desire to skip, I walked slowly down the steps to Panther's hiding place behind the lorry, crammed on my helmet, turned the key, stamped the kick-start and zoomed through the open barrier. A mile later I pulled over at the edge of the road and looked back towards the border post, the straggle of buildings dwarfed by the sharp shoulders of the mountains on either side. Seeing a cloud of dust heading my way and fearing it to be the guards coming to arrest me I held my breath and tried to look inconspicuous. The cloud of dust drove past. I was safe.

Hardly believing how easy the whole thing had been, I stood on a rock and drunk in the vista of a new world. Laos. I really was in Laos.

And what a new world it was. It was as if the mountains were the heavy velvet curtain of a theatre, drawn back to reveal a wholly different reality. On the Vietnamese side, the Truong Son Mountains drop sharply to the coastal hinterland where the land is cooled by sea breezes. In Laos the cordillera slips gently down to the baking plains, the oceanic breeze replaced by a withering heat. Now, just before the rains came, the heat was at its most incendiary and the forest before me shimmered in the noon inferno. Only six hours earlier I had ridden out of Phong Nha through a drizzly grey dawn, my fleece and motorbike jacket zipped up against the cold. Now I stood in a thin cotton shirt, pounded by forty degree heat.

Glance at Laos on a world map and it is reminiscent of a tree bent over in a westerly wind. The trunk – the southern panhandle of the country – is separated from Vietnam by the Truong Son and from Thailand by the Mekong. To the south lies Cambodia. Although parts of the canopy were also flattened by bombs, it was the trunk that the Trail crept through, filtering in at Mu Gia and a handful of other passes before crossing back into Vietnam south of Sepon.

By 1966 seventy five per cent of all Trail traffic was heading to South Vietnam through the Mu Gia pass. North Vietnamese soldiers trekked through the 'The Door of Death' to join, as one soldier put it 'the endless streams of heavily burdened trucks, bicycles, elephants, and people on foot, a procession of marching ants with no purpose except to move south.'

How different my own elation was to how those men and women must have felt as they crested the ridge of the pass and started their descent, knowing the most deadly part of the Trail was before them. I imagined what it must have looked like; the lines of lumbering Soviet-made trucks, columns of weary soldiers, the jungle stripped of all life by bombs and defoliants. Through the searing haze I could make out a single gap in the jagged ridges of limestone which rimmed the valley. From here, about twenty miles away, it was barely perceptible, but since all Trail traffic had to pass through this choke point before turning south, this unknown valley became one of the most bombed places on earth – one American pilot dubbing it, 'the most godforsaken place in the world.'

Much of the damage here was done by B-52s, huge bombers that dropped their payloads from 40,000 feet. A World War Two bomber might only drop 40 tonnes of ordnance in its lifetime but B-52s, designed for nuclear warfare, could carry 32 tonnes in a single load. First used over the Mu Gia pass in April 1966, they became a mainstay of US airpower in the war; the ultimate symbol of coldblooded, mass killing.

Still incredulous at having crossed the border I drove slowly down from the pass to the *ban* – Laotian for village – of Langkhang. In Vietnam there were people everywhere, yet Laos was deserted, the only sign of life a couple of Laotian trucks heading for the border. There wasn't even a chicken or a trotting cur to signify human habitation. Laos has a population of only 6.3 million scattered over a landmass almost double the size of England, and the majority of these people live in the lowlands around the Mekong. Up here in the wild tribal lands of the Truong Son, the population is much scarcer. Whereas in Vietnam people had crowded around me every time I stopped, in Laos I might go for a day or more without seeing a soul. Loneliness was a much more real possibility here.

A small border settlement, Langkhang is the sort of place you would only stop at out of necessity. A single tarmac road ran through the centre, flanked by a shabby collection of wood and concrete dwellings. Blasted by heat and boredom, even the stray dogs scratched their fleas with a sense of listlessness. Riding slowly into the village, past a petrol station and a new karaoke bar, I pulled Panther up outside a green concrete building. The sign read 'Hostel: Massage and Steam'. Two Vietnamese lorries were parked outside, the trunks of at least twelve forest giants lashed to each one. The drivers, I suspected, were in one of the hostel's scrofulous rooms enjoying a quick pre-border 'massage'.

The hostel was Vietnamese-run and the extended family of seven were sitting down to a lunch of rice, pork and cabbage as I arrived. At their behest I sat on the floor with them, politely refusing a bowl of pork, explaining that I was *ăn chay*. A sinewy young man on my right pulled out a bottle of homemade rice wine, poured a shot and handed it to me with a suggestive smile. A large tattoo of a fish swam down his muscular left arm and he had the air of someone it was unwise to disagree with. Anyway, why not – I had good reason to celebrate. By the end of lunch the bottle lay empty in the corner, and my head was spinning from the effects of three shots of the forty-per-cent-proof moonshine. I wouldn't be driving anywhere that afternoon.

It was too hot to do anything and I sat on the steps of the hostel watching the road, pondering the next few weeks. A baby girl tottered around me, sucking on the last pork bone and pulling at the pages of my diary with sticky fingers. Occasionally a four-wheeled drive belted past, but otherwise Langkhang was deserted, driven into hiding by the ferocious heat.

Not wanting to tempt fate, I hadn't let my thoughts wander to this side of the border in the last week. Every time my mind had strayed to sitting here in Langkhang, my Other Self had turned me back, bossily closing the mental gate and telling me to return in a week's time. Now the gate had been flung open and the Lao jungle summoned me like a siren. But the Lao jungle was a frightening place; thoughts of which had kept me awake at night in the months preceding the trip. Things could get a lot dicier from now on. At around three o'clock the arrival of the two jeeps broke my reverie and Digby, Cuong, George and Roger all piled out, looking dusty and hot. Boy, was it good to see them.

'You made it!' said Roger, giving me a hug.

'Ants!' said George, following suit.

'How was it?' asked Cuong.

Digby disappeared into one of the rooms without a word, still suffering from last night's hangover.

That evening we had celebratory *Beerlaos* outside the new karaoke bar, grimacing at the awful singing that was coming from within. I still had no Lao currency and didn't want to drive ninety miles to Thakhek, on the Thai border, in order to find the nearest ATM. I asked Digby if there was another solution.

'Look, there's a money changer there,' he said, pointing to a woman sitting near us, the only visible sign of her profession a bulging black bumbag around her waist.

The woman ushered me into a neighbouring shop and we squatted behind the counter, doling out notes. Minutes later I walked out a millionaire, having changed $400 into just over three million kip. With my budget of $25 per day, it should be enough for my first few weeks in Laos.

By 9 p.m. we had all said goodnight and gone to our rooms. Tomorrow the real adventure would begin.

CHAPTER 7

THE KID ON THE KARST

By 7 a.m. the following day our convoy was turning south out of Langkhang onto the red dirt of what had been Trail Route 128. The village's wooden shacks petered out and I followed the jeeps, pulling on my goggles and Buff face mask to keep out the clouds of dust. It was exciting to be crunching over dirt, to hear the rumble of the engines, to know that we were plunging into true Trail territory.

Until now I'd had an easy ride, clipping along smooth roads at a steady 20 miles per hour. For the next month tarmac would be a rare luxury. Instead I would be coaxing the old girl along rough dirt tracks and across myriad rivers. With her city tyres, it was going to be like trying to cross a ploughed field in Christian Louboutins. Excited, and a little anxious, I'd given Panther a once-over as the sun rose over the mountains that morning, checking the oil, filling her up and making sure the brakes and chain were OK. Her green neutral light had stopped working, but that wouldn't affect her performance. Most importantly, I let down the tyre pressure a few bars to give her more grip on the dirt. There was nothing else I could do – she was a twenty-five-year-old 90-cc Cub after all, not a KTM dirt bike.

The track ran south through a Lost World landscape of thick, tinder-dry jungle and pinnacles of slate grey karst. There were no gently sloping hills, just trees, shrubs and sheer, jagged walls of rock, dropped at random into the landscape. To our left rose a high ridge, its surface punctured with numerous caves and dark recesses. But the most arresting thing about this new landscape wasn't the jungle, or the rocks, or the billowing dust. It was the steady procession of smooth, gaping holes in the ground on either side of the road. Some were a few metres wide; some were large enough to swallow both jeeps. All had been gouged out of the earth by American bombs.

The craters were a reminder of the obsessive lengths the US went to in order to cut the Trail. Fearing a communist victory as much as his American allies, in 1964 Lao Prime Minister Prince Souvanna Phouma had given the US the green light for 'armed reconnaissance' flights over his country. From that moment on American pilots flew 580,000 attack sorties over Laos – an average of one planeload of destruction every eight minutes for almost a decade. Costing $2 million per day, by 1973 a stupefying total of 2,093,100 tonnes of bombs had rained down on this neutral country. Many of those killed had never seen a plane before, nor had they heard of communism or a country called America. When Hmong villagers first saw US planes on a secret runway in northern Laos, they peered under the fuselages to see what sex they were. Even with hindsight it is hard to comprehend how this tiny kingdom became a fulcrum of the Cold War; the most bombed country per capita on earth.

A few miles south of Langkhang Digby waved his arm and signalled for us to pull over.

'There are some caves in here where I found some old Vietnamese graffiti. Let's go in and have a look.'

The boys – bristling with khaki, maps, binoculars, cameras and sun hats – hopped out of the jeeps and shook off the dust. George and Roger looked like Scouts in their shorts and matching Keen sandals.

'Watch out!' barked Digby. 'This area's full of UXO, so be careful where you put your feet.'

Clambering up into the mouth of the cave, we scanned the dried leaves and rubble under our feet. Inside, the space opened up into a series of caverns, bats flapping overhead in the darkness, and in the pale light of Digby's torch we could make out rough charcoal graffiti. Cuong, whose father had died of bomb injuries and uncle had been a Trail truck driver, translated each one. Twenty per cent of drivers had died, but Cuong's uncle had survived. 'All night I am alone, dreaming of the beautiful Vietnamese countryside,' one poignant Vietnamese description read. Next to it were childish depictions of a sad face and a stick soldier, drawn by a young soldier far from home, cowering in the darkness from the unrelenting bombs. An adjacent scribble marked the 1969 Tet holiday; another was a line drawing of a soldier. Still more bits referred to 'heroes' and 'Mother Laos'.

The thousands of caves in this honeycombed karst landscape were vital to the success and survival of the Trail. Not only were they used as storage, but they provided shelter from the deadly iron rain. A few weeks later I met a former Trail truck driver who had survived his convoy of trucks being bombed by hiding in this very cave.

Phanop, the first *ban* we came to, was a single dusty street of ramshackle stilted houses on the bank of a shallow river. Pigs and chickens scrapped in the dirt and raggedly dressed children crouched on the riverbank, watching as we splashed through the water. They gathered around us as we parked, staring curiously with huge brown eyes. The adults were more circumspect, watching silently from the shadows of their bamboo balconies. For people who hardly ever saw *falangs* – foreigners – the arrival of our motley group must have been akin to ET walking into a pub in Somerset and ordering a pint of cider. I wondered if US jeeps had ever been here before, or if any of the villagers recognised them for what they were.

In the mid-sixties Phanop found itself awkwardly placed, directly on the main Trail from Mu Gia. The Americans bombed the valley so heavily, parts of the mountains themselves crumbled and for eight years the villagers hid in caves, their rice fields destroyed, their houses flattened. Four decades later the village was still a living war museum, the likes of which I'd never seen elsewhere. Spring onions sprouted in rusty cluster bomb casings, women leant against ladders made of aluminium fuel rods, boys paddled in canoes fashioned from discarded aeroplane fuel canisters, a chicken nested in a missile nose cone, rice seedlings grew in a rusty Vietnamese helmet. Under a hut a long-lashed brown cow chewed cud, its bell fashioned from an old mortar fuse.

We walked among the dilapidated huts, trailed by an expanding flock of children, giggling and pressing in behind us.

One pulled an ingenious toy made out of three plastic bottles and bits of rubber for wheels. With no Toys R Us to nip down to, children here have to be resourceful and imaginative. The adults remained aloof, smiling and nodding from the shade of their houses.

'There's so much stuff here, the villagers will be charging entry once the word gets out,' predicted Digby.

Halfway up the street we passed two five-hundred-pound bombs lying in the dirt outside a hut. A puppy chewed an old shoe on top of the rusting steel, its wagging tale beating on the shiny fuses.

'They're definitely live,' said George seriously. 'Those fuses are still intact.'

The Lao government made the collection of UXO for scrap metal illegal in the nineties, but many poor people still take the risk. In a *ban* like Phanop, finding bombs this size was like winning the lottery. At around $0.30 per kilo, their scrap metal value could feed a family for weeks. The owner was likely waiting for a buyer, or someone to work out how to defuse them. We walked quickly past, not quite knowing what it would take for them to blow us all sky high.

Farther on, outside a small wooden *wat,* temple, the faded green wing of a US F-4 fighter leant against a tree. Forty-three American planes were shot down by North Vietnamese surface-to-air missiles and anti-aircraft gunners over Mu Gia; this must have been one of them. The children peeped through an exploded hole in the middle of the wing, picking at the fraying metal. Apparently it had been left here to remind them of what had happened, although this seemed unnecessary given that their entire village was built out of war scrap.

In a parched grass field on the edge of the village we met a group of people returning from a fishing trip. Four lithe men of varying ages had nets slung over their shoulders, the youngest of whom had the most enviable pair of long, shapely legs. Beside them a little girl carried a wicker basket flopping with silvery fish.

Cuong addressed the oldest of the group, a small leathery man of about sixty, in Vietnamese.

'He Pathet Lao, he fight with North Vietnamese,' said Cuong, when the man understood him.

'*Xin chào đồng chí!*' giggled Digby. 'That means "Hello Comrade".'

The man smiled in recognition.

'He remember when that plane crashed, the one at the *wat*,' translated Cuong. 'It was in April 1969, before the rains. He say the pilot's remains are still at the crash site.'

The Americans still spend millions of dollars every year combing the jungles of Indochina for fragments of lost combatants, far more than the relatively small sums they spend on UXO clearance. If there really were the remains of a US pilot here it was big news. George, understandably empathetic towards the fate of his fellow airman, probed Cuong, who in turn probed the man. Everyone looked confused.

'Ah, I see! He say plane crash and catch fire, there was meat everywhere, the dogs took it...' said Cuong, grasping the real answer.

'Oh, Cuong! Too much!' groaned Digby, who was squatting in the dust.

George looked a little pale.

Unabated, Cuong continued, '... the dogs and wild animals ate everything, even the bones – except a gold ring which people in the village took. He say the Americans already been here and know about the crash site.'

With George and Roger present, the whole conversation felt less than comfortable.

As we parted company the old man told us to be careful where we walked; one of his seven children had been killed by a cluster bomb in this field a few years earlier.

Phanop was typical of the hundreds of Lao villages I would pass through over the coming weeks. Schools and sanitation were rare and the people lived simple, subsistence lifestyles. They hunted in the forest, kept pigs, chickens, goats and the odd cow, fished in the rivers and grew rice in their fields. To our western, urbanised eyes it might seem like a bucolic existence; an oriental version of *The Good Life*. But life in these remote villages is harsh and often short or, as one anthropologist put it, 'Hobbesian and brutish'. Medical care is, on the whole, non-existent, infant mortality and illiteracy are common, food is often scarce and malnourishment rife. And in the Truong Son region life is made harder by the pervasive threat of UXO.

The village was also representative of the complex web of Lao ethnicity. Based on linguistic diversity, the government of Laos divides its people into forty-seven recognisable ethnic groups. The most eminent voice on Lao anthropological matters, Dr Jim Chamberlain, puts the number at more than two hundred. In an effort to simplify this, Lao ethnic groups have historically been lumped into three categories based on the altitude at which they dwell.

First come the Lao Lum, the lowland majority who prefer not to stray above 300 metres. Depending on whom you speak to, these Theravada Buddhists make up between 52.5 and 65 per cent of the population.

Perching slightly higher up the mountainsides, at 300 to 900 metres, and making up around 25 per cent of the population, are the Lao Theung – literally translated as the 'Lao in the middle'. Often claimed to be the original inhabitants of Laos, these loosely connected Mon-Khmer tribes – among them Brao, Alak, Talieng, Ta Oi and Nga – were elbowed off the fertile Mekong lowlands by the invading Lao Lum.

In the loftiest reaches of the remotest mountains live the Lao Sung – the 'Lao up there' – Tibeto-Burman latecomers from China who hide in the mists above 900 metres and make up around nine per cent of the populous. Like the Lao Theung, these fiercely independent animists – the most famous of whom are the Hmong – are feared and mistrusted by the lowlanders for their strange dialects, penchant for animal sacrifice, wartime links to the CIA and perceived lack of civility. As one Laos-based British anthropologist told me, 'Ethnic minorities in Laos are seen as jungle savages who must be brought into the twentieth century, let alone the twenty-first.' Indeed, the very terms Lao Theung and Lao Sung have become derogatory, imbued with the sort of negativity that Europeans might call someone a 'gypsy' or 'tinker'.

The problem with this neat system of classification is that forced resettlement, intermarriage and a syncretisation of beliefs and traditions have made it increasingly meaningless. You might find Hmong people living by a roadside at 300 metres or Lao Lum cultivating upland rice at 600 metres or villages of mixed racial groups. Just by looking at the altitude on my GPS, I wouldn't be able to state the ethnicity of the village I was in. Very broadly, the minorities are poorer, smaller, darker skinned and have lower levels of literacy and life expectancy. Often they don't speak Lao at all. Some groups might be recognisable from their clothes, jewellery or style of houses, but otherwise trying to distinguish between this cocktail of genes is like trying to separate the eggs in a well-scrambled omelette. Even anthropologists who have worked in the country for years would struggle to walk into many villages and identify the people's ethnicity.

In Phanop, identification was impossible. Situated at 300 metres, the traditional boundary between Lao Lum and Lao Theung, the people here practised both Buddhism and *phi*, or spirit worship. As well as the *wat*, between the huts were smaller wooden spirit houses. Some were empty, others held offerings of water or dollops of sticky rice aimed at appeasing the *pha phum*, or spirits of the land. Officially banned, *phi* worship occurs all over Laos, even in the capital Vientiane. Without asking the locals, I had no idea from which ethnic group they came.

Every morning during the War, Misty pilots would take off from their base at Phu Cat in South Vietnam and fly over the spine of the Truong Son into Laos to check conditions on the Trail. Anti-aircraft gunners were their nemesis and pilots quickly learnt where the guns were, and which ones were the most accurate. As the War dragged on a legend had grown amongst the Mistys about a specific Vietnamese gunner, one of hundreds positioned near the Mu Gia choke point. Just as they entered Lao air space, a line of tracers would routinely burst from the summit of a distinctive pinnacle of rock and fall harmlessly behind them. The gunner's reliably poor hosing pattern became so legendary that Misty would send new pilots over him as a training exercise. He became known as the 'Kid on the Karst,' and in recent years the surviving members of Misty had become intent on tracking him down. They had no idea if he was still alive, or where he might be, but with Digby's help they had pinpointed the exact location of his gun emplacement.

A few miles south of Phanop we parked the jeeps and Panther under the shade of some trees at the side of the road. Across a wide, shallow river lay the Kid's karst, its base covered in scrub and jungle.

'Over beer and drinks at the club after a few hundred missions the legend of the Kid grew,' said Roger, holding the brim of his hat as he looked wistfully at the rock. He paused as two logging lorries tore past, their loads straining at rusty chains.

'We imagined how early every morning he'd haul up his daily supply of bullets and perch alone way up there. Sometimes the pilots would do a second fly-by, to let him expend his ammunition for the day. Then he could have the rest of the day off. It was far too hot to work in the afternoons anyway.'

'What are you saying?' asked George, leaning in – his hearing wasn't as good as it once was.

'Typical pilot, they never listen to Intel,' ribbed Roger. He continued. 'We made a pact at Misty, that we'd never call in a strike on the Kid. We never did, and as far as we know he survived the war.'

'How do you know it was the same gunner?' I queried.

'Well, we don't,' admitted George, 'but gunners had specific hosing patterns, and the gunner on that karst always fired in the same pattern, and always shot behind the plane. If we find him we want to fly him to America to one of our Misty reunions. It sure would be emotional.'

Earlier that day Roger had mooted an attempt to walk up to the top of the ridge, but Digby had said no, deeming the risk of UXO too high.

But now that the karst was so tantalisingly close, the thrill of the chase overcame good sense and the four of us waded across the river, watched by a brace of albino water buffalo. Cuong, sensibly, opted to stay behind with the jeeps. Walking in single file, the four of us followed a narrow footpath through the bomb craters and bushes, tinder-dry leaves crunching under our feet. Around us the trees reverberated with the metallic screech of cicadas and I could hear Roger's breathing in front of me. Tell-tale holes in the ground showed where local people had dug up bombies to sell for scrap metal.

'Stop!' commanded Digby from the front, ten minutes after we had crossed the river. There, inches from the path, lay a single cluster bomb, so small and rusty it was hard to comprehend the damage it was capable of. First used in Indochina in December 1965, forty per cent of the bombs dropped in Laos were these tennis-ball-sized killers. Released in hateful packages of around six hundred at a time, ten to thirty per cent didn't explode, leaving millions of these little puppies lying around the countryside. If there was one, there were bound to be more.

'Everyone stay fifteen metres apart, military style,' ordered Digby, serious for once. 'Then at least if one of us goes, we don't all go.'

Watching our feet intently we walked on, the path climbing to the foot of the karst. Thorn bushes pulled at our clothes and our feet slipped on the smooth, steep path. Twenty minutes later the walk became a climb, the path disappearing under rocks and piles of dry leaves. Unable to see what lurked beneath the leaves I now felt as if we were taking a stupid risk. I thought of the little boy I met the other day with MAG, and considered how much I didn't want to have my limbs blown off and die in an ambulance thousands of miles from home. Not that there was even an ambulance within half a day's drive of here.

In their eagerness Roger and Digby had pulled ahead. George and I paused, panting from heat and exertion.

'This is crazy,' I said to George. 'I'm going to go back down.'

'No, I can't really see that the reward is worth the risk,' agreed George, ever pragmatic. 'And my energy levels sure aren't what they used to be. I don't know if it's my age or the cancer.'

I loved the way George spoke; slowly, methodically, in that distinctive Detroit drawl. I couldn't imagine him ever getting stressed.

We turned around, keeping 15 metres apart as we started the nerve-wracking descent. It was smotheringly hot and the air rasped in my dry throat; goodness knows how many bombies were lying within 20 metres of us. We hopped between the rocks and dodged piles of leaves like children avoiding imaginary crocodiles. As we reached the sandy riverbank both of us breathed a sigh of relief.

'That was a little rash,' admitted George laconically.

Half an hour later a very red-faced Roger and Digby appeared out of the bushes, defeated by more bombies and brambles. Roger's elegant black silk shirt, handmade for him in Burma, was torn across the back. Stripping down to their shorts, they plunged into the river to cool off, laughing at our near miss. Finding more clues about the Kid would have to wait until another day.

George had dropped the subject of his cancer into the conversation a few nights earlier, when I had been relaying the story of my day with MAG. I told him about the two young men I'd seen whose father had been exposed to Agent Orange.

'Oh, I know all about that,' chipped in George, fixing me with his blue eyes.

'Before I joined Misty I used to have to fly cover for the planes spraying Agent Orange and other defoliants over the jungle. We always flew upwind, but traces of the stuff must have stuck to our planes. I didn't give it a second thought at the time, but a few years ago I developed non-Hodgkin's lymphoma. My oncologist says it was consistent with cancers caused by Agent Orange. I was given the all-clear just recently. I'm one of the lucky ones. At least ten other Misty pilots who were exposed to it have died of related cancers since, not to mention tens of thousands of other veterans.'

America's use of Agent Orange and other defoliants in Southeast Asia has to be the most unforgivable act of the War. Using Vietnam, Laos and Cambodia as a laboratory for chemical warfare, the USAF sprayed 72 million litres of toxic rain over the land from low-flying C-123 aeroplanes, poisoning water supplies and laying waste to thousands of acres of jungle. The point of the exercise was to strip the Viet Cong of their hiding places and lay bare their web of jungle trails, but ultimately it had little effect on their fighting capacity.

It did, however, affect more than five million Vietnamese, Laotians and Cambodians exposed to it, as well as thousands of US, South Korean, New Zealand and Australian troops who have since suffered from cancer and a host of other diseases. Worst of all, the deadly dioxin in Agent Orange worms its way into the DNA and poisons the genes for generations. The War Remnants Museum in Saigon is full of horrendous images of adults and babies born with monstrous defects caused by Agent Orange. And two generations on, the effects aren't abating. Da Nang in central Vietnam, where the chemical was stored and flown from, still has the highest incidence of congenital deformity in the world.

Yet efforts by US and South Korean veterans to extract justice from the American government and the chemical companies who manufactured it have largely failed. And an attempt in 2004 by the Vietnamese Association of Victims of Agent Orange to sue the same parties was dismissed a year later. To this day the Dow Chemical Company and Monsanto still claim that Agent Orange is harmless.

On the shady riverbank we ate a luxurious picnic of rye bread, reblochon, Port Salut, chèvre and salami, brought in cool boxes all the way from Hanoi's finest French Delicatessen. As we ate Digby pulled out a map of Laos, spreading it on the bonnet of one of the jeeps. The brown relief of the Truong Son region was riven with spidery lines made up of hundreds of thousands of red dots, so close together they looked like rivers of blood.

'This map is from USAF bombing records,' explained Digby as George, Roger and I leant over the map for a closer look.

'The Air Force kept records of the plane, the pilot's name, the latitude, the longitude, the date and the bomb damage assessment. Each of these red dots represents a single sortie. As you can see, the red lines follow the main branches of the Trail – it looks like you guys had a good idea of where you needed to hit.'

'Well, yes,' replied George, 'we got to know where the main truck roads were. What we didn't know was where all the smaller parallel routes were, and all the foot and bicycle trails. And they were building new routes all the time.'

When the US became too wise to one section of road, the North Vietnamese just extended the spider's web into another part of the jungle. As early as 1966 the communists were building sixty miles of new roads a month, much of it by hand – young men and women wielding shovels and pickaxes and moving tonnes of earth each day. Other unseen Trails were plied by an army of foot and bicycle porters; one celebrated *boi doi* pushed his bicycle 24,000 miles and hauled fifty-five tonnes of supplies over the course of the War. US intelligence couldn't keep up.

At two o'clock we packed the sweating cheeses away and continued on our way. The land was in a state of wilting catatonia, desperate for the respite of the impending rains. Leaves drooped and the singed earth was drier than the Sahara. Other than a handful of logging lorries, which enveloped us in billowing clouds of red dust, there was no traffic. The only other village we passed through was Xom Peng, prominent on old Trail maps as a *binh tram*, or supply base. Like Phanop, evidence of the War was everywhere: houses made of finest US aircraft aluminium, bomb casings, decaying fuel drums. Under the trees, children caught cicadas in plastic bags tied to the end of long poles. At the blistering end of the dry season, food was in short supply and the unlucky insects provided much needed protein.

Around mid-afternoon our progress was interrupted by a wide river crossing. At this time of year, when the water was at its lowest, four-wheeled vehicles could just about drive across, but it was too deep for motorbikes.

'You've got to take that,' laughed Digby, nodding towards an unnervingly narrow, unstable looking wooden canoe steered by a toothless old man wielding a single pole. Riding a moped across a river on a canoe was not something of which I had any previous practice. Nor was it a situation that allowed for a test run; get it wrong and Panther and I would be in the drink. Butterflies beat against my rib cage and I gulped nervously, but I had no choice. Either I man up and drive onto that canoe, or I stay on this side of the river indefinitely.

I watched the jeeps rumble across then rode down a steep sandy bank towards the waiting canoe. The old man held the meagre vessel steady as I crept Panther forward to the bow, walking my legs along the foot-high sides for balance, only a few inches spare either side of my tyres. I heard two extra passengers squat down behind me and with a thrust and a wobble the aged pilot pushed us slowly off the bank. Thrust, wobble, thrust, wobble – I gritted my teeth and swore quietly as we lurched forward, my fellow passengers laughing at my outburst.

'Think yogic, think yogic,' I muttered to myself. 'Just look straight ahead, balance and *don't move*!' I knew if I panicked and moved, all of us would be in the water.

Gripping the handlebars, hardly daring to breathe, I watched the opposite bank inch closer noticing, out of the corner of my eye, a large green lizard paddle past, eyeing me with a beady yellow eye. Sweat and suncream ran down my face, stinging my eyes and collecting in small pools at the base of my neck.

Finally the canoe slid onto the opposite bank and I paid the toothless man 6,000 kip – about eighty pence – pulled the throttle and rode shakily away, Digby cackling as he filmed my escape. That definitely counted as a significant small victory.

The architects of the government guest house in Bualapha must have once harboured delusions of grandeur. Pale pink stucco peeled off balustraded balconies, leprous patches of damp dappled the arches of ornate triple windows and the colonnaded entrance portico was ringed by the sort of bushes that suggest someone might once have done a spot of gardening. But nowadays it was a loathsome, feculent, rotting establishment seeping with canker and contagion.

The guest house had one redeeming feature – air conditioning – and it was this sole factor which led us to unload our kit into the festering interior. The only other accommodation option in town was a Vietnamese-run brothel where the pushy madam hired out her two daughters for $10 a pop, and the four windowless rooms stank of sex and cheap air freshener.

My overpriced $10 room at the government borstal was the sort of place you should only enter with a protective suit and a gas mask. The cheap plaster crawled with ulcerous patches of damp and disease, a plague of yellow and green bleeding into the blistered cream paint. Vomit-green sateen curtains hung off a plastic rail, underneath which were two single beds with thin, stained mattresses. A column of small red ants flowed across one of the beds into the bathroom; a dank affair consisting of a squat loo, a single bucket of stagnant, malarial water and a broken hose. The air was heavy with the smell of damp and drains, and fat mosquitoes lingered on the walls. Washing my hair under a trickle of brown water, I clamped my mouth shut for fear of giardiasis, botulism or worse. I'm no stranger to bad hotels but I would struggle to think of a less appealing place to lay my head for the night.

Since the guest house didn't appear to have any staff, let alone food, we walked down Bualapha's single street to have dinner at the brothel's restaurant. The two girls preened moodily in the corner while the painted madam grumpily served us Vietnamese beer and *pho*, apparently peeved to have lost our business.

Over supper I asked George and Roger how they had felt at the end of their year-long tours. Both had arrived here as young patriots, eager to fight the communist terror, confident that their nation was fighting a Just War. Thousands of veterans had returned home soaked in bitterness, remorse and disillusionment. I wondered how George and Roger had felt as their tours progressed.

'Well, I don't think our politicians did a very good job,' started George with typical understatement. 'It left an extremely bitter taste in my mouth. If we'd been allowed to bomb Hanoi and the northern ports, it might have been very different.'

Roger felt much the same.

Fearful of goading China and the Soviet Union into joining the fight, President Johnson refused to sanction ground or air attacks on Hanoi or Haiphong, the major northern port where supplies from Uncle Ho's communist allies were arriving. Many believed that a successful strike on that could have brought the North to its knees. Instead pilots like George were tasked with picking out impossible targets hidden under triple-canopy jungle. Such 'lousy tactics' were never going to win the war and alienated those who were risking their lives on the front line.

George and Roger may have felt anger towards the politicians, but they didn't go home and spend years wallowing in alcoholism and drug addiction. For thousands of American grunts returning from a year in 'Nam, life was never the same again. The war stripped away their youth and threw them into a meat grinder from which they never recovered. They went to Vietnam as eighteen-year-old American schoolboys, but came back embittered killers. In Mark Baker's excellent *Nam* one veteran writes how, 'We had a thing in 'Nam. We used to cut their ears off. If a guy had a necklace of ears it meant he was a good killer... it was encouraged to cut the ears off, to cut the nose off, to cut the guy's penis off... the officer expected you to do it or something was wrong with you.'

This wasn't a single, extreme, isolated experience. Neither was it confined to the GIs. As with any war, there were heroes and villains on all sides. The Viet Cong did unspeakable things to captured Americans. They forced allegiance from South Vietnamese villagers by tying up the local chief, cutting open his stomach and letting the pigs eat him alive. And during the 1968 Tet Offensive they murdered 3,000 unarmed civilians in the southern city of Hué. South Korean troops, 300,000 of whom fought on the American side, butchered thousands of innocent South Vietnamese villagers. But none of these incidents gained the notoriety of the My Lai massacre.

In a single horrific episode on 16 March 1968 a platoon of US infantrymen raped, mutilated and murdered an alleged 504 South Vietnamese villagers. 'Outstanding job,' praised General Westmoreland, head of the military in Vietnam, later that day. 'US infantrymen kill 128 communists in a bloody day-long battle,' shouted the *Stars and Stripes* magazine. But combat photographer Ron Haeberle's photos of the incident told a different story. So did the initially smothered reports of US helicopter pilots and GIs who had witnessed the killings. Of the twenty-six soldiers eventually charged, only one was actually convicted – unemployed college dropout turned platoon leader, Second Lieutenant William Calley. His punishment was a risible sentence of three and a half years under house arrest.

Thousands of veterans never recovered from what they saw and partook in. Of the three million US servicemen who went to Southeast Asia between 1964 and 1974, 150,000 have since committed suicide. Several hundred thousand more have ended up in prison or with life-long mental illness. I don't wish to diminish their experiences or personal bravery, but George and Roger were exposed to a very different war. Neither man endured the hell of Khe San or Huế, or saw tens of their friends die in front of them in a war they didn't believe in. As travel writer Norman Lewis wrote in *A Dragon Apparent* in 1949, 'Space, like time, anaesthetises the imagination. One could understand what an aid to untroubled killing the bombing plane must be.'

The air war had been a very different war.

We walked back to The Hell Hotel under a clear, starlit sky and I gingerly climbed into the bed with the fewest ants in it. First though, I checked under it for snakes, spiders, people or anything else of interest – a childish habit I've never grown out of. Closing my mouth and pulling the cotton sleeping bag tightly around me, I tried not to think of the malaria and the mould. Above me the air-conditioning unit rattled and wheezed. It was going to be a long night.

CHAPTER 8

THE RACE TO BAN LABOY

Between islands of sleep I decided that this would be my last day with the boys. This journey was about going solo. I couldn't hang on to their coat-tails forever. It was a hard choice; with Cuong translating in the villages and their joint expertise I was getting a mass of information. But I had lost that feeling of self-reliance and independence, wasn't thinking for myself and felt one step removed from Laos and its people. After three days on the road in Vietnam I'd learnt a useful smattering of Vietnamese, but after three days in Laos I'd stalled at *sabadi* (hello) and *khawp jai* (thank you). It was time to cast off the safety net of numbers and dive into Laos alone.

Over an early breakfast of *pho* and several strong Vietnamese coffees, Digby outlined the plan for the day – a sixty-mile drive on dirt roads to the town of Vilabury via a famous river crossing called Ban Laboy. A shallow ford over the Nam Ta Le River a few miles from the Vietnamese border, it had been a major target for two reasons. Firstly, the trucks were forced out of the tree cover to cross the water, thus making them visible to US planes. Secondly, it was the gateway to Ban Karai, one of only four passes over the Truong Son. Like Mu Gia, it was clobbered by US bombs.

'Ants, there are two routes from here – a longer, easier one and a harder shortcut,' Digby told me before we left. 'We're going to take the easy route. It's up to you which way you go.'

Exercising my stubborn streak, I waved goodbye to the jeeps ten miles south of Bualapha and turned east down the shortcut to Ban Laboy. I would either meet them there or at a hotel in Vilabury at the end of the day.

It was a still, sultry morning and the ridge of the Truong Son was blanketed by low-lying cloud. Off the 'main' road the route narrowed to a sunless track hemmed in by a towering bodyguard of trees. A tangle of greenery thrust inwards, primordially dense and stiflingly humid. Far above, the canopy fingered its way across the divide. In Vietnam there had always been some sign of civilization – people, tarmac, houses, buffaloes -but now it was just me, the Trail and the dark knot of trees. For the first time on my journey, I was seemingly alone in the jungle.

But I wasn't thinking about my isolation, or what might be lurking within that sylvan press. I was thinking about the mud. There had been no rain overnight in Bualapha but here, nearer the mountains, an unseasonable downpour had churned the rutted red earth into a vile sludge. In places the whole width of the track had dissolved into an orange lake.

I had never ridden off-road before and my steed was ill-equipped for sliding around in jungle mud. Mighty as Cubs are, there's a reason most people choose to do journeys like this on proper dirt bikes. They have large, knobbly tyres designed to cope with difficult terrain. They have advanced braking systems. They have proper suspension. They have the necessary engine power for steep hills. C90s have none of the above. Instead they have wheels as smooth and skinny as a child's forearm and brakes that would barely stop a bolting snail.

'Relax,' I told myself, as my wheels skidded unnervingly. 'Shoulders down, let the bike find its own way.' Wearing my shoulders around my ears wasn't going to help.

As it turned out, there were other humans here; by 9 a.m. I'd passed a handful of makeshift logging camps. Despite being a National Protected Area this was clearly the source of all the logging trucks I had seen. Men slept in hammocks under blue tarpaulins and women stirred pots over fires, eyeing me suspiciously as I passed. Whenever I stopped and switched off the engine to listen to the forest, the silence was shattered by the evil whine of chainsaws. Every few miles stacks of numbered logs awaited collection. Farther on, Komatsu diggers were at work widening the track, clawing at the soil and ripping down trees. Road building and logging often go hand in corrupt hand in Laos.

Soon the forest opened out into sun-baked paddy fields, separated from the track by a rough picket fence. A mile later oinking piglets scampered as I rode into a collection of stilted huts in a dusty clearing. A handful of people watched me from the shadows of their dwellings, some timidly returning my waves, others just staring in surprise. Judging by the lack of school or *wat* and the partly shaved heads of some of the children, this was a minority *ban*. Then, slowing to say *sabadi* and wave at a stooped old couple standing by the track, my wheels slipped on the lip of a puddle and I tumbled over the handlebars. There was a painful thud as my right shin hit something hard. Embarrassed, I dusted myself off and surveyed the damage, watched by the inscrutable old couple.

Panther lay on her side in a large puddle, her front basket bent and caked in mud. Shards of glass from the smashed left wing mirror glinted in the dirt. Hauling her upright, I saw her metal foot peg was bent backwards and a section of paint had been scraped off. She no longer looked like the pristine pink city girl that had left Hanoi ten days earlier.

That'll teach me to go around waving at everyone like an imbecile, not looking where I'm going, I thought.

By now about ten people had gathered around, watching intently as I opened the top box and extracted the toolkit. No one spoke a single syllable of English, but it's amazing how far you can get with sign language and a smile. A young man in dirty blue overalls took my hammer, kneeling down to knock the basket and foot peg back in to shape while I unscrewed the useless wing mirror. To explain that I was from *Ang* – England – I handed out postcards of the Queen, Buckingham Palace and Big Ben. A little girl in a ripped, dirty orange dress poked the Queen's face and said 'Mama' delightedly, as if recognising her. I doubt they had ever heard of England, let alone ever seen Her Maj. An old man then pointed to the mountains, made thundery noises and shook his head sympathetically, as if saying 'Don't worry, it's not your fault, it's the rain.'

With a cheery wave and a throbbing shin I set off, leaving them to puzzle over their unexpected morning interlude. The incident reminded me that an adventure isn't an adventure until things go wrong. Falling in that puddle had forced me into a pleasant interaction with the villagers, which I hope had brightened their morning as well as mine. If I ever pass by again, I hope to find the Queen's face still adorning several of the huts.

More cautious after my fall, I continued east towards Ban Laboy. Tall trees soared above me, still and silent. Butterflies fluttered overhead. There was a flash of midnight blue as two imperial pheasants bustled across the track, their glossy plumage catching the light. At midday, having covered a pathetic fifteen miles in four hours, I emerged onto the old Highway 20. Blasted through the mountains between here and Phong Nha in a superhuman three months in 1967, the road's name was a nod to the average age of the three thousand young men and women who built it.

Nowadays it was a little used yet spectacular track, the ochre earth studded with the remnants of original Trail cobblestones. Panther bucked and skidded as we twisted up steep ridges and plummeted down forested canyons, a speck beneath the formidable wall of the Truong Son; more impressive and impermeable than I had ever seen them. But all I could think about was whether the boys would still be at the ford, and if I would make it to Vilabury that night. It reiterated why I needed to travel alone; instead of going slowly and immersing myself in the experience, I was rushing. Rather than easing the bike up the steepest hills, I was thrashing the engine in first gear.

And when I arrived at Ban Laboy two hours later, I was irritated and hot and in no mood to appreciate the beauty and tranquillity of the river. I was annoyed about how much I'd had to push myself and the bike to get here, about my aching leg, about finding the boys parked on the far bank, and even more irate to see that they were packing up to leave. The river was too deep to ride the bike over so I sat in a sulk beside Panther, rubbing my aching leg.

The jeeps soon splashed back through the water and stopped on the pebbles beside me. George, Roger and Cuong said hello and asked if I was OK; Roger pulling a slab of cheese out of the cool box and holding it against my leg.

'Oi, don't waste that cheese. It's Port Salut,' said Digby, who hadn't even said hello. He wasn't one for sympathy.

'Bugger the cheese,' I replied moodily, pressing it harder.

With only four hours left before nightfall, there was no time for an altercation over the Port Salut.

'You're not going to get to Vilabury tonight,' said Digby. 'There are a few villages on the way you might be able to stay in though.'

His comment came down on me like a chequered flag. Pulling Panther around, I set off up the hill in front of them, flinging the bike through puddles and over uprooted cobblestones. I was determined to not only get to Vilabury, but to beat them to it.

For the first hour I fought both the mud and my own petty fury, but then the red mist turned to adrenaline and I began to love it. All I could hear were the whirring of the engine and my own thoughts; nothing else in the world mattered. Leaning around corners and thudding over potholes at the warp speed of 20 miles per hour, I felt like Valentino Cubossi.

Khammouane, the province I was riding through, was spliced by hundreds of rivers and streams rushing down from the mountains to join Mother Mekong. That day alone, I must have crossed fifteen of them. A few had some sort of makeshift bridge – questionably stable structures made of bamboo or galvanised metal – but on the whole it was a case of assessing the depth, pulling the throttle and hoping for the best. The key was to wait until another moped arrived and observe their tactics. Failing that, I had to wade in and check the depth, then opt for the best course.

As an off-roading novice my technique left a lot to be desired. About halfway across a river or stream there would be a loud hissing as the engine hit the water, followed by a clunk and then silence. Getting off and kicking the gears into neutral, I would heave Panther to the other side, my Gore-Tex walking boots filling with mud and water. Incredibly, the bike always revived at the first kick-start. What a marvellous little machine she was.

Towards late afternoon, as thunder pealed around the mountains and a few fat drops of rain hit my nose, I came to yet another river. A beautiful teenage girl was waist deep in the brown murk, elegantly washing her long black hair. There were no other mopeds in sight and it didn't look deep, so I pulled the throttle and gunned it across. Halfway, there was the usual hiss, clunk and then silence. Leaping off, I forced Panther through the mud and over two submerged logs, letting out an unsavoury Monica Seles-style grunt as I propelled her over the last log. Muddy, wet, sweaty, grunting, brutish – how uncivilized I felt compared to my silent, graceful witness.

'What a bike!' I exclaimed, as Panther hummed to life on the other side and we rode away, waving to the bemused girl.

Traffic was minimal; a few mopeds per hour, the odd grazing cow and a handful of *tok toks* – a prehistoric-looking tractor-trailer hybrid common in much of Southeast Asia. These would chunter past me loaded with passengers sheltering from the heat and raindrops under brightly coloured parasols.

'*Pai sai* – where are you going?' they would shout as I rode past.

'Vilabury!' I'd shout back, my answer lost in the noise of our passing engines.

The few villages I saw were simple collections of stilted wood and bamboo shacks populated by pot-bellied pigs and filthy children, the adults always outnumbered by their offspring.

At some point I crossed the unmarked provincial border between Khammouane and Savannakhet. And by 5 p.m. I was on the home run to Vilabury, chasing the lengthening shadows through a darkening tunnel of trees. There was still no sign of the jeeps and despite nearly three hours of solid riding since the ford and no food since breakfast, I was buzzing with adrenaline and admiration for the bike.

Then, without warning, Panther faltered, as if gasping for breath. 'Oh no, not the petrol,' I cringed.

My whole family has a talent for running out of petrol; some sort of aversion to the mundanity of the filling-up process. I could have bought a litre in a village that afternoon, but in my fervour hadn't wanted to break my rhythm. The petrol gauge was under the seat and the only way of checking the level was to stop, take off the panniers and lift up the seat; a boring waste of time. Instead I chose to carry on, confident that I would have just enough fuel to reach Vilabury. I feared I was about to pay for my impatience.

Panther gasped again and shuddered to a halt on the dirt track. A quick check showed the gauge to be lying despondently below the red. On tarmac the bike had a range of 120 miles – more than I would ever need – but the day's rough riding had sliced that in half. I had well and truly run out of petrol.

Without the noise of the engine I was immediately aware of how alone I was. The safety of the town was just ten miles away, but it was getting dark and I hadn't seen anyone for an hour. As I pondered my next move, however, a moped miraculously materialised out of the gloom. It halted beside me and two thirty-something Vietnamese men – lighter-skinned, slightly taller and with narrower eyes than their Lao neighbours – stepped off. As I pointed out my problem, the two men nodded and agreed to siphon a litre of fuel out of their bike into my empty tank. Then another moped turned up. This time two young Lao men stopped to watch the show, lighting up cigarettes as they did so. Programmed by English sensibilities, I flinched at the proximity of the naked flame to the exposed petrol.

Midway through the exchange, one of the Vietnamese grabbed my right boob, grinning.

'Oh, for God's sake!' I said, firmly removing his hand. 'You're kindly helping me with petrol, now's really not the time to be grabbing my boobs.'

For a second it crossed my mind that I was deep in the Lao jungle, at twilight, with four strange men. But like the earlier cash offers, it felt more like an annoyance than a real danger. Instinct told me they wouldn't take it any further.

At that moment, a familiar engine noise signalled the arrival of the two jeeps.

'I ran out of petrol!' I laughed, as they pulled up behind the three bikes.

'Are you OK?' asked Roger, leaning out of the front passenger door

I insisted they go on, saying I'd catch them up. Roger, who had children my age, looked concerned, as did George and Cuong. Digby remained silent. Roger later told me that Digby hadn't wanted to interfere, knowing how intent I was on doing this journey solo. Perhaps that explained his strangeness at Ban Laboy.

'Go on! It's fine, really,' I urged, and off they roared down the track.

The boob incident forgotten, I thanked the men and offered them a few dollars. When they refused I cranked Panther's 7.5 horsepower into action, thanked them and sped off in chase of the jeeps, squeezing past them a few miles farther on. For the next hour I had the most joyous ride, storming along the dirt, weaving between potholes, mud and dust spraying up behind my wheels – sheer exhilaration. When I hit the tarmac road of Vilabury's main street I stood up on the pegs and whooped in excitement.

I'd made it! What a day! A victory indeed.

By the time the jeeps drove through the hotel gates I had already unloaded the bike and drunk half a warm *Beerlao*.

'How old is your father?' asked Roger, as he carried in his dust-coated bag.

'Seventy-three, the same age as you. Why?'

'Well, if I was your father I'd be really proud.'

I was very touched.

If I had been a young American in the sixties, I would probably have been one of the thousands marching on the White House, yelling for the War to stop. I am against everything the conflict represented: foreign imperialism, the death of six million Indochinese, Agent Orange, the blanket bombing of neutral countries. George and Roger had been part of that conflict, had guided thousands of tonnes of bombs on to the land we now stood on. But that was all a long time ago. In the context of the sixties, the Cold War and the Cuban Missile Crisis, George and Roger, and millions of other Americans, believed they were doing 'the right thing'.

In the same way, British Tommies who fought the Germans on the Western Front thought they were doing the right thing. Paul Tibbets, the pilot of the B-29 plane that dropped the bomb over Hiroshima, thought he was doing the right thing then and to the day he died. All of them were fighting for a cause they believed in, doing as their countries had asked them. The men who fight in wars are not the war itself. As Bao Ninh wrote in *The Sorrow of War*, 'The ones who loved war were not the young men but the others like the politicians... not the ordinary people.' And for Roger in particular, the war still wasn't over. Guilt, compassion and God had drawn him back here year after year. I'd become very fond of them both.

The next morning, after an unhurried intake of saccharine 3-in-1 Nescafé and greasy omelette, the boys packed up the jeeps to leave.

'Ride safe,' said Digby, pecking me on the cheek and clambering into the back seat.

'Don't forget to put oil in the bike and check the chain,' added Cuong, ever the mechanic, from behind his black wrap-around sunglasses.

'Please email when you can to let us know you're still alive,' said the Mistys, looking like a pair of worried grandfathers.

A moment later I was alone; a solitary figure waving as the green jeeps vanished down the road to Sepon. No tears or sadness, just an acceptance that the next chapter had begun.

The previous day's jungle TT had taken its toll and my aching ribs, swollen shin and stiff arms were in no hurry to go anywhere. Panther was in need of a good clean and service, my sodden boots could do with drying out, it was high time for another *cắt tóc'* and I had some much needed mapping to do. Riding could wait for a day, or perhaps even two.

Locals have long known this district as Muang Ang Kham – place of the gold valleys – and Vilabury is quite literally sitting on a gold mine. In the early eighties Soviet geologists found villagers panning for gold using chunks of shrapnel and bits of US plane wreckage. A decade later, when the Laos government had lowered the red tape enough to let foreign investors in, Australian surveyors started sniffing around. In 2002 they opened Laos' first modern mine, the Sepon gold and copper mine. I say modern because the site, situated on an ancient trade route between Thailand, Laos and Vietnam, had first been mined for copper 2,000 years ago.

Ten years on the open cast mine, a few miles south of Vilabury, has transformed the place from a UXO-ridden backwater to a rapidly growing town; an island of health and safety in the middle of the wilderness. The main street hums with Toyota Hiluxes and minivans full of Laotian men in orange overalls and yellow hard hats. Sold to a Chinese company for more than a billion dollars in 2009, the mine is now one of the country's biggest employers. It pours over $100 million per year in tax into the coffers of the Lao government, and at dusk each day an armoured convoy rumbles through the town carrying the daily booty of $800,000 worth of copper. Gold bars are flown to Vientiane from the private airstrip within the mine.

From a ruined house on a hill above the mine you can see the huge scale of the operation: beeping lorries, trundling earth-movers, scurrying men, processing plants, accommodation, canteens, car parks. The hills for miles around bear the scars of new excavations, suggesting there is some truth to the rumours that the gold is running dry.

To assuage its conscience the mine does nice things like fund archaeological digs and wild elephant counts, and teaches its employees English. One of these men, Phouvath, a twenty-four-year-old welder, lived with his new wife Kula at the hotel and was on a two-week stand down from work. A pocket-sized Lao with pale skin, almond-shaped eyes and a girly voice, Vath – pronounced Vat – spoke good English and went everywhere with a yapping Bichon Frisé. Named after a Korean cartoon character, the revolting mutt had suppurating eyes, a pink topknot and its own basket attached to the handlebars of Vath's moped.

Vath, like so many Laotians, was both kind and horizontally laid back. In the two days I ended up staying at the hotel, he, Kula and the four other live-in staff spent a large proportion of their time engaged in the art of idleness. All of them had very specific jobs: Kula and another pretty teenage girl cleaned the rooms, the quiet old man was the outdoor cleaner, the plump middle-aged lady was the cook and the shy, one-eyed man did 'lights and maintenance'. But since I was the only guest they weren't exactly run off their feet and most of their time was

133

spent sitting under a shady pergola, listening to Lao pop on their mobile phones, gossiping and eating.

The Lao have long had a reputation as fun-loving idlers. In the fourteenth century Fa Ngum, the founding monarch of the original Kingdom of Laos, described his people as preferring to go to 'festivals than into battle'. Henri Mouhot, the French explorer often mistakenly credited as 'discovering' Angkor Wat in 1860, wrote of the Lao, 'Their poverty results from excessive indolence, for they will only cultivate sufficient rice for their own support. This done, they pass the rest of their time in sleep, lounging in the woods, or paying visits to friends.' Almost a century later Norman Lewis echoed this, observing, 'It is considered ill-bred and irreligious in Laos to work more than necessary.'

Today it seems the same still holds true. The government and a clique of Vientiane-based, western-influenced businesses might be busy making money out of the country's natural resources, but the average Lao is busier lying in a hammock. It's as if achievement is measured by who can do as little as possible, for as long as possible, in as much shade as possible.

This lethargy was something I ruminated upon as I passed through endless villages of dozing adults. In our culture, the fine art of doing nothing has been lost in the stampede to achieve and accumulate. But isn't idleness in fact a form of wisdom? For fifty weeks of the year many of us set the alarm, put on a suit, cram onto the Underground, hunch over a computer, go to the gym, go to bed, set the alarm, put on a suit and tie... All so that one day we can retire, relax, lie in a hammock, do nothing. Most Lao have skipped the suit and tie bit and gone straight to the hammock.

But in the West, on the whole, idleness is a choice; a luxury of age and wealth. In Laos, it was hard to delineate between enforced and chosen sloth; was it boredom or contentment I saw on people's faces? In the past Laos was an isolated, mountainous kingdom, bursting with natural bounty. Today the forests and their wildlife are diminished, the culture diluted with western influences and much of the land poisoned with UXO. In most rural areas schools are scarce – a recent Asian Development Bank report put literacy rates for Lao ethnic minorities at 33 per cent – and, beyond growing the basic necessities for survival, there is little else to do. With very little money, little or no education and, in many cases, no language skills beyond their own tribal dialect, what other options do they have?

Ten years ago, when Vilabury was little more than a village, the smart pink hotel where I was staying had been one of the first. Now there were several newcomers and I was a rare pay-per-night customer; most of the hotel's dwindling income came from charging rooms out at 30,000 kip – £2.30 – per hour. But a clean, mould-free room was yours for £4 a night – heaven compared to Bualapha's hell.

To supplement their meagre incomes, the staff made full use of the available natural resources. While I cleaned and serviced Panther that morning, the cook caught geckoes with a noose tied around the end of a long stick. She was surprisingly adept, plopping her wriggling catches into a dirty white bucket, where a terrified clutch of the creatures sat frozen in terror.

'They're delicious with mangoes and chilli,' chuckled Vath, seeing me wrinkle my nose.

When lunch was served a few hours later, I could make out the tails and feet amidst the slices of tart green baby mango, and politely declined a taste.

The next day the cook appeared looking triumphant, clutching a bulging dishcloth crawling with ants.

'It's a red ants' nest,' said Vath gleefully. 'She found it in some bamboo.'

Soon after, the cook waddled out of the kitchen holding a steaming pot of green goo, hundreds of ants' legs sticking out like tiny red candles. Everyone sat under the pergola and tucked in hungrily.

'They're cooked with jackfruit and chilli – try some,' offered Vath, chewing on a mouthful. The others laughed.

'No thanks.'

Then, remembering my 'Yes' rule, 'Actually, yes please. I'll try a little bit.'

Digging a spoon into the pile I lingered a little too long on the forest of legs, antennae and abdomens, then – closing my eyes – popped the whole entomological lot in. It was spicy, slightly crunchy, tasty and not remotely vegetarian. *Goodness knows what gastronomic depths I'll have plumbed by the time I leave Laos*, I thought. Would nothing with legs or wings now be safe from my carnivorous ravages?

It wasn't just the hotel staff who enjoyed a bit of wild food. Among the mangoes, garlic, tiny red chillies, squirming black catfish, knots of rice noodles and bags of peanuts on offer at the tin-roofed food market was a dead civet. Slung over a cardboard box like a discarded jumper, the dead cat stopped me in my tracks. It seemed so wrong to eat such a beautiful wild creature. But poverty and the country's once abundant forests have given the Lao a taste for jungle fare and I never once went to a market without seeing at least one dead rare animal, caught for the pot. Porcupines, snakes, hornbills, bamboo rats, monkeys, parrots, frogs, civets; anything with fur, feet, feathers or claws was game.

On my second night in Vilabury I wandered up the main street, past the Vietnamese *cắt tóc'* – the best yet at £2 – past the moped mechanic, past the shack selling stickers of Lenin, Che Guevara, Trotsky and Uncle Ho. At the first galvanised metal and wood restaurant-shack I came to I sat down and ordered *cao neo* – sticky rice – a *Beerlao* and stir-fried greenery. In the corner a man and two teenage boys lay on a communal bed watching a Thai soap opera, while the wife stood up to cook.

It would have been another unmemorable meal had it not been for a splenetic row that erupted between the two boys. For half an hour they circled the restaurant spitting fury and invective at each other across the empty bamboo tables, ignoring the mother's pleas to calm down. It culminated with the elder boy flouncing out, and the younger collapsing into howling sobs on the bed. The Lao are generally gentle people, who give great importance to the philosophy of *jai yen* (cool heart) and *bo pen yang* (no worries); it was the only time I ever saw a Lao lose their temper. I can only imagine it must have been over a girl.

As I walked back to the hotel a moped slowed and lingered on the road near me, and I could feel a man staring at me through the darkness. Pretending to ignore him I quickened my pace, turned into the hotel gate, walked to my ground-floor room, closed the door behind me, locked it, and pulled the chain across. Leaning against the door in the dark I listened as the moped pulled up outside and footsteps approached across the courtyard and along the corridor, stopping outside my door. The owner of the footsteps then started banging on my door, shouting in what sounded like Vietnamese.

Perhaps the sensible thing would have been to ignore him until he went away. But the fact he'd had the gall to follow me to my room infuriated me, and this was one unsavoury male encounter too many. So instead of quietly waiting for him to give up and take his lechery elsewhere, I undid the chain and opened the door.

A five foot nothing of a man of about fifty stood before me, a cigarette in one hand, the other fist raised mid-hammer. He was swaying slightly and doing that disgusting suggestive pointing thing. I don't remember anything about his features, just that everything about him repelled me.

'NO! Fuck off!' I screamed, slamming the door in his face.

Immediately the footsteps retreated down the corridor and I heard his moped pull away. I doubted he'd be coming back for more.

CHAPTER 9

ALL ROADS LEAD TO SEPON

In spite of my proclivity for travel, my navigational skills are somewhat lacking. I can read maps, but somehow I rarely end up where I intended. My mother, who could get herself home from Novorossiysk blindfolded, is forever amazed by this, and never tires of asking, 'But how *did* you drive all the way home from Thailand?' The answer: I was travelling with Jo then, and Kazakhstan has only one north–south road.

Navigating the labyrinthine Ho Chi Minh Trail solo was a little harder. In the early days of the Trail it wasn't uncommon for *boi dois* to get lost in the jungle and never be seen again. And while Vietnam now has good maps and signed roads, the part of Laos I was travelling through was surprisingly uncharted. There were no publicly available paper maps of Laos with anywhere near the level of detail I needed. And the only things marked on Google maps were international borders and the occasional bigger town like Sekong. Otherwise the Truong Son region of Laos was a big green and white blank.

Fortunately Don Duvall, the American biker I had met the previous year, has taken this matter into his own hands. Dubbed the Midnight Mapper, Don has spent the last decade mapping Laos from the back of his Honda dirt bike: to date recordeding more than 50,000 GPS points and producing an unrivalled digital map of the country. His findings, in the format of a $50 SIM card compatible with handheld GPS units, would be an invaluable asset to my journey. Some might say, 'Pah, that's cheating. She should be using a compass and the stars,' then throw down this book in disgust. But if I had opted for the old-fashioned method, I might have gone the same way as those early *boi dois* and still be lost and starving in the jungle.

Two mornings after I'd waved goodbye to the boys I sat in the empty hotel restaurant roughing out my route through Laos. When my GPS unit was connected to my laptop I could view Don's data through a mapping software programme, allowing me to plot my route much more effectively. The tiny screen of the unit was only really good for glancing at when you were riding, to check you were going in the right direction, or to look up place names and local detail.

In conjunction with Don's modern map, I was using a copy of an old map of the Trail, obtained from the Ho Chi Minh Trail Museum in Hanoi the year before. The detailed map, drawn by a Vietnamese military cartographer, was entitled 'Truong Son Strategic Road System – Ho Chi Minh Road: In the Anti-American Resistance War of Vietnam People to Save the Country (1959–1975).' It showed a web of red and black numbered roads, communication networks, a petrol and oil pipeline, airfields, the Trail command's headquarters, *binh trams* and footpaths running through Vietnam, Laos and Cambodia.

My choice of route was governed by man and nature. In the five decades since the end of the War much of the old network had been reclaimed by the jungle, particularly the smaller footpaths. Other stretches were in restricted border areas, blocked off by mining, logging and controversial dams, or too heavily contaminated by UXO. Using the old Route 128 – known as 911 to the Americans – as a backbone, I would ride south via Sepon, Nong, Ta Oi, Kaleum, Sekong and Attapeu. Here I would turn west towards the Mekong, along the old Route 18, before crossing into Cambodia near Si Phan Don. I had no fixed schedule, I'd just get on Panther every day and ride, deviating when and if I felt like it.

At 9 a.m. it was already murderously hot and even the mild exertion of loading up Panther sent trickles of sweat running down my back and chest. By now the packing process was a familiar routine and took no more than five minutes from room to riding. Before leaving my room I would strap on my concealed money belt and bumbag; then in one go lug my panniers, backpack, jacket and helmet to the bike; cram the backpack into the top box, on top of the resident toolkit and C90 Haynes Manual, and hoist the eight-kilo panniers over the seat, securing them with two bungees. The final piece of the packing puzzle was to load the front basket; home to the tyre pump, spare inner tubes, water and snacks.

As I was attaching my panniers Vath, off to a local wedding in his best white leather shoes, the newly washed mutt panting in his basket, came to say goodbye Afterwards I paid my tiny

£12 hotel bill, wrote the staff a thank you note on a postcard of the Queen and set out for Sepon, thirty miles to the south.

There hadn't been a single C90 wing mirror in Vilabury and my efforts to gaffer a small make-up mirror to the handlebars had failed. With one wing mirror, a broken odometer, no neutral light and scraped paintwork, Panther was accumulating a litany of minor injuries. As recompense, she was sporting two new stickers of Che Guevara and Lenin, and my bashed shin was feeling considerably better.

Following the old Route 128 south I passed a string of very poor *bans,* deserted in the heat, the stilted houses built around gaping rubbish-filled bomb craters. Red UXO warning markers poked out of the dust and wooden noticeboards displayed faded pictorial posters warning people against picking up bombies. UXO was a huge problem in the province of Savannakhet, particularly on this old Trail route. When Truong Son commander Dong Sy Nguyen visited the area during the war he wrote, 'Almost all the trees are withered away and there remains only dry trunks under the blue sky.' A Swedish explosives expert who had worked for the mine told me that in a single day the previous year he had found two five-hundred-pound bombs, a mortar and a phosphorus bomb, all within metres of the tarmac road I was now riding on.

Ten miles from town I came across a very different sort of gold mining. Around twenty men, women and children were dotted across the wide, shallow water of the Nam Kok River, busy in the various stages of small-scale gold extraction. They were diving, shifting rocks and panning in the water for specks of the metal in wide aluminium bowls.

Parking Panther under the shade of some trees I sat on the pebbly riverbank to watch, my presence eliciting ripples of curiosity. Nearest me, a group of three young women laughed when I said *sabadi*, returning my greeting with smiles and looks of surprise. Thumbing my phrasebook to find the word for 'gold' I asked them if they had found any. They shook their heads – not yet.

In the shallows nearest me two tiny girls, no more than five, expertly rocked and circled their pans, lifting them close to their faces to inspect the grey sediment. Beside them the three women – fully clothed and soaking – tugged at rocks to loosen the fine silt on the riverbed beneath. In the middle of the river a small, lean, muscular man sang and laughed as he dislodged rocks with his feet, his eyes red from the water. His teenage daughter, again fully clothed, dived next to him in a rudimentary mask. Everyone returned my *sabadis* cheerily and continued with their work. More groups of people arrived: a family of four on a moped, a single barefoot man with a pan under his arm and three older women on foot, wearing *sins* – traditional hand-woven sarongs – and chequered headscarves. The latter's dress, wider faces, higher cheekbones and darker skin suggested they were of a different minority, although I didn't know which.

From Moses to Midas and Croesus to Columbus, humans have been obsessed with gold. The shiny metal has cast a perfidious spell over us for millennia, building empires and destroying civilizations. These poor villagers were no different, although they wouldn't even be building houses with their meagre finds. The tiny amounts of gold they pulled from the river were simply a means of survival, a way of feeding their families in the dry season when the river was low and food supplies scarce. These were the same people who went out with cheap Vietnamese metal detectors in search of scrap metal, a valuable 'dry season crop'. Searching for gold, as opposed to potentially fatal bombs, was both safer and more lucrative.

After about half an hour, one of the young panners closest to me beckoned me over and smiled as she pointed to the bottom of her pan. She crouched on her haunches, a floppy camouflage hat casting a shadow over her small pretty face, her black and white striped shirt soaking and muddy. A crumb of gold, about a fifth of a gram, glowed in the sunlight. At the time of writing gold is worth $1,800 an ounce, which would make this speck worth about $12 on the market. She wouldn't have received anywhere near this price from the Vietnamese middle-men these villagers sold it to, perhaps as little as $2. But that would be enough to feed her family for several days.

Wrapping her find carefully in a cotton rag, she put it in her shirt pocket and sat on the pebbles with the other women for some lunch, ushering for me to join them. Plastic bags of *cao neo* and spicy sauce were pulled out, to which I added bananas, a bag of peanuts and chunks of sugary peanut brittle. Grubby hands dived into the bags, deftly rolling the rice into balls and dipping them into the sauce. Gums were smacked, peanuts crunched and there was much chatter and conviviality, my seven companions giggling as I ate, one of them filming me on her pink Nokia. If only I could have understood what they were saying; at times like this the language barrier was a frustrating obstacle.

The only *falangs* that villagers in this area ever saw were aid workers in white Land Cruisers and American MIA teams leaping out of helicopters. A lone female traveller was cause for much confusion – where was I from? How did I get here? Why was I alone? By way of explaining my arrival I wheeled Panther down the bank, causing nods of understanding and a few giggles. One of the men circled her approvingly, as if eyeing up a prize buffalo, exclaiming *Xin chào!* – 'hello' in Vietnamese' – when he saw the white Hanoi plates.

By the time I left it was 1 p.m., the hour of mad dogs and Englishmen. Although today not even the dogs were venturing outside. I rode on through a bomb-blasted landscape of desolate villages and cracked paddies. The tarmac shimmered with mirages and even the wind felt hot, as if I was riding into the open door of an oven. After an hour I had to escape. In the next *ban* I stopped at a thatched hut which doubled as a home and the village shop. Pulling off my boiling motorbike gear I bought a warm Pepsi and sat fanning myself on the ladder. A mother and daughter sat cross-legged on the floor watching me, the mother in a dirty T-shirt and *sin,* the daughter in tight jeans and green Adidas tracksuit top.

'*Hawn!*' I sighed, reverting to the English habit of discussing the weather. 'Hot!'

'*Hawn! Hawn!*' They agreed, smiling.

The hut was typical of shops in rural Lao, by day a shop, by night the family home. About fifteen square metres, the bamboo floor was covered in woven matting. In one corner was a television, in another the family's rolled up sleeping mats. The back wall was neatly stacked with shelves of *Beerlao*, Pepsi made in Vientiane, nuclear-coloured orange juice, cigarettes, sachets of shampoo and pots of Pond's skin-whitening lotion. It wasn't exactly ruthless commercialism. Most of the time shopkeepers would be stretched out on the floor like Siamese cats, dozing in the heat.

Through sign language I learnt that the mother was forty-one and the pretty sixteen-year-old girl one of her six children. The mother was so small and thin she didn't look capable of having given birth so many times, her awful teeth the only real indicator of her age. The daughter's face was slathered in whitening cream, giving her the appearance of a poorly-made up extra in a zombie film. Such treatments are sold all over Asia, the skin-whitening market in the Asia-Pacific region now valued at $13 billion according to *Asian Scientist* magazine. While we pale Brits want to have honey-hued skin like Beyoncé, Asian women aspire to Geisha-like complexions, supposedly a sign of urbane affluence. Dark skin is seen as common, the reserve of poor agricultural labourers. In India it's even possible to buy vaginal whitening creams, the advertising tagline stating that, 'Life for women will now be fairer and more intimate.' At best the products are baloney, at worst they're horribly damaging, stripping the skin of pigmentation and leaving women with blotchy, uneven complexions.

Evidently the mother thought my Lao could do with some improvement. Watched by a swelling audience of local children, she took out her till – a plastic basket full of kip notes – and embarked on a rudimentary counting lesson. It reminded me of something I'd felt a lot on this journey, that travelling alone in a country where you don't speak the language reduces you to the level of a child. I was no more than a dumb curiosity, unable to communicate properly, ignorant of the language and the nuances of social mores. Often, when people didn't know what to do with me, they would hand me their babies or send the children to play with me. In the absence of linguistic communication it was a way of breaking down barriers. Perhaps every race has an innate belief that all foreigners are stupid, especially ones that turn up on their own on old pink mopeds.

At the village of Nabo I turned east along the Sepon valley, the high ridges on either side blanketed in a heat haze. A few miles later a straggle of half-built concrete houses and wooden shacks marked my arrival in the town of Sepon.

Sepon – or Tchepone as the Americans referred to it – became a White House obsession. By the late sixties the small town, eighty miles south of Mu Gia and a mere thirty miles from the border with South Vietnam, was the epicentre of the Ho Chi Minh Trail. Hemmed in by thick jungle and high ridges, the valley was a hornet's nest of caves, supply bases, truck parks, ammunition stores and anti-aircraft emplacements. It was also the alleged location of the 559 Headquarters, an underground redoubt believed to be the largest Trail command centre outside North Vietnam. The Americans knew that if they wanted to cut the Trail and win the war, they had to take Sepon.

Yet while the US was unloading tonnes of bombs on to Laos every hour, the 1954 and 1962 Geneva Accords still meant that not one American soldier was allowed to set foot on Laotian soil. Covert US Studies and Observation Groups (SOG) teams had been sneaking around lower Laos for years, but the White House couldn't risk the press getting the slightest whiff of this. A full-scale US ground invasion of Sepon was hence out of the question. As American journalist Henry Kamm wrote, 'Tchepone became to many Americans and South Vietnamese military leaders what Moby Dick was to captain Ahab – the object of an obsessive, destructive quest.'

The answer, the White House believed, lay in President Nixon's policy of Vietnamisation, 'To expand, equip and train Southern Vietnam's forces and to assign to them an ever-increasing combat role, at the same time steadily reducing the number of US combat troops.'

The plan was simple. South Vietnamese ground troops, supported by US air muscle, would nip into Laos, take Sepon, rip the Ho Chi Minh Trail at the jugular and march victoriously back into South Vietnam. With all their supply bases and command centres in ruins, the North Vietnamese would run cowering back to Hanoi and the war would be over. No US troops would so much have put a big toe on Laotian soil and all the dirty work would have been done by the US-trained Army of the Republic of South Vietnam. What could possibly go wrong?

Well, rather a lot as it turned out. It might have looked good on the back of a cigarette packet, but the plan – known as Lam Son 719 – was an ill-conceived disaster from the outset. Not only would the battle take place in hostile enemy territory, but the ARVN was an unproven, undertrained force riddled with communist double agents. By the time the South Vietnamese started to advance west along Route 9 in early February 1971 Hanoi knew exactly what was going on. Gathering over 30,000 troops in the Sepon valley, the North's plan was to 'let them in, but not let them out'.

Two months later Sepon had been reduced to a cauchemaresque mangle of craters and burnt-out houses. In forty-five days of bombardment this small valley in Laos had been hit with more tonnage of explosives than was dropped on any German city in World War Two. A bullet-ridden wall of the old *wat* and its miraculously intact golden Buddha were among the only things left standing.

The communists had indeed 'let them in'; ARVN tanks advanced fifteen miles into Laos, and two battalions of ARVN briefly 'took' Sepon. But the advance soon turned into a chaotic rout. By the end of March the ARVN had lost an estimated half of their 15,000 men and the ridges around Sepon smouldered with the wreckage of over a hundred US and ARVN helicopters. One of the defining images of the battle is ARVN soldiers hanging off the skids of US choppers in their desperation to get out.

Although the North Vietnamese also incurred heavy losses, it wasn't the hammer-blow that Nixon had hoped for.

Four decades on, the new town of Sepon is a growing settlement of 10,000 people fed by gold, timber and aid money. Half-built concrete houses sprout by the roadside and the main street hums with traffic. But reminders of the war are never far away. Stacks of rusting aircraft bombs lie outside cafes, fishermen paddle down the Sepon River in canoes made from discarded aeroplane fuel canisters, the bombed remains of the original French bridge lie forlornly next to its Russian-built replacement, and the town crawls with the white Land Cruisers of western aid agencies.

Riding slowly down the main street, I looked for a hotel amongst the usual jumble of shops, cafés, mechanics, orange 'Unitel' posters and stacks of empty *Beerlao* crates. The first I spotted was a smart Panther-pink building in a courtyard with neatly planted flowers and a newly fitted basketball hoop. Not only did the owners speak a few words of English, but the extensive menu – written in Lao and English – included bacon and pancakes. My spotless pink room had soft white sheets, hot water, a comfortable bed and air conditioning; all for £5.

Such luxury was thanks to frequent visits from American Missing in Action (MIA) investigation teams. As of June 2013 there are still 310 American MIA cases in Laos – many of them air crews from Lam Son 719 – and the US government will spare no expense in their quest to bring them home. Four times a year, teams of fifty specialists descend on Laos for a month, hire every helicopter in the country and comb the jungles for the bones and teeth of ex-servicemen. It's not only in Laos this happens. American MIA teams can be found in Vietnam, Cambodia, Korea, Japan and every other former war zone where Americans fought and died, fulfilling their motto of 'Until they are home'. Even a single tooth will be put in a coffin, draped in the American flag and flown to Hawaii with full military honours, to be identified by a forensic anthropologist. Digby had bumped into one of their teams in Bualapha a few months earlier, and another lot were due to arrive in Sepon the following month. With their specially imported bacon, basketball games, high-level security and helicopters, they must be quite a sight.

The lure of refrigerated *Beerlao* and pancakes made my hotel a favourite haunt of Sepon's foreign aid workers and I spent the evening in the unlikely company of four French, English, Welsh and Armenian UXO clearance specialists. One of them, Roly, was a pale handsome young Welshman who worked for Belgian NGO Handicap International as their Senior Technical

Advisor. Roly was a former British Army Bomb Disposal Officer, one of those ineffably brave men who spend their life neutralising and disarming mines, mortars, submunitions, aircraft bombs, rockets, artillery, grenades and cluster bombs; their CVs reading like a tour of everywhere you'd never want to go. At only thirty-two he had already served in Iraq and spent two years working for the Mines Advisory Group in Lebanon, calmly undoing the destruction of war, fuse by fuse. In Laos alone he had to deal with over 150 different types of ordnance. Bomb disposal isn't for those prone to histrionics and Roly spoke in a controlled serious way, modestly underplaying the dangers of his chosen occupation.

'I'd love to glamorise it and say how dangerous this is, but if you know what you're doing it really isn't. You only make mistakes when you're in a hurry.'

The blond Englishman sitting opposite me was less amiable. Overweight, sunburnt and cantankerous, he spent the evening sitting sullenly in the corner, interjecting grumpily. It was obvious none of the others liked him.

'I've been stuck in an office in Burma for six months, but today I got out in the field and blew up 132 cluster bombs,' he boasted, in explanation of his fuchsia face. 'We were the first people to go and clear in the area in four decades.'

When I asked him how the team was received by the villagers his reply was surprising.

'They didn't seem that pleased actually, they were more worried that we didn't do anything to upset the village *phi*.'

UXO is still a huge problem in Laos. There might be more of it in Vietnam, but in poorer Laos there are fewer internal resources to deal with it. More than 20,000 people have been killed or injured by UXO since 1975 and a *quarter* of the land surface remains contaminated. Around two hundred people are still dying every year, nearly all of them subsistence farmers in the Truong Son region. Of these, forty per cent are children.

Nowhere is more affected than this battle-scarred valley. Of all the Lao killed or injured since 1975, a quarter of them were from this region. But UXO doesn't just kill and maim, it renders agricultural land useless and disables socio-economic development. Although Savannakhet is rich in gold, copper, gypsum and tobacco, its development has been crippled. People aren't able to farm their land properly and schools, roads and hospitals can't be built without the land first being cleared of UXO. The legacy of nearly a decade of constant bombing is a significant reason why this resource-rich country still languishes near the bottom of the global economic table.

Astonishingly, the Lao government didn't do anything about UXO clearance until the mid-nineties. Impoverished, cut off from western aid at the end of the War and faced with such a monumental problem, the communist government chose the easiest solution – nothing. The tardiness could also have been something to do with the fact that the worst-affected areas were the mountainous, remote lands of the unpopular, feared minorities. Shell-shocked, hungry, displaced villagers were left to deal with it as best they could, with often fatal results.

Two decades on, Handicap and MAG are two of about fifteen UXO clearance agencies in Laos. Some of these, like UXO Lao and the Lao Military, are governmental organisations funded by major foreign entities like DFID, AusAid, USAID, Irish Aid, UNDP, the European Union and the Canadian International Development Agency. Others are foreign NGOs, funded by parties such as DFID and the EU as well as individual charitable donors. The third group are commercial profit-making companies – both local and foreign – who clear UXO for mines, hydropower projects and public works such as road building.

UXO clearance is a frustratingly slow process costing millions of dollars per year. Each organisation has to pay for expensive – often foreign – technical staff, local demining teams, specialist metal-detecting equipment, vehicles, medics, drivers and translators. The UXO is cleared by hand with detectors unable to differentiate between a rusty nail and a lethal Blu-26 cluster munition. Remote terrain is inaccessible during the worst months of the monsoon, and even the biggest NGOs may only manage to clear a few hundred hectares per year.

You might well ask how much the American government is doing to help. Not enough would be the short answer. Even though Washington is giving increasing priority to clearing ordnance of US origin worldwide, they currently donate a piss-poor $9 million a year to UXO clearance in Laos. In 2012, during Hillary Clinton's much-publicised visit to the country, she pledged a further $100 million over the next ten years. It may sound impressive, but you can bet your Great Aunt Ethel that it's a fraction of what they're spending on searching for MIA in Southeast Asia each year.

In bed that night I lay awake in the stifling heat, my mind buzzing with the evening's conversation. This was the fourth time I had been to Laos, but I still found the scale of its destruction bewildering. The more I knew about it, the more unreal it seemed. Few people in the West had even heard of

Laos in the sixties. It was a sleepy Southeast Asian backwater with one traffic light, less than three million people, no national newspaper and only 400 miles of paved road. A 1962 *Time* article wrote that, 'Though it has a king, a government and an army and can be found on a map, Laos does not really exist. Many of its people would be astonished to be called Laotians, since they know themselves to be Meo (Hmong) or Black Thai or Khalom tribesmen.'

But by 1964 the CIA's secret air base at Long Tieng, north of Vientiane, was one of the busiest airports in the world. And tens of thousands of North Vietnamese soldiers were fighting on Laotian soil. Yet as far as the outside world knew, there was no war here. It was a secret war, fought by a secret army in a land few people had heard of.

Four decades on, Laos remains an unknown war. Many Americans wouldn't be able to show you Laos on a map or tell you one thing about it, even though their bombs will be killing the Lao people for decades to come.

CHAPTER 10

GIRL ON A PINK MOPED

For such reputedly gentle people, the Lao have a surprising fondness for noise. Televisions blare horribly and Lao pop music is played as loud as the cheap speakers will allow, regardless of what time it is. The current favourite was a shrill female vocalist who wailed over the tap-tap of a repetitive four–to-the-floor beat. Played at 6 a.m. at full volume, it made for an effective alarm clock.

An hour later, having stocked up on fuel – 30,000 kip (£3.75) for a fill-up – water and bananas, I drove east out of town in the direction of the Vietnamese border. Already a heat haze hung over the adjacent ridges, the sun leaching all colour out of the landscape. Traffic was light: two white UXO Lao Land Cruisers, beaten-up Honda mopeds crawling along under 100-kilo loads of green bananas, and a Toyota pick-up truck carrying wooden chairs, a table, a fridge and two cud-chewing brown cows.

At Ban Dong I stopped for a Vietnamese coffee, rocket fuel laced with viscous condensed milk. As I drank it, a small

Vietnamese woman pulled up beside Panther on a moped. Or at least I think it was a moped, for it was piled with such a peculiar paraphernalia of objects you could barely see the wheels. The woman was perched on an inch of seat in front of a muddle of fishing nets, cooking pans and pink plastic bonsai trees. Either side of her, panniers made of chicken wire and wood bulged with flip flops, sandals, packets of instant noodles and more cooking utensils. Another basket attached to the handlebars contained plastic helicopters, spotted headbands, T-shirts and tracksuits. Somewhere in there she probably had an inflatable shark, a kitchen sink and an antique hatstand.

In the dry season the eastern side of Laos is full of these moped supermarkets. Many of them are Vietnamese farmers who supplement their income at the leanest time of year by selling a variety of wares to rural Laotians. Some specialise in speakers, others in pots and pans, some – like this lady – in absolutely anything. It's an ingenious idea which fulfils the needs of both parties. Although why anyone would need a pink plastic bonsai tree I wasn't quite so sure.

Ban Dong was the scene of Lam Son 719's most vicious fighting and Hanoi had commemorated their victory by building a large museum in the village. The pink pagoda-like structure was entirely at odds with its surroundings, as if the Imperial War Museum had been built in a Norfolk village. Behind a shiny pair of locked blue iron gates the spotless concrete forecourt was stuffed with Huey helicopters, the crashed remains of a B-52, Zil trucks, M48 tanks and bombs of every description. Everything was polished, perched on concrete podiums and surrounded by carefully planted flowers and shiny golden chains. It must have cost the victors more than a few billion dong.

As I was wondering how to get into the apparently closed museum, a smartly dressed young woman appeared on a moped and let me in, opening the darkened rooms with a few words of faltering English, a jangle of keys and a clicking of light switches. In the entrance hall a large poster proudly depicted Savannakhet's tourist attractions: rivers, waterfalls, temples, monkeys and... wait a minute, were they dinosaurs splashing about in that waterfall?

'Yes, we have many dinosaurs here,' said the woman, beaming proudly.

I presumed she meant dinosaur remains, but didn't want to quibble. As for western tourists in Savannakhet, in my experience they were almost as rare as dinosaurs.

Even though most of the descriptions were in Vietnamese, the photos alone told the story of Lam Son: convoys of trucks on bomb-pitted roads, skies swarming with American helicopters, smiling young North Vietnamese soldiers sitting on the captured ruins of South Vietnamese firebases, upturned tanks. Other photos depicted life on the Trail: elephants padding through the jungle carrying ammunition, pretty female porters shouldering boxes of bullets or baskets of rice. The happy, victorious faces told the official version of the war, the one where everyone died joyfully and skipped between the bomb craters. Not the one Bao Ninh dared contradict in *The Sorrow of War*.

I wondered what had become of those young faces, how many had survived the disease, the hunger, the bombing. How many had gone on to live happy lives.

To my delight, the last room of the museum contained a 3-metre high map of the entire Trail network, from north of Phong Nha right down to Saigon. Dating from the time of the War it was by far the most comprehensive map I'd seen, and the only one with any detail of the Trail in Cambodia. Excited by the discovery I took a number of photographs, sure it would prove a useful reference later on. A tangle of red lines tumbled through the Truong Son and beyond, so thick around Sepon and Ban Dong it was hard to tell them apart. Among them ran the thick black line of the Petrol Oil and Lubricants pipeline, constructed with the help of Soviet engineers between 1965 and1968.

War doesn't only need weapons and men, war needs fuel. Before 1965 *boi dois* had carried gasoline south inside nylon rucksacks, their backs becoming burnt and blistered from petrol poisoning. As the War escalated, thousands of barrels were transported by truck or floated down rivers. Later, in 1968 the North Vietnamese opened a 3,000-mile pipeline, running all the way from the northern port of Vinh to the heart of South Vietnam. It was an exceptional feat of logistics and engineering; in a matter of three years they had progressed from carrying gallons of fuel by hand to a pipeline of dazzling sophistication.

By the time I left the museum it was the midday inferno – far too hot to ride – so I retreated to a wooden shack opposite and sat in the shade. The lean-to doubled as a shop, café and home, and three generations of the resident family were similarly stricken by heat; too hot even for curiosity. An old couple dozed on a bamboo platform; the man snoring lightly, the woman's head lolling uncomfortably on a plastic water bottle which crackled every time she moved. Beside them snoozed two small children, their parents idling on the bench next to me. Several times, a young woman paraded past with a purple parasol, her whitened face as pale as flour, her skin shielded from the sun by cream socks, tight blue jeans and a zipped-up red Adidas top. On the curb in front of me a masked couple loaded their Daelim moped with an inestimable weight of bananas before stuttering off, both of them folded between the seat and the handlebars.

An hour later I rode due south to Nong, my tyres kicking up a wake of red dust. Between banana plantations were swathes of burning forest where flames licked the edge of the dirt. Farther on the fires had burnt out, leaving a landscape of blackened tree stumps and ash-filled bomb craters, eerily reminiscent of the War.

Despite its alarming appearance the fires were intentional, designed to clear patches of forest in order that the ground could be replanted with rice, maize and other cash crops. Known as slash-and-burn, swidden or shifting cultivation it's a practice that has been setting the hills and mountains of Southeast Asia ablaze for thousands of years. Traditionally the reserve of upland minorities, who used it as a way of rotating land use on poor mountainous soils, in today's Laos you see it at every altitude. Sadly though, the government has used this controversial practice as both a scapegoat for the country's rampant illegal deforestation and as an excuse to resettle and homogenise the more remote mountain tribes.

Resettlement is a word you hear too often in Laos. It started in the early eighties, when the fledgling communist government began to forcibly relocate what remained of the mountain-dwelling Hmong. They said it was to protect the forests from their slash-and-burn practices, but everyone knew it was a ruse to move them to lower altitudes in order to keep an eye on them. As allies of the CIA, tens of thousands of Hmong had died fighting the communists. Thousands more had fled to refugee camps in Thailand and a new life in America. Those who were left were killed, resettled and persecuted by the new government.

Soon resettlement became an official policy, aimed at absorbing the ethnic minorities into majority Lao culture. Later it spread to anyone in the way of new roads, mines, hydropower projects, hotels and logging concessions. In 2011 one hundred and two families in Vientiane were hoofed out of their homes to make way for luxury villas and a conference centre, dumped miles away with no compensation and little land. Around the same time five villages in Luang Prabang were forced to move in order to make way for a vast new golf course, a local official allegedly pocketing $2 million to ensure it all went smoothly. Stories such as this are horribly common in communist Laos, where there's no such thing as private land ownership, leaving the victims powerless to resist. Although there are efforts to change the laws, the process is proving slow and beset by strongly entrenched opposition.

I leant forward and rode past the burning forest as fast as I could. In areas along the Trail it's common for these fires to set off buried explosives and most farmers leg it as soon as they've thrown the match. Even small domestic fires are potentially dangerous, let alone acres of burning forest. In Tamluang, one of the villages I rode through that afternoon, a Blu 26 cluster bomb had lain unseen under the soil for decades until the heat of the fire a family was huddled around ignited it, killing four children and maiming three others in one deadly instant.

It was 4 p.m. when I reached the first stilted huts of Nong. This small *muang,* or town, sits on the northern bank of the Xe Banghiang, one of the multitude of rivers that winds its way from the Truong Son down to the Mekong. To get to the next town of Ta Oi meant fording the 400-metre river and driving through 50 miles of extremely remote jungle. Not only was Ta Oi known as tiger country until very recently, but the ethnic groups in this area had had little contact with foreigners. It was only just passable on a dirt bike; whether Panther could make it was questionable.

Thirsty and unsure of how to get to the river crossing, I stopped outside a corner café to look at the GPS. Outside it a small masked woman was barbecuing pig's ears, yellow fat dripping through the grill onto the burning charcoal. Hearing a loud 'Hey!' as I turned the engine off, I noticed two things at the same time. The first was that I had pulled up next to a Yamaha moped piled with luggage. The second was that two people were excitedly waving from a wooden table behind the stinking smokescreen.

Other travellers! On a moped! Dumbfounded, I jumped off Panther to say hello.

'Olivier,' said the man, coming over to shake my hand. 'And this is JJ,' he added, nodding towards his companion, a pretty Asian girl. 'Wow, I never expected to bump into a girl on a pink moped!' he exclaimed.

Olivier was Swiss, at least six foot four and equipped with biceps that could wrestle an anaconda. Half of his black hair was scraped back into a ponytail, the rest shaved into an undercut.

The single word *Boracay* was written across his white vest top. I tend to think of the Swiss as grey-suited bankers, the sort of people who like to measure things and arrange their socks in colour order. Everything in Switzerland is so neat, even the cows look like they've been trained to graze in formation. But Olivier was ebullient, twinkly-eyed and excitable, nothing like his stereotypical countrymen. His South Korean girlfriend, JJ, was about half his size, slim and delicate looking with long black hair.

Both of us were equally amazed to bump into the other and rushed to hear each other's reasons for being in Nong.

'Oh my God! Your bike's even shitter than ours, I don't believe it!' laughed Olivier, speaking English with a slight American twang.

'Er, that's the Pink Panther you're talking about. She's the best motorbike in Southeast Asia. What's your bike like?'

Their choice of steed was a newish 110-cc fully automatic Yamaha Nouvo, a twist and go with wheels no bigger than dinner plates. It was the sort of squealy moped spotty seventeen-year-olds in shell suits race around English towns on.

'Terrible!' he said delightedly. 'We bought it in Saigon a few months ago for $450 and we've already melted the engine twice. We spend most of our time at mechanics.'

Considering their combined weight, the 2,000 miles they had travelled and their choice of moped, this was no surprise.

'You should have gone for a Honda C90,' I said smugly, patting Panther's seat lovingly. 'She hasn't put a foot wrong since Hanoi.'

Retreating to the shade of the café, we sat down to hydrate and swap tales from the road. Olivier was forty-four, although he seemed ten years younger. For a decade he had been drifting around Asia, living on Thai islands, doing the odd bit of interior design and IT consultancy. He was one of the transient tribe of young Europeans who go East to find themselves. But after a while they find that years of drifting have left them with a sense of purposelessness. The novelty of escape has worn off. The adventure has become normality.

'I'm bored of living out of a suitcase,' Olivier admitted. 'I find that I'm doing more and more extreme things in order to get a kick out of it. But I can't imagine going back to Europe. Poor JJ, she'd only left Korea once when we met in Boracay last year, now she's bumping across Southeast Asia on a moped with me.' JJ giggled and looked adoringly on, clearly not the least bit worried about her new-found adventures. Olivier and JJ had a useless map of Laos, no GPS and no idea of how to get across the river. It was amazing they'd travelled so far.

'We've heard there's a bamboo bridge somewhere, but no one seems to know where it is,' said JJ.

As she said this the masked woman threw a gelatinous mess of bile-coloured pig's intestines onto the barbecue. They slithered between the grill and filled the café with a fresh cloud of porcine smoke.

'I'll show you,' I offered, wincing at the smell.

According to the GPS the bridge was only three miles west of here. Since I also planned to go to Ta Oi in the morning I could do with knowing where it was. We decided to go and check it out, then find somewhere in Nong to stay for the night.

In the late afternoon the river was at its busiest, fulfilling the multiple functions of community centre, laundry, supermarket and swimming pool. A gang of skinny teenage boys were jumping between rocks and casting fishing nets off the bridge. Smaller children paddled in the shallows and splashed around with bamboo floats. Farther up, a bare-breasted woman kneaded a bundle of soapy clothes on a smooth boulder. The bridge, a handmade fragile-looking structure propped up by thousands of spindly bamboo poles, stretched for four hundred rickety metres across to the far bank. A few boys were walking across it trailing fishing nets, and a single moped was rattling over the bamboo slats balancing an unstable load of cut logs. It didn't look like it was capable of taking much more.

After a dusty, sweaty day on the Trail a dip in the cool river water was an irresistible prospect. Since Lao women generally swam in all their clothes or covered up with a *sin*, a bikini was out of the question. The challenge was how to get out of my jeans and into a sarong without showing so much as a suggestion of *falang* thigh. As if reading my mind, all the men within a 50-metre radius dropped what they were doing and gathered in a neat semi-circle to watch me change. They sat cross-legged on the smooth rock, water dripping off their toned bodies, seventeen eager faces hanging on my every move. As tempting as it was to shock them with a striptease, I modestly slipped off my jeans under my sarong and kept on my T-shirt. Disappointed, they turned their attention to Olivier and JJ, shuffling closer for a better view.

'Oh my God!' said Olivier, whipping up his swimming trunks under a towel. 'They're trying to see my dick. I had this all the time in Vietnam, men making pervy comments about JJ and me, the fact that I'm a tall western guy and she's a small Asian girl. It got pretty annoying.'

Mission accomplished, we slid off the rocks and into the cooling water, T shirts, sarongs and all. Such relief.

We left the river at sunset and checked into Nong's only guest house, another lurid Panther-pink affair, the entrance of which was marked by a pair of five-hundred-pound bombs. In the dusty school playground opposite, about fifty uniformed children stood in a circle holding hands, singing what sounded like *Auld Lang Syne*. Behind them several serious-looking Lao men in World Vision International shirts watched the children with folded arms. An evangelical Christian relief organisation, World Vision is the world's largest international children's charity. Although their website states that they 'do not proselytise or work with those who insist on proselytism' there is an undeniably strong evangelical element to their work.

Nong is one of the poorest districts in Savannakhet, where Christianity is a little-known religion and *phi* worship still dominates. Given the choice of no education at all or a Christian school that provides paper, pencils and books, it's obvious which is going to win. World Vision may not be preaching hellfire and damnation at assembly every morning, but Jesus & Co would certainly have been making regular appearances on the curriculum. Not being a believer myself, I can't help feeling cynical about such organisations and their homogenising effects on dwindling minority cultures.

On the steps of the guest house I met more aid workers, three Laotian men who worked for the Asian Development Bank. One of them spoke basic English.

'What are you doing here?' I asked nosily.

'We're starting an agricultural development programme – racing goats,' he replied seriously.

'Racing goats? Really, the ADB is training people to race goats?' Development was at times misguided, but funding a programme to breed thoroughbred goats? I made a galloping motion with my hands.

'No!' he threw back his head and laughed. '*Raising* goats.'

'Ah, yes, that makes more sense.'

That evening Olivier, JJ and I ate greasy noodle soup at a Vietnamese *pho* stall, the only place open on the main drag. On the next table a group of young men were hunched over bowls, shovelling chunks of meat and noodles into their mouths with wooden chopsticks. At their feet two mangy dogs lay hopefully on the dirt floor. Halfway through our second beers a terrific electrical storm broke out, the clatter of rain on the metal roof so loud we were forced into silence. Curtains of water began pouring off the buildings and flooding the street and bursts of pink and purple lightning flashed across the sky, momentarily freezing telegraph poles, houses and palm trees in a phantasmagorical pink light. An hour later the storm had moved on and we picked our way back to the guest house, mud squelching under our flip flops and oozing between our toes. It didn't bode well for the state of the Trail the next day.

Studying the old and new maps that night it looked as if, as well as the road south over the bamboo bridge, there was a second road I could take. Skirting north of the Xe Banghiang River, the road ran east through the jungle for about twenty miles before dropping south to Ta Oi. I knew that the first route across the river was extremely hard. The only thing I knew about the second route was that it passed near La Hap, a significant intersection of the Trail and one time location of the front line headquarters. What the road was like today, I had no idea.

Whichever route I chose, I knew it was the boonies; dense jungle inhabited by little-contacted ethnic minorities, elephants and even the odd Indochinese tiger. There had been little or no UXO clearance in this wild region and the nearest significant town was Salavan, at least a day's drive by four-by-four. If there was anywhere on the trip I didn't want to have an accident, it was in this malarial belt of jungle south of Nong.

Unsure of which route to take, I emailed the American biker Don, asking him if he knew anything about the second road to La Hap. The next morning, thanks to Nong's 3G signal, I picked up his reply on my iPhone.

'The real Trail rider would always take the road to La Hap. I've done it at night – imagine what it would have been like with an AC-130 circling overhead.'

His email was enough to convince me: La Hap it was.

CHAPTER 11

THE ROAD TO LA HAP

The following morning, in the cloying heat, I lugged my kit out of the hotel and prepared Panther and myself for the jungle. Oil – check; 6 litres of water – check; peanut brittle – check; tyre pressure – check; spare batteries for GPS charged – check; iPhone charged – check. With everything ready, I knocked on Olivier and JJ's door to say goodbye.

'Oh that's a shame you're leaving, we'd have liked to have come with you,' said Olivier, rubbing the sleep from his eyes.

For some reason it felt churlish to explain that I wanted to travel alone, so I muttered something about reaching Ta Oi before nightfall and said perhaps I'd see them there. As lovely as they were, I needed to go solo.

On the way out of town I stopped to buy some petrol at a wooden hut, the roof of which was held up by a pair of painted green cluster bomb casings. Beside it the rusted top of a tank turret lay in the mud. A masked woman appeared and hand-pumped 3 litres of fuel into my tank out of a thirty-five gallon oil barrel. To be safe, I filled a 2-litre water bottle and strapped it to the metal rack between the seat and the handlebars. Today was not the day to be running out of petrol again.

The first half an hour was disappointingly easy; hard laterite road running though young banana plantations and more patches of recently burnt forest. Then, as if hearing my masochistic discontent, the road plunged into bamboo forest, narrowing to a deeply rutted footpath. Years of monsoons and heat had shaped it into a Himalayan diorama of deep crevasses and narrow ridges, last night's rain churning it into a gelatinous bog. Slowing to a speed of five miles per hour, I steered along a narrow strip of harder dirt which ran tightrope-like between the goo.

After a few miles I came to a confusing confluence of paths around a deserted village. Five empty, unusually small bamboo, wood and thatch huts stood among the trees, all of them resting on cluster bomb casings. A 5-metre-wide bomb crater lay between two of them. There was no indication that humans lived here anymore and it felt eerie, as if someone or something was watching me from the trees. It must either have been a village that had been resettled by the government or one which was only lived in for part of the year.

Even with a GPS it's possible to get disorientated. Every track I took out of the village turned into a dead end or became too narrow to ride along. Each time, I hauled Panther around yet again, doing ten-point turns for fear of her wheels hitting concealed bombs. Finding myself back among the huts for the fifth time I turned off the engine and took off my boiling bike gear for a proper look at the GPS. At that moment a young woman wearing a black sarong walked up a steep hill out of the forest in front of me, five full gourds of water strapped over her shoulders, a blackened tobacco pipe hanging out of the corner of her mouth. Seeing me, she stopped dead in her tracks and looked startled, unsure of her next move. I smiled and said *sabadi,* at which she broke into a run and bolted past me into the trees, the gourds rattling as she fled.

Five minutes later two more young women walked up the hill carrying wicker baskets filled with leaves on their backs. I said *sabadi* and shot them my most 'I'm a friendly foreigner' smile. But alas, they thought differently, hitching up their sarongs and speeding into the thickets of bamboo, like deer startled by a wolf.

Bewildered by these reactions I tried another path. This time it took me out of the weird village into a womb-like tunnel of bamboo, immediately recognisable as a main artery of the Trail. The edges of the narrow track were gouged with truck-sized bomb craters, out of which grew smooth clumps of bamboo. Within twenty minutes I had passed the mangled, rusted remains of three Trail trucks and numerous old fuel drums, untouched in four decades. Nowhere else on my journey did I feel such a pull of the past, such a sense of what had happened here. And, as in the village, I had that feeling of being watched, as if the ghosts of dead *boi dois* were peering at me from behind the bamboo. I knew what Don meant when he'd told me to imagine driving a truck down here at night, pursued by the infrared beams of AC-130 gunships.

According to the North Vietnamese, of all the weapons deployed against the Trail, the Lockheed AC-130 Spectre gunship was the most damaging. Until their introduction in the late sixties the USAF had relied on flares to illuminate their night time raids, giving drivers plenty of time to hide their trucks or dive for cover. But Spectres were fitted with low-light televisions, heat-sensitive infrared sensors and the 'Black Crow,' a device able to detect the sparks in truck engines. The combination of these new weapons enabled them to pick off whole convoys with terrifying accuracy, the motto of the gunship crews being, 'You can run, but you will only die tired'. Trail truck drivers were so terrified of this killer that there were cases of them refusing to get behind the wheel.

With typical cunning the communists set to work on outfoxing this formidable new adversary. Spectres were beasts of the night, their vampiric infrared sensors only valuable under the cover of darkness. If the trucks could somehow move during the day, the gunships would become redundant. The solution was the construction of almost eight hundred miles of hidden roads, called 'K roads,' disguised by elaborate trellises and tied-together tree canopy. These new roads meant that trucks were able to drive from just south of Ban Laboy all the way to lower Laos, invisible to the prying eyes of US pilots. As a diversionary measure, like lambs to the slaughter, unfortunate drivers were ordered to act as sham targets, steering old and damaged trucks along the original roads at night. Once again Dong Sy's Trail army had emerged victorious.

Stopping beside the bombed-out shell of one truck to take a photograph, I saw a group of people about 50 metres away walking towards me along the track. The second they spotted me, they turned on their heels and melted into the forest. Nowhere else in the world had this ever happened to me, and I found it utterly bamboozling. The 'natives' might have fled at the sight of Pizarro, Stanley and Columbus, but for it to happen now is highly unusual. Television has beamed western culture into the remotest of societies. Missionaries have traipsed across every continent. Aid has taught people to raise goats and send their children to Christian schools. But in this pocket of the Truong Son, the western world was still something to be feared and run from. I wished I'd been able to ask them what they were running from, to hear their conversation around the fire that night. Was their reaction connected to the War? Did they see me as some sort of devil or evil *phi*? Did the presence of foreigners signal mines, logging or resettlement? Or was it simply a fear of the unknown, an inability to comprehend who and what I was?

Apart from these few terrified people the track was empty, winding through dense, humid jungle. The only suggestion of life was that same musky animal scent I'd noticed near Dong Loc in Vietnam, perhaps a bear I thought. At some point I crossed the unmarked border into Salavan province.

The farther I went, the harder it became: steep hills, horizontal slabs of slate-grey rock, deep ruts and that nefarious orange mud. We bumped and slid down, revved and clanked up. Panther's poor little engine strained and wheezed and her tyres span in the mud, struggling for hold. Several slopes were so steep and rocky I paused at the top, wondering how on earth we would do it. Resting Panther on her side stand I walked ahead, picking out the best path, usually a narrow strip of harder mud right at the edge. Wedging my right boot on the back brake, holding the front ones on with my right hand and dragging my left boot in the mud for extra braking and stability, we would jolt down. Go too slowly and I'd lose balance, too fast and I'd lose control and risk going over the edge

On the hardest, rockiest inclines I put both feet down, took my weight off the seat and heaved her up with all my strength, the engine struggling in first gear.

It was the toughest riding I had done yet. *Keep buggering on*, I told myself, and metre by metre, mile by mile we nosed forwards. All I could think about was that moment, those rocks, that deep rut, which gear I was in – nothing else mattered except that place and that instant in time. As hard as it was I felt fully engaged, spurred on by the same fire of determination that had ignited in me on the road from Ban Laboy.

Around lunchtime I stopped at the top of a hill and turned off the engine. Pulling off my helmet, gloves and jacket I sat down on the track. I was hungry, dehydrated and drenched in sweat and my head pounded from the effort. Without the buzz of the engine I felt very alone, a long way from anyone or anything familiar. Dark walls of smooth bamboo, tall trees and lianas hemmed me in, silent except for the screech of cicadas. Usually I could hear at least one bird, or the mournful call of a distant gibbon, but this time there wasn't a single bird singing or monkey howling.

What if it means there's a tiger nearby? I thought, searching the darkness of the trees for movement. What if all the tigers had retreated to this part of the mountains, far from roads and people, and built themselves a fortress in the jungle? I imagined stern-faced big cats walking on their hind legs, patrolling a bamboo perimeter fence with old Kalashnikovs. The thought, however comic, was enough to make me down a dehydration salt, wolf down some peanut brittle and ride on.

In reality though, there was nothing comic about the rapid decline of the Indochinese tiger. When Norman Lewis travelled through Indochina in 1949 he wrote of the jungles being full of tigers, gaurs – ferocious wild buffaloes – storks, ravens, vultures, peacocks, parakeets and monkeys. Tigers were so plentiful in Dalat, Vietnam, it was rare to go outside at night without either seeing or hearing at least one. Two decades later, they were said to roam the battlefields, feasting on the rotting flesh of unburied corpses and allegedly attacking the odd GI. Occasionally bored Marines would go on tiger hunts, using their helicopter rotor washes to drive the animals into the waiting guns.

As recently as 2007 the Laos *Lonely Planet* wrote that tigers were still so common around the town of Ta Oi that people avoided venturing out at night. In the same year Cuong and Digby were warned by local people not to camp in the jungle there because of the danger of an attack. Around the same time, just south of here in Kaleum, people had tied a cow outside the village at night so the tiger would eat it, rather than them. Later on I met a UXO clearance specialist who had been driving to Kaleum in 2003 when a big male tiger jumped into the road right in front of their car.

But hunting, poaching and development have led to the calamitous decline of the once widespread Indochinese tiger. In the last decade their population has fallen by more than seventy per cent. The World Wildlife Fund puts their numbers at three hundred. The NGO Panthera are less optimistic, believing there are only a handful of them left in the whole of Vietnam, Cambodia and Laos. The reality is no one quite knows how many survive. But whatever their numbers, their future looks depressingly dismal.

It was on the road to La Hap that I felt Panther falter for the first time, as if the old lady was feeling her age. Forcing her up a steep muddy hill, engine straining in first, the bottom of the cylinder barrel caught on a rock. She toppled sideways beneath me, the spare fuel bottle ripping open and leaking away over the scalding hot engine. This time the kick-start only worked on the sixth attempt, the engine spluttering to life with a reluctant rattle. Even with my amateur understanding of mechanics I could tell something was wrong. The Panther I'd ridden out of Hanoi had made a contented purring sound. Now she sounded more like an old man choking on a bag of nails. I just hoped she would make it to Ta Oi.

Around 2 p.m. I rode up a hill, around a corner and into a *ban* of about thirty stilted huts in a clearing. The relief to see people and life! Pot-bellied pigs, ribby dogs and scrawny chickens scrapped in the dust. Naked children with swollen stomachs stared open-mouthed as I rode past. There was no *wat,* no electricity, no school. A pitiful shop sold bottles of Pepsi and not much else. Thirsty and exhausted, I stopped to stretch my legs and gulp down a tepid Pepsi, my presence attracting the villagers like iron filings to a magnet; within five minutes I was in a circle of fifty agog faces.

But it wasn't a friendly gathering, my smiles and *sabadis* were returned with silent, hostile stares. Then, emboldened, a few of the young men started nudging each other and laughing. One, a shark-eyed character with a bolt through his ear and a ripped black T-shirt, pointed at me and said something which caused the whole village to break into laughter. Not the sort of laughter that made me want to join in and stay for a nice friendly cuppa, but a jibing unpleasant cackle. Of course it could have all been harmless; a cultural misunderstanding. But instinct was all I had, and instinct told me to wave a cheery goodbye, pull the throttle and get the blazes out of there, with a final glance over my shoulder to check I wasn't being followed.

A mile beyond the village I came to a fast-flowing tributary of the Xe Banghiang. There was no bridge or canoe, just a rocky ford about 40 metres wide. A bare-breasted old woman washed in the clear water, looking at me inquisitively as I rode past. Pointing to the river, and then to the bike, I gave her a questioning thumbs up. She nodded. Well, there was only one way to find out. Panther's wheels shed clods of mud as they splashed through the shallow water. But halfway, I paused. In front of me was a deep gulley, too deep to cross without a ducking.

At that moment a man on a moped rode into the river from the other side. Seeing my predicament, he stepped off his bike and waded towards me, bending down to pick up a sturdy bamboo pole that lay in the pebbly shallows. Out of nowhere appeared two young boys, who the man efficiently marshalled into action. In an instant the bamboo pole was through Panther's front wheel and the four of us were hoisting her over the gulley, the boys and me holding either end of the pole, the man holding her aloft by her top box.

As I thanked them, three Vietnamese men arrived riding Honda Dream mopeds, each one stacked with cellophane-wrapped speakers, aluminium cooking pots, spades and bundled-up jute sacks. Their loads were five feet wide and at least 100 kg each and they took it in turns to push each other across the river, pans clanking and speakers wobbling. Then off they zoomed into the jungle, their mastery of the crossing putting me to shame. It struck me, not for the first time, that the riders of Vietnamese moped supermarkets might just be the best off-road bikers on the planet.

To my astonishment, a mile later the track emerged out of the jungle onto a wide, perfectly smooth, tarmac road. So new the tar was barely dry, line-painting teams were asleep on the verge, buckets of paint lying idly next to their bare feet. Local villagers looked oddly out of place as they walked barefoot along the boiling tarmac, bundles of firewood and woven baskets strapped to their bony backs. Behind one group of women two old men teetered drunkenly, gripping each other by the shoulders. The few villages at the roadside were newly built. The stark huts were constructed in oppressively neat lines, their uniformity and proximity to the road classic indicators of resettlement.

It later transpired that the road had only been finished a week before and ended at the Vietnamese border at Samuoi, less than twenty miles from where I had first hit the tarmac.

Riding slowly south, I marvelled at the incongruity of this symbol of modern Laos. Ta Oi had always been such an inaccessible region; a place where tigers roamed and little-known minorities still practised animism. In the mountains to my right were still people who fled at the sight of a foreigner, but here I suddenly was riding along a gleaming belt of asphalt. Somehow it didn't compute. It was like seeing the homeless man who lives on your street corner turn up one day in a pinstriped suit.

Half an hour later I reached the edge of Ta Oi town. Beneath the tarry veneer of development it was the same as any other rural Laotian *muang*: scruffy wooden huts, scrappy metal roofs, stacks of empty yellow *Beerlao* crates, a smattering of

Vietnamese *pho* stalls, shops selling dusty nets of Chinese-made footballs, sachets of Sunsilk shampoo, motorbike oil, Angry Birds T-shirts and cigarettes; and the ubiquitous choice of two basic guest houses-cum-brothels. It was a curious thing about Laos that even the smallest, grottiest, remotest *muangs* had a guest house, even if it was only four tumbledown walls and a mattress full of lice.

Supper was *pho* and *Beerlao*, accompanied by a mad – or drunk, or both, I wasn't sure which – toothless man who babbled on at me in Lao. At my feet lay the oddest mongrel I'd ever seen: a basset, Jack Russell, Heinz 57 cross with hound's feet and the elongated body of a sausage dog.

Afterwards I sat on the tiled balcony of my £3, ant-infested guest house – the marginally better of the two in town – smoking cheap Lao cigarettes and watching Ta Oi shut up shop. A Vietnamese woman in floral pyjamas wheeled a barrel of petrol into her hut; a boy closed up his family's shop with wooden planks; a young woman gathered her washing in from where she had hung it on a barbed-wire fence. At that moment a second guest arrived, an older Lao man whose four-by-four was branded with the logo of a Lao commercial UXO clearance company.

'Where have you come from?' he asked in good English.

'Nong, via the La Hap road.'

'Oh! That road, so much UXO there.' He shook his head and tutted. '*So* many big bombs up there.'

As we stood talking a logging lorry crawled past, followed by another, and another, and another.

'Where do you think all those logs are coming from?' I asked the man.

He looked awkward. 'I don't know.'

Immediately I regretted asking him. Under stated Laotian law it is illegal to export unprocessed timber out of the country. But these lorries were heading over the Vietnamese border in direct contravention of this, under the flimsy cover of darkness. Wherever the wood was coming from, and wherever it was going, it was almost certainly a below-the-belt deal involving a chain of liberally greased palms. Asking questions like this was unwise; in Laos you never knew who was on the government's side.

All night those lorries rumbled past, each one heading for Vietnam creaking under the weight of at least ten vast trees. Around 3 a.m., the road went quiet again. It made me sick to think how many acres of virgin forest that single night's haul represented.

Something was definitely wrong with Panther, and I had a suspicion it was major. So as the sun rose above the roofs the next morning, I opened my toolkit, turned to the 'Routine Maintenance' section of my Haynes Manual and set to work. Apart from checking the oil, chain and tyres, it was the first time I'd given her an attempt at a service. I knelt in the dust, flipping the pages, examining diagrams, picking out spanners. Passing men stopped to watch. They leant over my shoulders, hands clasped behind their backs, commenting to each other on my progress. Occasionally one of them would interject, passing me a different spanner or offering to help me unscrew an unwilling bolt.

I did everything I could: changed the oil, tightened the brakes, removed and cleaned the air filter, hosed off the mud, oiled the chain. It was satisfying to realise how easy it all was, how quickly you learn when you have to, how usually it's not a matter of 'can't' but simply 'haven't tried'. But when I started her again an hour later, she sounded just as bad.

'*Pai sai*?' asked the young owner of the guest house as I rolled up my tool pouch.

'Kaleum.'

Kaleum was another small town about thirty-five miles south of Ta Oi, reached by a narrow jungle track.

'No!' He shook his head, pointing between the rocks in the dirt and my bike, before patting his new Honda Wave and giving a proud thumb's up.

Perhaps he was right. Panther was sounding more like an ancient *tok tok* than a prize C90, another day of rough riding might be too much for her. But impatience and denial drove me on.

A friend at university once told me that the most likely phrase to come out of my mouth was 'Shall we go?' I would always want to go to the next pub, the next club, the next after-party. Even on this long, immersive journey I was finding it hard to escape from the constraints of time, from my own irritating desire to move on, to get to the next place. Perhaps it's a part of my rabidly 'itchy feet syndrome,' that desire to move, to be somewhere else. Or you could blame my genes; my fearsome Irish granny had holes in her left sleeves from pulling them back to look at her watch with such frequency. But there was also the boring matter of a return flight home, of *having* to be in Saigon by a certain date. Even in Ta Oi there was that ticking mental clock, the feeling that with so far still to go, I couldn't afford to lose a day. I would deal with the problem later.

On the outskirts of Ta Oi I turned south to Kaleum on the packed, levelled earth of another infant highway. What was marked on the GPS as a small track through the jungle was now a gaping laceration in the landscape. It was wider than an English A-road, yet we were in one of the least-inhabited corners of Laos. It was soon evident that this was where all last night's logging lorries were coming from. Hundreds, if not thousands, of hardwood logs were stacked by the empty roadside, each one numbered and colour-coded ready for collection. At what seemed to be the central depot queues of trucks waited for their loads to be craned on, directed by men in yellow hard hats. This was logging on an industrial scale.

With surging international demand for hardwood furniture, the forests of Laos are a veritable goldmine. Posing as timber dealers, undercover agents from London-based NGO, the Environmental Investigation Agency (EIA), were recently offered a thousand cubic metres of rare Lao rosewood for the incredible amount of $38.5 million. Teak, keruing and yellow balau fetch between $250 and $1,000 per cubic metre. Such high prices are driving the systematic and illegal destruction of the country's forests.

In 2011 the EIA produced a damning report on the extent of illegal logging in Laos. The report showed how a coterie of well-connected companies routinely makes illicit deals with the highest echelons of the Lao government. These deals strip the jungle around new roads, dam sites and mines, making a mockery of laws about quotas and export. One of the worst culprits is the Lao conglomerate building the road I was now riding on, responsible for destroying thousands of hectares of virgin forest and making millions of dollars in the process. But since the boss of this company is the adopted son of the Lao President, it's unlikely they'll be stopping any time soon.

Writing in 1641, Dutch explorer Gerrit van Wuysthoff said of Laos, 'The mountains that surround it on every side fortify the land marvellously against the enterprise of foreigners... whole forests of full grown timber trees grow at the foot of these mountains, seeming to have been planted intentionally to serve as a rampart against the great falls of rain which would cause great damage if there were not this natural obstacle.'

Nearly four hundred years later, his words have never been more poignant, and seeing all those felled trees made me despairingly sad. Their demise represented so much: deforestation, global warming, soil erosion, loss of habitat for countless species, the resettlement of powerless minorities. And the only people it benefitted were a few sickeningly corrupt individuals. Development is one thing, raping your country of natural resources quite another. It was eye-watering to think that a handful of wealthy people were selling off these forests in order to buy a bigger car, build a bigger house or buy their wife a diamond necklace. Looking at the undulating, verdant, superabundant forested hills that flowed into the distance I wondered if – a decade from now – a single tree would be left standing.

Aside from logging lorries the only other traffic was a man on a moped, his head and face swathed ninja-like in a black scarf, a rifle slung over his shoulder. He slowed to look at me as he passed, then twisted the throttle, vanishing in a shroud of orange dust.

Halfway to Kaleum I passed a single *ban* perched on the edge of a small river. Two yellow Komatsu diggers idled beside a half-built concrete bridge. For tens, perhaps hundreds of years that village had stood in an isolated clearing deep in the jungle. But now the road ran straight through the middle of it.

I crossed from Salavan into Sekong province. One of Laos' smallest, poorest, least populous and most ethnically diverse provinces, Sekong was formed in 1984 when Salavan province was split in two. Hugging the south-eastern border with Vietnam, most of the province is mountainous highlands populated by Mon-Khmer minorities such as Alak, Talieng, Nga and Katu. UXO and poor infrastructure mean tourists very rarely make it here.

Farther on, a second *ban* sat pathetically in the middle of a new coal-mining operation, owned by the same company as were building the road. Lines of lorries rolled past, spilling coal dust onto the already black road, the drivers leaning out of their windows to shout at me. On a hill above the *ban* diggers and thirty-five-tonne Terex earthmovers ripped at the earth with monotonous efficiency. Below, naked children played in the dirt, their bodies smeared grey.

Lost in the maze of roads hewn by the new mine, I flagged down a four-by-four to ask the way to Kaleum. The driver, an engineer for the company, spoke a bit of English, and was amazed that I had come all the way from Hanoi.

'But this bike so old,' he said, before driving off, his wheels spraying two children with coal dust as he went.

At 4 p.m. I crested a hill and saw the Sekong River winding around Kaleum in a basin below me; a sleeping cat curled around an ankle. Wood and metal roofs poked through a blanket of trees, and waterfalls of foliage tumbled down the high banks into the river. All around it were forested hills, tinged blue in the mist.

But all this would soon be gone, flooded by the waters of the Sekong. Upriver from here a Russian firm had just been given the go-ahead to build the Sekong 4, one of seventy-two dams currently being planned for Laos. By 2014 nearly five thousand villagers in the Kaleum district will have been forcibly relocated to make way for the headwaters of the dam. In a few years from now the scene below me would be no more than a memory.

The government of Laos sees hydroelectricity as the gilded bootstraps with which the country can pull itself out of poverty. Laos, they say, will become 'the battery of Southeast Asia'. The electricity from its rivers will power Thailand and Vietnam, the revenue funnelled back into much-needed development and infrastructure. Of the seventy-two planned dams, twelve were already under construction and twenty-five in the advanced planning stages. But conservationists argue that the dams will stop the flow of sediment, hinder rice production, prevent fish migrations, flood vast areas and lead to the forced resettlement of thousands of people. Kaleum was the tip of a very dirty iceberg.

Hungry and dehydrated, I rode down the final hill into Kaleum. According to the GPS, just this side of town was a 'restaurant with a great view'. Bumping down a dirt track, I turned Panther into a compound of sorts. There were a few simple huts, bamboo racks of wooden longboats and what looked like a long dining table. The view over the river, forest and mountains was indeed a good one, but there was no sign of either food or diners.

A small Lao man in a white aertex shirt walked out of one of the huts.

'Hello, can I help you?' he asked.

'Ah, you speak English!' I exclaimed, noticing a scar across his cheek. 'Is this a restaurant by any chance?'

'No, it's a geologist's camp. But come and sit down and have some water if you want.'

My hunger had reached the stage where all I could think about was ingesting calories. But stumbling across a geologist's camp and a rare English speaker had piqued my curiosity.

The man, Pong, and I sat at the wooden table, while a shy young woman brought us bottles of water. Trying not to sound overly interested, I asked him about the camp. It belonged to an Australian mining company, he told me, who were prospecting along the banks of the Sekong for gold and other precious metals. A team of Australians had just left and Pong, who'd trained as a geologist in Soviet Uzbekistan, had just started a twenty-eight-day shift. I asked him if they'd found gold.

His mouth curled into a greedy smile. 'Oh yes. Lots – and copper, zinc, lead. We'll start drilling upriver at Ban Bak next year.'

He walked over to a wooden rack beside the table, filled with lumps of rock. 'The Sekong River is very rich in gold, just look at some of these.'

I stood up to have a closer look, the golden seams glittering seductively as I turned the rocks in my hands. From there, I could see three Komatsu diggers parked on the opposite river bank.

'We're not the only ones looking for gold here,' said Pong, following my gaze. 'That's a Lao company. There are Chinese and Vietnamese here too. Everyone's looking for gold.'

'What about the dam. Has the resettlement started yet?'

'Yes, it's already begun.' He pointed to some houses near the diggers. 'That used to be a Katu village, they've already been moved.'

Pong, who was from Vientiane, told me nearly everyone in this area were Katu and Nga minorities. Many would be resettled to neighbouring provinces, far from their ancestral lands, innocent victims of the government's ruthless quest for development.

Warming to company, Pong asked me to stay for some food – insipid omelette and a plate of plain rice, which I consumed in a most unladylike manner.

'Do you like your job?' I asked Pong, between my final mouthfuls of rice.

Again that greedy smile. 'Oh, yes. Of course, it's looking for money.'

At that moment, I couldn't help thinking of Gollum.

The last few days had made me feel achingly sad for Laos; the rapacious mining, the resettlement, the ongoing legacy of the war, the dams, the spoliated forests. But it didn't mean that I wasn't enjoying the journey, that the experience wasn't everything I'd hoped it to be. The more I saw of this dark underbelly, the more impassioned I became about digging deeper, discovering more, exposing what was really happening here. I wanted people to see beyond the temples and boutique hotels, glimpse how this magnificent land was being ravaged by a tsunami of corruption and consumerism. Being able to write about what I was seeing and hear the stories that normally go untold was more stimulating and rewarding than any night in a five-star hotel.

CHAPTER 12

PANTHER REVOLTS

Kaleum, like a Monet, is best when viewed from a distance. Down among the bowels of the town it was the usual muddle of metal and wood huts, rubbish, feral dogs, old tyres and empty *Beerlao* crates. A single dusty street ran past a school, a police station – the first I'd seen in Laos – a Vietnamese *cắt tóc'* and a few shops. Turning off the dusty main street down a rutted track, past stares and wonky wooden huts, I parked Panther outside a decrepit concrete hovel. The steps leading up it were cracked and dirty, the land around it piled with rubbish. Even a remote outpost like Kaleum had a hotel, and this was it. Appearing from a hut behind the building, a rotund transvestite indicated I hand over 60,000 kip – £5 – gave me the key and pointed me to Room 1.

Those are the remains of the last guest, I thought darkly, sidestepping a festering damp patch in the concrete hallway. My room wasn't any better. The only features were two stained single beds with faded Mickey Mouse sheets, swags of spiders' webs and the rotting corpse of a gecko beside the light switch.

Locked doors marched up the dark hallway. Aside from me, the hotel was empty.

Intent on washing away the day's sweat and grime, I picked my way across the rubbish dump to the washing facilities, a concrete block divided into four disgusting cubicles. Each had a shit-splattered hole in the ground, a tap and a bucket of stagnant brown water. Grimacing, gingerly pushing open each door, I chose the cubicle that looked the least diseased and hosed myself at speed.

Retiring to my room early, I checked under the bed, wrapped myself in my sleeping bag liner and read Norman Lewis under the light of my head torch.

It was Sunday night, but Kaleum was in party mood. At about ten o'clock the clamour of cicadas was joined by the thud-thud-thud-thud of Lao pop. All night bawdy voices and laughter floated through my open window. Around midnight some of the revellers decided to race their mopeds along the hotel corridor, banging on my thin wooden wall as they passed. At 2 a.m., 4 a.m. and 6 a.m. the pop music was still blasting, fuelled – I suspected – by *yaba*, a type of methamphetamine that has become a worrying problem in rural and urban Laos.

Underslept and slightly grumpy, I dragged my panniers out to Panther at 7 a.m., relieved to find she hadn't been stolen or vandalised. The transvestite was delicately laying strips of raw water buffalo meat on a satellite dish to dry, waving at me in doing so. As I closed my top box two policemen came riding up the track on a moped. Very young, thin as rashers of wind, they looked odd in their pressed green uniforms and shiny shoes, as if they were simply playing at being policemen for the day.

'*Sabadi*,' they said, as the elder of the two opened an official looking briefcase. 'Where you from? Where you go? Why you here? Passport please,' they asked in pidgin English. I handed over my passport and they leant over it, flicking through the stiff pages importantly, puzzling at all my visas and stamps. I wondered if I'd asked Pong too many questions yesterday and he'd reported me to the police. Kaleum, with its gold, logging and impending dam, was a highly sensitive area.

It was a dangerous time to be critical of the government's policies. Sombath Sompone, a well-known Laotian civil rights activist and critic of land and resettlement policies, disappeared in Vientiane in December 2012. Caught on CCTV being stopped by police and bundled into a pick-up, his disappearance is widely blamed on the government of Lao. Amnesty International, Hillary Clinton, the UN and Desmond Tutu have all campaigned for his release, but six months on, there's still no sign of him. The rumours are that he was shot a few days after his disappearance. The incident has had a huge impact on the efforts of foreigners and more moderate Lao to speak out against the government's land, environmental and resettlement policies. Everyone is afraid of ending up like Sombath.

The same month Sombath vanished, Anne-Sophie Gindroz, Lao country director of Swiss NGO Helvetas, was given forty-eight hours to leave the country after openly criticising the government. And earlier on my journey, I'd been put in touch with a Laos-based Australian anthropologist who had been too afraid to talk to me by phone or email about land policies here. It was too dangerous, he said. If I wanted to talk to him, we'd have to do it in person. I have also been given advice and information by several other foreigners working within Laos, none of whom are able to be named in this book.

Technically, as someone writing about the country, I should have been accompanied at all times by a Lao government official. But that would have been a) boring b) hugely inconvenient c) expensive d) impossible. Not wanting to attract suspicion, I'd hence been careful not to seem too interested in controversial topics, not to tell anyone I met I was writing a book and not to write anything inflammatory on my blog, Twitter or Facebook page. In answering the policemen's questions I played the stupid foreigner card, smiling innocently and saying how much I liked Kaleum. After a while they became bored, handed my passport back and rode away.

After some persuasion Panther started, coughing into life at the eighth kick and rattling and sputtering up the main street. I stopped at a tin-roofed shack for breakfast, interrupting the one-eyed cook from her morning dose of the Karaoke channel. Loath to leave the television, she shuffled into the dark interior, returning with black coffee, *pho* and fried eggs, which I shared with a pathetically thin dog.

My plan today was to find a way across the Sekong River by boat and ride twenty miles along the northern bank to Ban Bak, the village the Australians were due to start drilling in the following year. One of the biggest and most important supply bases on the Trail, Ban Bak had been hit by a brutal bombing campaign in the winter of 1970–1971 and the area was allegedly still thick with wreckage. Rumour had it there were the remains of a crashed USAF F-4 in the vicinity, and

Digby, Don and a handful of other Trail hunters had all been there. I was keen to go too.

Panther, it seemed, was less keen. Numerous attempts at her kick-start produced no more than a loud pop, then ominous silence. I had seemingly done the impossible; I'd killed my C90. Dialling Cuong's number, I explained her symptoms and asked his advice.

'It sounds like the cam chain,' he diagnosed. 'You'll never find decent mechanic in Kaleum, get the bike on a truck to Sekong and find a Vietnamese mechanic there. Whatever you do, find a Vietnamese mechanic, Lao ones no good.'

Sekong was the provincial capital, about fifty miles from here. Getting a truck would be expensive. Digby called back a few minutes later.

'Look, if the worst comes to the worst we can always send you a new engine. There are worse places to be holed up for a few days than Sekong.'

Strangely, instead of worry, I felt a frisson of excitement. Seemingly disastrous situations like this often lead to memorable incidents. Or as motorcycling legend Ted Simon is fond of saying: 'The interruptions ARE the journey.' Whatever my immediate future, it would likely be interesting.

Watched by the one-eyed cook and the transvestite from the hotel, I pondered my predicament beside the stricken Panther. Almost instantaneously, a man walked up to me and said in faltering English,; 'You need mechanic? I'm Vietnam. There's Vietnam mechanic just up the road.'

What incredible luck. I wheeled Panther a hundred metres up the road to a tin and wood shack, where a sinewy young man was crouching next to a moped amid a scattering of tools and slicks of black oil, his long legs folded under him like a cicada. With a bit of sign language and the help of the Haynes Manual we established what the problem was, and he set to work, squatting beside Panther, unscrewing her oily innards into a green plastic bowl. Cuong was right, the cam chain was broken, as was the cam sprocket. It was going to take at least two hours to fix.

Like a worried parent at their child's bedside, I looked over the mechanic's shoulder as he hammered, scraped and screwed; chain-smoking and listening to Euro house as he worked. An indecipherable, half-finished tattoo crawled over his right shoulder and a heavy silver chain hung around his thin neck. At the back of the hut, next to their bamboo bed, his young wife sliced chunks of raw fish on a grimy chopping board.

By this point it was 9 a.m. and next door to the mechanic's hut another party was going on. Fifteen men and women sat around a wooden table, the floor piled with discarded bottles of *Beerlao*. Lao pop crackled out of blown speakers in front of which several of the women danced. Others sat and smoked large bamboo bongs. I suspected this was the effect of impending Armageddon, and that the people of this doomed town would be getting stocious until the moment they were hauled from their homes.

On the other side of the street the occasional customer came and went from a Chinese shop which sold phone credit, T-shirts, bits of bicycle, motorbike parts, oil – you name it. School children slouched by, dragging their flip flops in the dust, the girls shading themselves under pretty parasols, their feet protected from the sun by thick white socks. Somewhere nearby a pig was being slaughtered, its dying squeals piercing the morning air.

Having nothing better to do on a Monday morning than watch a pink moped being fixed, some of these passers-by paused to watch. One was a Vietnamese man who spoke basic English.

'Are you here on a picnic?' he asked. 'You know, tourism.' Well, I guess you could call it that.

Another passer-by was a young woman in a hand-woven blue *sin* who handed me her bamboo bong. I took a deep inhalation, filling my lungs with strong tobacco smoke before passing it back to her with a choked *khawp jai*. On she walked without a word, as if handing her bong to a *falang* on a Monday morning was an entirely normal procedure.

By 11 a.m. the mechanic had replaced the cam chain and cam sprocket and reassembled the engine. I held my breath as he tried the kick-start. Nothing. Not a whisper. Damn it. Echoing my disappointment, a small boy toddled out of the hut opposite, pulled down his tracksuit bottoms and pissed in the gutter.

Unscrewing the other side of the engine, the mechanic spilled more of Panther's guts into the green bowl. The broken cam chain had, in technical terms, really screwed up the whole engine, damaging the piston, valves and cylinder head. He could fix her, he said, but it would take another five hours.

Resigning myself to a day in Kaleum, I wandered off to get cool drinks for the mechanic and his wife. By now the pile of empty *Beerlao* bottles next door was nearly touching the bottom of the table, and most people were slouched in their chairs in the advanced stages of inebriation. As I walked past, the conscious ones let out a chorus of *sabadis*, excitedly waving me in, where a red-eyed, shirtless man handing me his bong. Two women swayed next to the speakers, so drunk they could barely stay vertical. The younger of the two, a moon-faced woman in a red apron, accosted me, thrusting a glass of warm beer into my hand. *Well, why not,* I thought, and drank some – to cheers from the assembled revellers. Egged on by the others, the two women grabbed me, gyrating against me, groping, whooping. First a transvestite, now a lesbian sandwich; what was it with this town? I danced for a while then extracted myself from their grasping fingers, their shouts and laughter following me down the street.

Lunch was fish curry, eaten cross-legged with the mechanic and his wife on their bed – although I call myself a vegetarian, I'm actually what a friend once described as a 'fish and chipocrite': eating fish, but not meat. In their early twenties, the young couple were from Huế, the old Vietnamese Imperial Capital. They had already spent two years in Kaleum, living in this cramped hut, saving everything they earned in order to return to Vietnam and start a family. Although Laos is a poorer country than Vietnam, prices are much higher. Hotels, fuel, food, beer, hairdressers, mechanics, phone credit – all are significantly more expensive than in Vietnam. This, combined with a lack of good local mechanics, meant they could earn much more in the heat and poverty of Kaleum than at home in Huế.

At one o'clock the sky turned black and curtains of rain sent everyone scuttling for shelter, heads bent under plastic bags and parasols. Only three tiny, naked infants remained. They threw themselves into the newly formed puddles with glee, berated from the shadows of the Chinese shop. After half an hour the storm moved on, leaving Kaleum to roast once again.

With time to kill, I worked on my plan to get to Ban Bak. Down by the river a few broken-down wooden boats were pulled up on the bank, their owners smoking lackadaisically in the shade. No, none of them could take me across the river. The language barrier made it impossible to argue. Walking a hot mile to the geologist's camp, Pong said he couldn't take me on one of their boats either, adding it was too difficult to get there by road.

On the walk back, in need of a treat, I stopped at the *căt tóc'* and was fussed over by three pretty Vietnamese teenagers from Da Nang. For a facial, hair wash, face, shoulder and neck massage, it was a whole 30,000 kip (£2.50).

Oddly, every time I wandered off from the mechanic's, the younger of the policemen popped up. He'd be pretending to buy a drink at the same time, or coincidentally down by the river when I was asking about boats. He had a lot to learn about the finer art of sleuthing.

As the shadows lengthened and the party next door finally dwindled, the mechanic screwed Panther's last few bolts in, turned the key and tried the kick-start. This time her engine leapt to life, purring like the Panther of old. Writing out the bill with oily hands, he explained all the parts he had replaced: cam chain, cam sprocket, cylinder head, gasket set. All that, plus a whole day's labour came to 206,000 kip – a mere £17. Pulling a wad of notes out of my bumbag I thanked him heartily and rode Panther away, smiling widely.

It was too late to go anywhere, so I retired to the one-eyed cook's restaurant for a beer and some writing, delaying the inescapable reality of having to spend a second night in Kaleum's only hotel in the company of the dead gecko.

Travelling makes me superstitious and sharpens my ear to the whims of Fate. And the following morning I had a sense that Fate, or the Universal Mind, or whatever you prefer to call it, didn't want me to go to Ban Bak. I had found no obvious way across the river, the road on the other side was allegedly terrible and I was reluctant to destroy Panther again. Moreover, others who'd gone there had either spoken Lao, like Don, or taken a translator. On my own, it was likely I wouldn't see anything except bomb craters and oil barrels, neither of which were a novelty. Instead, I slipped a thank you note and a USB key full of electronic music under the mechanic's closed shutters and rode up the hill out of Kaleum, pausing at the top for a last look down at the town. From here, distance once again evoked a sense of romance, of a lost world floating in the mist.

At the coal mine, I turned south towards Sekong on a sandy, rocky, isolated track through deep jungle. Every square inch was pullulating with arboreal life; a matted wall of variant greens which pressed against the edges of the track: magnificent trees with smooth silvery trunks, lianas, ferns, hundreds of different types of bush, grass, shrub and tree. I wish I'd known their names, but with literally hundreds of species of flora in a single hectare of jungle, identifying them would have taken a lifetime. Hampered by deep white sand, which spilled over my boots and seeped into my lungs, I rode slowly, listening for any irregularities in Panther's engine, savouring the beauty and serenity of the jungle.

My musings were interrupted by a passing logging truck carrying five enormous yellow balau trunks worth, I estimated, between $25,000 and $75,000. A few miles on, the jungle opened into a village, the entrance to which was marked by two things: a rusty green sign announcing this was the Bor Namoun Protection Forest, and a sawmill. Behind the latter's high walls were neat stacks of cut and processed timber. Beyond its gates, the sawmill had turned the village into a dumping ground. Hundreds of trunks lay in untidy heaps, like bodies cast into a mass grave, and piles of sawdust and burnt offcuts smouldered between the stilted houses. The children's faces were coated in a patina of green snot and dirt, and rags hung off their bony shoulders.

When I stopped at a tiny shop for a drink a teenage girl materialised from the next-door hut. She was ethereally beautiful, with dark luminous skin, high cheekbones and a sultry gaze. In her delicate hands she held a two-foot bamboo bong, which she drew on at habitually regular intervals. Taking off my baking jacket and helmet and turning Panther's engine off, I asked her for *nam*, water. '*Baw mi*,' she replied in an idle whisper. After 'hello' and 'thank you,' *baw mi* (don't have) has to be the third most used phrase in the Lao lexicon. *Pai sai?* (Where are you going?) comes a close fourth. Instead I pointed to a bottle of the nuclear orange juice and sat on a bench to drink it, rubbing the sweat and dust off my face and neck with my Buff.

The girl sat opposite, her black eyes observing me over the rim of the bong. Her long fingernails expertly poked and kneaded the burning metal pod of tobacco that protruded from the bottom, the water gurgling with each new inhalation.

A curious mix of child and adult, her stained teddy-bear-print T-shirt and youthful skin were at odds with her sensuality and rabid tobacco addiction. When a second girl with a baby came and sat down, the two exchanged baby and bong: the new girl smoking, the original one pulling up her T-shirt and attaching the child to her breast. *How old are you?* I asked her with the help of my phrasebook. *Sip haet* – eighteen – she responded in that same enervated whisper, as if even raising her voice was too much effort. This was her second child, she said. If she conformed to statistics, she would have at least five more.

Beyond the village, as far as I could see, all that remained of the once dense jungle was bald earth, sickly saplings and dead shrubs. Colourless and deathly silent, the denuded hills made me think of a beautiful young woman – like the one I'd just met – who had suffered a devastating attack of alopecia. In the midst of it was a small *ban,* an island in a sea of desolation. A bent metal sign read, 'Conservation and Management for the sustainable use of the Huay Ko watershed: Improving biodiversity conservation through livelihoods development. Project partner: Department of Forestry, Xekong Provincial Agriculture and Forestry Office, WWF. Donor: The John D. and Catherine T. MacArthur Foundation.'

Pinned to a noticeboard were two yellowing MAG UXO posters warning people of the dangers of cluster bombs.

A group of children gathered as I took photographs, smiling big beautiful smiles and putting their hands together in prayer-like *wais*, the traditional Lao greeting. When I said *sabadi* and did the *wai* back they all fell about giggling; such innocent mirth in such a forlorn place. With no animals to hunt, no berries, roots, flowers, bark or herbs to gather and nowhere for their spirits and ancestors to live, what was their future?

Riding away from the *ban* I began to cry; not tears that slid silently over my cheeks, but great gulping sobs. I cried for the loss of the forests, for the way the Lao government was pillaging its country at the cost of its poor rural populations, for the future of this beautiful land. I loved so much about Laos, but at that moment I never wanted to come back. Sobbing miserably I rode on south through the ruined forest, Panther's tyres crunching on the sand. It was the low point of my journey so far.

Farther on a few pregnant sploshes of rain fell on my face, threatening a downpour which thankfully never came. If it had, there would have been no trees to shelter under. Then, abruptly, the track hit the tarmac road into Sekong and I joined a steady trickle of mopeds, bicycles and Land Cruisers heading towards town.

CHAPTER 13

THE BOMB BROTHERS

Fate had served me well, for in Sekong, quite by chance, I met Mick. Lured by the only Wi-Fi in town – the first since Vietnam – Mick, his son Tim, their translator Somsack and I were the only guests at the Hongkham Hotel, a shiny new-build with a polished golden sign, marble steps and staff who slumbered in reception. At $20 it was steep, but for Wi-Fi, a real shower and laundry, it was worth it.

I bumped into them in reception, loitering by the glass doors. Mick was about sixty, with short silvery hair and downward sloping features. Heavy-lidded green eyes slanted towards a greying Dick van Dyke moustache. He would have fitted perfectly as a caped and booted extra in *The Mask of Zorro*. His son Tim, who was here for the school holidays, looked older than his twelve years, his dark eyes and shock of black hair inherited from his Vietnamese mother, Mick's third wife. Somsack was a tall, pale, quiet Lao in her mid-thirties. While the other two were wearing T-shirts saying 'PCL Phoenix Clearance Limited: Landmine and Bomb Disposal,' he wore a second-hand US army camo shirt, the words 'KING' and 'US ARMY' on the two breast pockets doctored to read 'FUCKING US ARMY'. In Laos it was probably a frequently felt sentiment.

'We're clearing a new German-funded road up in Dak Cheung at the moment. We just came down to Sekong for a day to get more supplies, it's pretty basic up there,' explained Mick in a gentle Kiwi lilt.

My ears pricked. Dak Cheung, a remote outpost perched up in the mountains near the Vietnamese border, was where I was heading next. For no reason at all, ever since I had first heard Digby mention its name the year before I'd wanted to go, envisioning a magical kingdom tottering on mist-wreathed peaks. Even Digby hadn't been up there, and at 1,300 metres it would be the highest point of my journey. The last significant *ban* before a pass over the mountains into South Vietnam, it had been on a key Trail route.

The four of us had dinner in the hotel's dark and airless restaurant, where our attempts to order from the lavishly illustrated menu were met with a wall of *baw mis*. Somsack ordered for us, speaking English and Lao with a French accent, the result of having been brought up in Paris. In 1976 his Royalist parents had been forced to flee the retributions of the new communist government, escaping across the Mekong to Thailand in the middle of one night. As she waded across the river with a handful of belongings Somsack's mother was pregnant. They eventually made it to France, and it would be thirty-three years before her unborn son saw his homeland for the first time. Although he had now lived in Laos for four years, Somsack still seemed more

European than Lao, and was known by his compatriots as the 'black *falang*'.

Over plain rice and omelette Mick told me fragments of his own extraordinary life story, which involved more near-misses than a world cup qualifier. An EOD (Explosive Ordnance Disposal) expert, he had served in both the New Zealand and Australian armies, the latter sending him to Cambodia as part of a peace-keeping force. It was 1993 and the heavily mined country was still recovering from years of war and the brief but genocidal grip of the Khmer Rouge.

'On my first day there one of the Cambodian government staff we were working with stepped on a mine five metres from me and lost his leg from the knee down.'

Soon afterwards he had nearly been killed when on a recce at Angkor Wat, one of the few cultural relics not destroyed by the Khmer Rouge.

'I was walking into one of the temples one morning when I noticed dew glistening on a wire two inches in front of my nose. Stopping dead and looking to my right, I saw that a mortar was fixed at the end of the wire; one more step and I'd have been toast.'

A few years later he had returned with the UN to work on landmine clearance.

'It was unbelievable. I'd have one or two landline casualties in my car *every day*, either people bleeding to death with missing limbs, or just bits of dead people. My driver drove into a minefield by accident once. I told him to stop and ordered everyone not to get out of the car. But he panicked, got out, and was promptly blown all over us.'

Mick had been clearing mines and UXO in Laos since 1997, for the government, a handful of NGOs and now as the boss of his own commercial clearance company.

'When I came here in 1996 I was employed by the government to train their first demining teams. None of them had ever worn shoes before. They'd turn up late, running down the street in bare feet. I'd have to force them to put their boots on.'

I asked him what he knew of the Trail around here.

'You won't find Sekong on any Trail maps as it was only formed in the mid-eighties, but the Trail ran right through here and over the river towards Dak Cheung.'

'My grandfather was a Ho Chi Minh Trail bicycle porter,' piped up Tim, who had been engrossed in a game on his iPad.

'Poor man,' picked up Mick. 'He was on the Trail until just before the end of the War, carrying ammunition to the anti-aircraft guns. He always said the worst things were the mud, hunger and disease, that the bombing was generally predictable. He was a really nice man who suffered very badly from his experiences on the Trail and hardly ever spoke about it. He drank himself to death in 2004.'

Mick was a great raconteur, speaking with an engaging geniality that belied the horrors he was recounting. I wanted to hear more, but over the course of the afternoon I had started to feel ill, and by nine o'clock had to go to bed. The three of them were leaving for Dak Cheung first thing in the morning so we made a plan to meet at the only guest house in town, a Vietnamese place on the main strip.

'It's a bad road up to Dak Cheung,' Mick warned. 'I doubt a foreigner on a scooter has ever been up there before. But if you make it, you'll meet my brother John – you'll like him.'

The next day, I was ill – a clammy, dizzy, malaise. I was in no state to ride up to the Dak Cheung plateau, a 70 mile, 1,200 metre climb east from here. All day I lay in my hotel room, thankful for the air conditioning, my sweat leaving dark patches on the white sheets.

Again the following morning I awoke soaked in perspiration, dizzy, my head thumping. But impatience won over reason and an hour later I was clunking along the main street towards the river dosed up on paracetamol, coffee and rehydration salts.

The 'ferry' across the muddy, 300-metre-wide Sekong River was a pair of old pirogues hammered together with ten warped planks to form a rough platform. Just wide enough for three mopeds, it was steered by a young masked woman who took your 5,000 kip – 45p – then crouched at the back to steer the noisy outboard motor. Riding Panther up a single, buckling plank I clicked her into neutral and wedged my boot on the back brake, keen to avoid an early morning dip in those murky waters. Two young Vietnamese men on new Hondas rode onto the ferry beside me. 'Hanoi!' they exclaimed, noticing my number plate. We chuntered across, the two men chatting and pointing at my bike. Halfway over one of them pointed downwards and shook his head; oozing oil and belches of blue smoke were coming from my exhaust. A check over on the far bank showed her engine oil levels to be zero. I would have to turn back.

There were at least six moped mechanics on Sekong's main street and all of them looked equally shambolic. Young shirtless men crouched beside the carcasses of half-repaired machines, their muscles flexing as they worked. Bits of engine, spare inner tubes and cartons of oil hung off the walls and lay in the dirt around them. Choosing one at random, I asked the small spotty teenage mechanic if he was Vietnamese. He nodded. Tapping out sentences on Google Translate and flicking through my Haynes Manual, I explained Panther's troubles. He pointed to the cylinder barrel, typing 'need new one' on my iPhone with a grimy index finger.

'How much?' I typed back.

'300,000 kip; five hours.'

'OK.'

It was 8.30 a.m. and already Sekong was like a frying pan. Too weak and hot to do anything, I sat on a stool and watched as he screwed and hammered, deftly dismantling Panther's interior into a cardboard box. The hours ticked by. Mopeds buzzed past, the women sheltering from the sun under parasols. Two white UXO Lao trucks sped by and a blacked-out Hummer patrolled up and down ostentatiously. A bored policeman stopped to watch, leaning on a wooden pole in his green uniform. Sitting there I mused how, like ET and Elliot, Panther and I were sickening in tandem. We weren't having the best of weeks.

At 11 a.m. I attempted a short walk around Sekong. It was the biggest town I'd been to in Laos, distinctly cosmopolitan compared to the wild highlands that surrounded it. It had real petrol stations, with forecourts and pump attendants; concrete houses; chemists; Vietnamese restaurants, one of which specialised in dog; a large *wat* compound, with golden Buddhas and frangipani trees; a UXO Lao office; five hotels and a new bank. Strings of large, half-built houses spoke of new money.

In the market, among the usual foodstuffs, two baby green parrots huddled in a plastic box, cawing pathetically and pecking weakly at a mouldy banana.

At 2 p.m. the mechanic wrote out the bill, holding up Panther's broken parts like dirty washing: cam chain, cam sprocket, crank shaft, gasket set and cylinder barrel. I thanked him, handed over 300,000 kip – £25 – and left.

With Dak Cheung a day's ride away, it was too late to leave now. Instead I checked into a cheap guest house on the main street and lay on the hard bed listening to the *whumph whumph* of the ceiling fan. Several times I dipped into Norman Lewis and his anachronistic descriptions of noble savages and indolent locals, before slipping back into a feverish doze.

Feeling much improved the next morning I checked Panther anxiously, rode down to the river and up the buckling plank, paid the woman another 5,000 kip and wobbled across the water. At a collection of hovels on the far bank I stocked up with 4 litres of water and a bunch of stubby thumb-like yellow bananas. Young women peered shyly from the shadows, waiting for business from passing truck drivers and Vietnamese men on their way to the border.

The road was in the embryonic stages of construction and a few tantalising miles of sticky new tarmac gave way to flattened and freshly dug earth, thundering steamrollers and scatterings of diggers, lorries and earthmovers. A gang of skinny muscular old men removed rocks from the soil by hand, their backs shining with sweat. The forest on either side of the road was partially logged, and the only *ban* was empty, its newly built cookie-cutter huts waiting to house resettled peoples. Then, cresting a low hill, I caught my first sight of the mountains I had to cross to reach the plateau. Mist had blurred them to a shadowy massif but they were imposing nonetheless.

By mid-morning I had climbed a thousand metres, grinding steadily up and around the slopes in second gear, my wheels spinning through deep sand. Below me spread a panorama of hills, their thinly forested flanks shorn with ugly patches of slash-and-burn. A few Land Cruisers dashed past – Norwegian People's Aid, Care International, BSL (a Lao commercial UXO clearance company) – forcing me into the rocky sides, enveloping me in blinding, choking sandstorms. Farther on, a UXO clearance team slept at the roadside, their legs dangling over the sides of army-green hammocks.

At midday the road levelled out onto a wide plateau of heat-scorched grass, pine trees and bomb craters – the old French airfield of Chavan. So different was the cooling breeze and oddly familiar pines that it felt like another country. I glanced at my GPS; it read 1,165 metres.

A former *binh tram* and the intersection of two major Trail routes, Chavan had undergone heavy US bombing raids and remained pitted with craters. Varying in size from 3 to 10 metres, each one now hosted a clutch of bushes and trees, their roots penetrating where the bombs had broken up the rocky laterite surface.

Beyond Chavan a decent graded dirt road climbed and dipped through dry patches of grassland, pines, tranches of jungle and acres of recently planted coffee plantations. Exhilarated to have climbed so far, I pulled the throttle and pushed Panther on. Groups of small whippet-thin women padded along barefoot in brightly woven *sins*, carrying baskets of goods on their backs. *Sabadi*! I'd wave. *Pai sai?* They'd shout back. Later, a lone man loped along with a rifle and *pa* – machete – slung over his shoulder, four lean curly-tailed hunting dogs trotting at his heels. Occasionally I would pass stilted *bans* clustered on dusty red hillocks or around the edge of the road. Distinguishable as belonging to the minority Talieng people by their low-eaved, tightly thatched roofs, they were noticeably unfettered by rubbish, with neat bamboo picket fences around some of the huts. Several were thick with the intoxicating jasmine-like scent of flowering coffee trees.

On the final stretch to Dak Cheung, large areas of slash-and-burnt jungle smouldered by the roadside. In all likelihood it was being cleared for more coffee saplings, which relished the altitude, cooler air and loamy soil of the plateau. Burnt trunks lay in piles, the boundaries with the living forest marked by singed toppling trees, their smooth silvery trunks and fanning canopies making them look like rows of blown-over parasols on a windy beach.

At 4 p.m. the first huts of Dak Cheung came into view and I whooped and pulled the throttle up the final hill onto an unusually wide flat empty dirt street. Visually, there was nothing unusual – wooden huts, a few small concrete houses, rubbish, orange earth, foraging pot-bellied pigs, some recently erected power lines. But the place felt different – wilder, emptier, colder, higher, more remote. A light wind sent dust eddies scurrying across the road, and gunmetal grey clouds hung low in the sky; tumbleweed and swinging saloon doors wouldn't have looked out of place. I'd arrived at the Wild East.

Firstly I wanted to find an old F-4 jet engine that I'd heard lay somewhere behind the main street. Riding slowly between houses, I caught sight of it on some short grass beside a crooked hut. It was an impressive object; a 3-metre-long cylinder of rusting engineered metal; a million dollars of fins, bolts, rivets and tubes lying twisted and forgotten in someone's back yard. I walked around it, fingering the metal, imagining what had become of its two-man crew. Being shot down in this featureless sea of thick jungle and hostile mountains, deep in enemy territory, was every American pilot's nightmare. When I arrived home I tried to research the story of this engine, but I never did find out how it ended up there or who the pilots were.

I arrived at the guest house at the same time as the butcher. A small woman in a woollen hat pushing a wooden handcart, she had a flat aboriginal face that looked too old for the peeping baby strapped to her back. Getting off Panther I watched with queasy fascination as she poked a metal bowl containing the remains of a freshly butchered pig; a macabre jumble of greying skin, staring beetle eyes, bloody haunches and rigid trotters. A thin Vietnamese man, who I presumed to be the guest house owner, was elbow deep in a plastic bucket of slimy intestines. He weighed several disgusting handfuls and poured them into a plastic bag, nodding at me as he did so.

The guest house, the only two-storey house on the main street, was a bijou place built around a gated courtyard. The bottom half was whitewashed concrete, the top floor clad in wood with shuttered windows and a sloping metal roof. A fabulous yellow *Brugmansia* clung to one wall, hung with foot-long trumpet-like flowers. With no sign of Mick, Tim and Somsack, I parked Panther at the back of the yard and set about giving her a minor service. The brakes and throttle felt loose and unresponsive, both of which were easy to remedy, and the oil levels and chain tension needed checking. Filthy anyway, I knelt on the ground and unrolled my tool bundle, turning to the 'Routine Maintenance' section in the Haynes Manual. Still smelling faintly of butchery the Vietnamese man squatted beside me, picking up tools and gently nudging me out of the way. In the last few weeks I'd learnt that the sight of a woman with a toolkit was too much for most Lao and Vietnamese men. They couldn't resist watching, prodding, checking, taking the spanners out of my hand to unscrew bolts themselves. Kind as their intentions were, it was frustrating. I wanted to do it myself, to learn. Gently, but firmly, I reclaimed the spanners and tightened the necessary parts, the man sitting on his haunches to watch.

As I was finishing up, Mick, Tim, Somsack and their Lao driver drove into the yard. They had been setting up a temporary camp for their demining team eight miles away.

'You made it!' said Mick, giving me a welcoming hug. 'We've reserved you a room, they're 80,000 kip (£6.60) each.'

A minute later a chrome-laced chopper sputtered into the yard, its rider looking as if he'd come direct from the ashes of the Apocalypse.

'It's Mad Max!' I exclaimed, laughing.

A wild-looking man of about fifty, he wore a battered open face helmet, large goggles and a dust-streaked waistcoat bulging with pockets. His right forearm was black with tattoos and a large machete was strapped across the handlebars. Most impressive of all was his resplendent Wyatt Earp moustache, which could have stopped a covey of cowboys at 30 metres.

'G'day!' he cried, grabbing my hand in a leather glove. 'I'm John, Mick's brother.'

'Nice bike,' I said.

'Chinese made, 125-cc. Bought it in Vientiane for $1000. Not bad, hey?'

Like a pair of grizzled bikers we opened cans of tepid Vietnamese beer, lit cigarettes and stood by our steeds, while the others went to their rooms to shower. On the ground behind us two captured porcupines cowered in a cage, all flattened spikes and twitching noses.

I asked John about his tattoos. 'These two are my favourite,' he replied, pulling up his shirtsleeves to show a man in army uniform next to a bull terrier's head. 'This is my grandfather, a World War One vet. He survived the Somme, Passchendaele, Messines, two bullet wounds, being blinded in one eye by barbed wire and a broken back. But he still lived until he was eighty-six.'

He moved his fingers across to the bull terrier. 'And this was Buster my dog. Gee, that dog thought he was human. He'd have a beer with me when I got home from work and if I took him to a party and anyone lit up a fat hooter, he wouldn't leave them alone until he'd had a blowback. He'd then lie on a beanbag with his legs in the air.'

John spoke in a broad Kiwi accent, punctuating his stories with a wheezing, Mutley-ish laugh. I liked him immediately.

'Check out what we found today – Megatron's penis.' More laughter.

I followed him to his room, where he showed me a three-foot-long rusting metal cylinder with wires sprouting out of one end. I'd seen replicas before, but never an original one.

'It's one of Operation Igloo White's sensors. We found it when we were clearing today.'

Operation Igloo White was the linchpin of America's efforts against the Trail from 1967 to 1972, an advanced electronic war that cost $1 billion per year to operate. Disguised as plants, thousands of sensors like this one were dropped from the air at strategic points along the Trail. Burying themselves into the ground they collected seismic, acoustic and chemical data on enemy truck and troop movements. The information was relayed to orbiting planes and the futuristic Infiltration Surveillance Center (ISC) at Nakhon Phanom in Thailand, the biggest building in Southeast Asia. 'We wire the Ho Chi Minh Trail like a drugstore pinball machine, and we plug it in every night,' said a US Air Force Officer in 1971.

The data they collected was used to direct bombing raids. One of these was the campaign against the huge NVA supply base at Ban Bak in the 1970–71 dry season, discovered by the 'pinball wizards' due to irregular convoy movements picked up by the sensors.

Unable to tell the difference between trucks, people, animals, thunder, earth tremors or wind, the sensors weren't infallible and the North Vietnamese soon found ways to fool them. Herds of cows were driven past, old truck engines started nearby and bags of urine hung in the trees. Still, along with the AC-130, Igloo White was the best weapon the US had. But since the pilots, CIA and USAF endlessly squabbled among themselves over bomb damage statistics, and their figures differed wildly to those of the North Vietnamese, its exact impact remains impossible to assess.

For supper the five of us – Mick, John, Tim, Somsack and I – walked to a small busy brightly lit restaurant on the main drag. For the first time in Laos, it was cold enough to wear my fleece. With wooden floors and benches, coloured tablecloths and low-hanging bulbs, it felt like a cosy mountain cabin; an unexpected hub of people and life. John was already on his fourth beer by this stage, sucking each one down in a few thirsty gulps, crushing the cans in his still-gloved hand.

'D'ya know why I've got this moustache?' he asked, leaning towards me conspiratorially. Not waiting for a reply, he pulled back the whiskery curtains and grinned a gummy toothless smile. 'I bloody hate dentists!' he said with a tarry laugh. 'I haven't been to one for decades; it's the only thing in the world I'm scared of.'

The more beers John drank the more he talked, his blue eyes darting, his moustache bouncing excitedly as the words tripped over themselves to escape. He told me how he had worked as a civil engineer in Christchurch all his life and couldn't understand why people wanted to travel abroad before they'd seen every inch of their own country, as he had; that he had never left New Zealand until four years ago, when Mick persuaded him to come out here to work with him in Laos. He told me how stunned he had been by the size of the billboards when he first arrived in Bangkok; about his house and adopted dog in Vientiane; that there were seven snakes in Laos whose bites would kill you in minutes, and that snakes were the one thing the rural Lao were really afraid of – oh, and those giant centipedes, which were wont to chase you; and that his big brother Mick was the best EOD expert in the world. After a few more beers he drew breath and asked me my route south from here.

I told him.

He leant in close. 'You *have* to go to the Cu Chi tunnels just outside Saigon and fire an M60 machine gun. It's one dollar a bullet so put aside *at least* three hundred dollars. It's the best thing you'll ever do. It's better than sex, isn't it Mick?'

Mick nodded. With four wives and seven children between them, they knew what they were talking about. John reiterated his point several more times, insisting I go. I promised I would.

The following day John and I chugged down the main street, taking a right down a sandy track towards the Vietnamese border and PCL's clearance site. It was a beautiful morning. Clouds scudded across a cerulean sky and high-forested peaks rose majestically in all directions. The two of us rode side by side, Mad Max and a girl on a pink moped – an unusual sight in these parts.

'You must really confuse people,' said John as we passed a thatched Talieng village. 'Not only are you a *falang* on a pink bike, but you're a girl.'

Proving his point perfectly, two barefoot men hugged the verge and shouted *Poo-so*! – Girl! – as we buzzed by.

The PCL demining team's temporary camp was on a grassy knoll at the roadside next to a small fast-flowing river. They'd been staying here for two weeks while they cleared this section of road of UXO. Ten Lao men in Guantanamo-orange overalls lay in hammocks or squatted on the ground under a blue tarpaulin. In the middle, two women scrubbed pots next to the ashes of a fire. Mick and Somsack were already there, briefing the men on the day's work while Tim sat in the car playing games on his iPad.

The men, aged between twenty and forty, were all Talieng – small and mahogany-skinned with flat noses and shapely mouths – recruited from the nearby village of Dak Vang. Most of the villages around here were called *Dak*, a minority word meaning 'water' for all the rivers and streams in the area. The smallest, who was about five foot three, had an effeminate face and wore oversized rounded sunglasses à *la* Elton John circa 1975. Another sported a diamanté earring and a red Adidas baseball camp – the rebel of the group.

'We always employ our deminers from the area we're clearing,' said Mick. 'That way they've got a vested interest in doing the job properly. We go to local villages and talk to the *nai bans* – village chiefs – asking them who might be interested.'

'In a poor remote area like this with few opportunities for income, you must be inundated,' I said.

'Ha! You'd be amazed. Even though we train them up and they're likely to get snapped up by UXO Lao afterwards, they're not that keen on the idea of work. We have to look pretty hard sometimes.'

All of the men carried guns – crude homemade muzzle loaders and old Soviet AK-47s – which they used to go hunting after work every night.

'What are they after?' I asked Somsack, who was inspecting one of the AKs.

'Bamboo rats, snakes, porcupines, deer, civets, lizards, parrots – anything. They just told me they found some fresh panther poo here when they set up camp yesterday, so they took turns to guard last night in case it was still in the area.'

I was amazed to hear there were real panthers around rather than just the two-wheeled pink variety. 'What would they do with it if they saw it?'

'Try and catch it apparently,' said Somsack, shrugging.

Just then a Vietnamese moped supermarket buzzed past under a stack of mattresses, cooking pans and clothes. The young baseball-hatted driver waved as he went by.

'You know half of those guys are Vietnamese secret police,' said John. 'Laos has always been a popular hiding place for Vietnamese on the run from the law, and since those guys ride all over, Hanoi employs them to keep a note of everything they see and report back anything unusual. There will definitely be a file on a white girl on a pink moped somewhere in Hanoi. That guy's probably stopped around the corner to write notes on what he's just seen.'

I later asked Mick if he had heard the same.

'Oh, absolutely. Some of them are just poor farmers trying to make an extra buck in the dry season, but a lot are employed by Hanoi.'

With a few hours to kill before they started clearing I went for an exploratory ride deeper into the mountains. The narrow sandy path wound through a paradise of lush valleys, pine forest, gin-clear streams, groves of bamboo, fans of elephant grass, cascades of pink flowers and mountains clad in virgin jungle. Elated by such pristine beauty, I stopped above a plunging valley to savour an unbroken view across tens of miles of forest and peak. The GPS read 1,400 metres, and still at least 500 metres above me towered a high mountain, which no one I asked knew the name of. Jungle as dense as moss covered every metre of its steep slopes and off its shoulders rippled a sea of undulating hills draped in a luxuriance of greens. There were no power lines, no villages and – for the first time in Laos – no sign of deforestation. Standing there, drinking in the beauty, I fell in love with Laos again. It was one of those views I know I shall never forget.

Back at the camp the team had started work and a half-mile stretch of road was dotted with orange figures sweeping the ground with clicking, beeping metal detectors. As protection against snakes, all of them had socks pulled up over shin guards. I walked up the road with Mick and John, watching as the men worked.

'This is why I want to train dogs to work here,' said Mick, as we watched Elton John carefully digging up an old nail with a trowel. 'I've used them for mine clearance in Cambodia and they're incredibly effective. You see, a dog can tell the difference between metal and explosives, which a detector can't, so you don't waste time digging up pointless bits of metal like this.' He held up the offending nail. 'I've proven that a dog can find UXO sixteen times more effectively than a human. If we introduced dog teams to Laos, imagine how much faster the country could be cleared. That's why Somsack is here; he's a specialist animal trainer as well as our translator.'

'Really?' I replied.

'Yup, he's worked in France, Bangkok and LA training animals for films. The last thing he did was train the monkeys for *The Hangover Part II*. His house in Savannakhet is full of animals he's rescued from markets here – toucans, dogs, monkeys, civets. The idea is that we bring over half-trained Belgian Malinois from Cambodia and Somsack finishes the training here.'

'So what are you waiting for?'

'Mainly the fact that it's expensive to buy, import and train the dogs, and we need to raise the funding to do it.'

'What's the oddest thing you've ever found with your detectors?' I asked Mick.

'Skeletons filled with gold in Cambodia. People would swallow their jewellery to stop the Khmer Rouge soldiers finding it, but a lot of them were caught and killed. One of our Cambodian deminers put on a gold necklace he found in a skeleton one day. The others on the team all told him not to, that it would be bad luck, but he ignored them. He stepped on a landmine two days later.'

It must have been twenty-eight degrees, but the story made my hairs stand on end.

'Illegal Vietnamese gold miner,' posited John, lighting a cigarette, as a rattletrap of a moped clanked by, festooned with spades, metal bowls and buckets.

'All the rivers around here are running with gold; the place is crawling with Vietnamese. They might be here under other auspices, but they're really after the gold. Our guest house owners for example, they've got some homemade gold-mining equipment next to those poor porcupines. They're all at it.'

'Go and run your hands through that river next to the camp,' suggested Mick. 'You'll find gold, I guarantee.'

I did as he said, crouching in the clear water and running my hands through the silt, pulling out a handful that shone with mineral wealth. Picking out the biggest specks, I showed my booty to Mick.

'There's a way of telling if it's gold or pyrites,' he said, taking out his knife and placing my findings on the blade. 'They look very similar but gold spreads, pyrites shatters.' With a smaller blade, he crushed the lumps on his knife. Half of them splintered, but the two biggest bits – about 3 mm across – spread like butter. Tiny as it was, I felt a primal thrill; that spell of gold. I looked at it, glinting in my palm and thought of gold rushes and greed: wagons rumbling across the Kansas plains, Spanish galleons groaning with bullion, El Dorado. What a strange allure this metal had. It was probably worth about £5, but it was real gold and I'd found it.

As the sun set we sat in the courtyard of the guest house drinking *Beerlao*. The owner's wife settled on a step behind me to absent-mindedly pick through my hair.

'Did you see those two Lao guys who turned up here this morning wanting to talk to John and me?' said Mick.

I hadn't.

'That was really odd. They said they knew of a US plane that had crashed on a mountain near here carrying a hundred and thirty kilograms of gold. No one had ever managed to get to the site because of UXO and the fear of booby traps. They wanted us to come and clear the area so they could get to the gold and said that if we helped them, they'd give us a share.'

It sounded like something out of Indiana Jones. 'But why on earth would a US plane be carrying so much gold?'

'The CIA used to pay their secret Hmong army in gold. The plane could have been carrying the gold from Saigon up to the Hmong headquarters at Long Tieng in the north. It's very possible that those men were telling the truth, but there was something really shifty about them and John and I both felt it was some sort of set-up. Maybe they'd have got us to clear the site and then killed us. Maybe it was someone trying to entrap us for some reason. Who knows, but it was dodgy, and I want nothing to do with it.'

The conversation turned to Cambodia. I would be crossing the border in a matter of days and I was keen to hear more about Mick's experiences there.

'Cambodia is still traumatised by the memory of the Khmer Rouge. It's the only country in the world where second-generation post-traumatic stress disorder (PTSD) has been recorded. Seventy per cent of Cambodians are still under thirty – the old people who survived were either very lucky, or party to the slaughter.' He took a slug of his beer and carried on. 'When I was there with the UN in the nineties, killing was endemic. One guy we were advising was known as "Dr Death". Twice I was with him in meetings when he pulled out his gun and shot someone over a minor disagreement. He didn't think anything of it, killing was a way of life.'

He was on a roll now, memories of Cambodia flooding out. I listened, transfixed, as the woman continued to pick at non-existent nits in my hair.

'I once had a meeting with a former Khmer Rouge general who even Dr Death said was a psychopathic killer. His staff were so terrified, they'd crawl up to him on their hands and knees to ask questions. That man was pure evil; he'd eaten the livers of so many of his victims that the whites of his eyes were yellow.'

The Khmer Rouge was a regime which scoured the very depths of depravity and barbarism. Accounts of cannibalism during those four murderous years aren't uncommon. Guards would cut out and fry their victim's livers; the starving were known to hide dead family members in order to eat their flesh. I didn't doubt Mick's story for a second. Later, a doctor friend of mine informed me that ingesting a surfeit of haematologically rich livers would lead to an excessive production of bilirubin, a pigment which causes jaundice and a condition known as unconjugated hyperbilirubinemia. The idea of it was nauseating.

'What about these days? Is the countryside still packed with landmines?' I asked him.

'Parts of it, yes. Originally between four and six million were laid and, despite a lot of clearance, there are still between three and four million left. A few hundred people still get blown up every year. If I were you, I'd stick to the path. It's just not worth the risk.'

They were words I'd recall frequently over the coming few weeks.

I had become attached to the PCL family. They were such characters, brimming with so many mind-boggling stories. I was struck by what a clearly devoted father Mick was, how kind and warm he had remained in the face of so much death and trauma, and how close he and John were. After the week I'd had – Panther's problems, my illness, my sadness at what was happening to Laos – being with these swashbuckling brothers was a much needed tonic. Had I succeeded in getting to Ban Bak, our paths might never have crossed.

CHAPTER 14

DOWN FROM DAK CHEUNG

'What on earth have you got in all those pockets?' I asked John as I zipped up my panniers to leave the next morning. Whenever I looked at him, he was pulling something new out of his Tardis-like fisherman's waistcoat.

'Everything you need to survive in Laos,' he said proudly. 'Compass, camera, pen, baseball cap, dust mask – a must for Laos.'

Like a game show exhibitor, he extracted and held up each object as he talked me through them. 'Binoculars, water purifying system, sachets of instant three-in-one coffee, cigarettes…'

He unclipped the silver Zippo that doubled as a belt buckle. '… lighter, multi-purpose knife…'

Now we'd moved on from the pockets to an extra layer of supplies strapped around his waist. 'Pliers, dog beater – in case you get attacked – water canteen, cup and a machete made out of the finest bomb steel.'

'Do you think you'd survive a nuclear war?'

'Definitely,' he chuckled. 'I think I'd do pretty well with the cockroaches.'

The Dak Cheung party was over. Mick and Tim were leaving for Vientiane, I was heading south to Attapeu and John and Somsack were staying behind with the clearance team.

'Be careful of the road down to Attapeu, it's about sixty miles from here,' said Mick as he loaded equipment into the Hilux. 'Some of it's OK, but there's a lot of deep sand and big rocks.'

The driver, a small plump Lao who couldn't speak any English, looked at Panther and shook his head – a by now familiar reaction. *Surely nothing could be worse than the road to La Hap?* I thought.

'You've gotta take my picture with James May's key and send it to him. I love Top Gear!' insisted John. He posed, all moustache and goggles and pockets, then fished something out of his waistcoat and handed it to me. It was a spent 12 millimetre artillery shell.

'For good luck,' he said. 'Oh, and watch it when you're riding across the old airfield at Chavan. I went for a walk there recently and found a lot of cluster bombs lying around.'

We all said goodbye and with a slight lump in my throat I rode away from the guest house, waving as I went.

My descent from Dak Cheung was the beginning of my journey out of Laos. From here it was down: down to the town of Attapeu, across the scalded plains of Champasak, and south along the Mekong into Cambodia. To get to Attapeu town I first had to retrace my steps to Chavan, then drop down into Attapeu province, Laos' most south-easterly, on what was left of the old Trail Route 128. Bordered by both Vietnam and Cambodia, Attapeu had been the southern terminus of the Laotian trail, the point at which the flow of men and supplies turned east into South Vietnam, or continued south into

Cambodia. If they made it as far as Attapeu, the *boi dois* knew the worst of the journey was behind them.

An hour out of Dak Cheung I stopped at a roadside shrine to the *phi*. Incense, water bottles, bananas and cigarettes had been placed on a small wooden platform at the edge of the forest, the earth around its base strewn with further offerings. A narrow river gurgled in a ravine below. It was either a grave or simply somewhere people asked the *phi* for safety while travelling on the mountain roads. I took a few photos and kicked Panther into action. But the lever slipped uselessly between first, second and third. The gear mechanism had gone. Without gears I couldn't move an inch. Flicking to 'Chapter 1: Engine and Gearbox' in the Haynes Manual, I was confronted with a terrifying-looking exploded diagram of the inner workings of a C90 gear system. Since the geary bits are inside the enginey bits, it meant taking apart the whole engine to see what the problem was. I'd become pretty good at basic tweaking but I feared this was beyond me.

Crouching in the dust, I fiddled with my spanner set and peered at the diagrams. Several overloaded pick-up trucks rattled by, the drivers and passengers all hanging out to shout *Pai Sai*?

'Attapeu!' I shouted back hopefully, not wanting to ask for help yet.

They laughed and burnt past without taking their feet off the gas, engulfing me in a storm of dust. So much for chivalry in Laos.

Temporarily defeated, I sat down and wondered what to do. I knew Mick would be coming this way soon, but relying on him felt defeatist. I would *have* to try harder. Forcing myself to study the problem anew, the cogs of my non-mechanical mind creaked into action. Perhaps the problem was simpler. Perhaps it was to do with the gear lever itself, rather than the actual gear-changing mechanism. Perhaps...

Midway through my ruminations a cloud of dust signalled Mick and Tim's arrival.

'Oh dear, what's happened this time?' asked Mick, looking amused.

An all-round engineering and gadgetry genius, he diagnosed the problem in an instant. A few more minutes and I might have diagnosed the problem myself. It was a simple matter of the bolt on the gear lever having shorn off, meaning the gears were unable to catch. We stole a bolt from the number plate, secured the plate with cable ties and within five minutes the problem was fixed.

While we were doing this, Mick's driver was busy offering incense and a delicately unwrapped chocolate bar to the spirits, muttering to himself as he did so.

'It's the spirits!' I said to Mick. 'I stopped to take photos but didn't offer them anything in return. That'll teach me to take and not give anything back.'

I peeled a banana and added it to the spirits' collection, apologising for being so rude and asking for protection on the road ahead. Then once again we said goodbye and I watched as Mick's Hilux vanished down the hill.

At Chavan I rode slowly between the craters, my eyes scanning the ground for stray bombies. By now this had become second nature. Every time I stopped for a pee I stayed on the track, checking the ground around me for UXO and the nearby shrubbery for snakes and spiders. It was a habit that would stay with me for several months after I arrived home. A handful of small brown cows grazed, their bells tinkling as they picked at the poor grass. Black holes in the ground were gossamered with the webs of spiders I'd rather not meet. Now the track narrowed, dropping due south through cool dark heavily scented pine forests and across parched grass clearings. Again that feeling that I had been transported to another land, that this couldn't really be Laos.

Amidst a barricade of pines I passed a grubby couple squatting on the path, roasting skewered bamboo rats over a small fire.

'*Pai sai?*' they asked, waving a blackened toothy rodent at me.

'Attapeu!'

Around the corner the forest was burning on either side of the track. Fire licked the edge of the path and the air was fragrant with pine smoke. Fearful of explosions I pulled the throttle, accelerating through the smoke and encroaching flames.

Minutes later I was clunking down a steep rubbly hill into a grassy clearing when I inexplicably lost balance and tumbled sideways into the dirt. Wincing, I picked myself up. Blood was seeping out of a two-inch slash on my left shin and my panniers lay on the ground, both ripped open along the top seams. I couldn't afford to make such silly mistakes, next time it might be more than just a cut. Hopping and swearing, I led Panther down the hill, pausing to clean the cut and smoke a nerve-calming cigarette. Having secured the panniers with an extra bungee, I rode on, trying to ignore my throbbing leg. The only thing for it was to laugh; first a breakdown, now a fall – this was turning out to be an eventful day.

The road snaked up and over hills, a saffron streak slicing through the green. On either side were red UXO markers. Above, grey clouds smothered the last chinks of blue. Farther on, in an avenue of trees lined with purple flowering rhododendron bushes, I met a UXO clearance team; men in blue overalls carrying buckets, spades and metal detectors.

'*Pai sai, poo-so* – where are you going, girl?' they asked.

'Attapeu!'

One of them spoke a little English. 'Attapeu?' he said, raising his eyebrows. 'Oh, it's ninety kilometres from here, road is very bad. You might have to sleep in jungle tonight. And be careful, road ahead is full of holes where we've dug up bombies and metal.'

I asked him if this was part of the Trail. If Attapeu was that far away and the road was this narrow, I must have taken a wrong turn.

'Yes,' he nodded, 'lots of UXO. Stay on the track.'

I asked him what they were clearing for.

'New bauxite mine,' he replied.

I later heard that there were thought to be 12 trillion tonnes of bauxite in this part of Laos. Mining it would mean more environmental damage and resettlement. Poor old Laos.

I bumped on slowly through the trees, steering between freshly dug bombie-sized holes and protruding rocks, the track narrowing to a footpath, trees knotting over my head. At this pace I wasn't going to get anywhere near Attapeu tonight. I only had half a litre of water left, a few bananas and half a tank of petrol, and a thunderstorm looked imminent. Sleeping in such a heavily bombed bit of jungle wasn't something I wanted to do, and I was wary of sleeping in a village where there was no guest house. Don, the American biker, had told me some villages 'weren't always what they seemed,' and that he'd had most of his kit stolen in one once. And a female Lao sociologist – also a biker – had said a lone white female appearing out of nowhere and asking for somewhere to sleep could send the wrong message. She had often travelled alone in rural Laos and told me she was frequently asked, 'Aren't you afraid of being raped?' If I wanted to sleep in a village, she said, go with a translator. Ironically, if I had to sleep out, the jungle was probably the better option.

To my utmost surprise the dark path popped out onto a wide graded dirt road. A group of women walked by, bent against the dust and a rising wind. Racing the storm and time I leant forward over Panther and twisted the throttle, nearly jumping out of my skin as a deafening thunderclap cracked over my head.

Something at that moment made me remember it was Easter Sunday. It was 3 p.m. About now, back in England, my parents would be belting out hymns in church and my nephew and niece would be tearing open Easter eggs, their faces smudged in chocolate. How far away that all seemed from my present situation – not enough food and water, no idea where I would sleep tonight and about to get drenched by a tropical thunderstorm. But I was happy; happy to be alone, happy to be pushed like this, enlivened by the adventure. Easter eggs could wait until next year.

It was on days like today that I really revelled in the solitude. I was engaged, focused, determined. On my own, there was no one to help me and no one to complain to. If I was with Marley I probably would have grumbled about my leg hurting, the thunder, being tired. But so what? So what if my leg hurt?

What use would telling him achieve? So what if I was tired or hot or cold? He couldn't change that. As I rode I considered how complaining has become so endemic in our western spoilt society; it's too hot, too cold, too crowded, too expensive; I've got a headache, I'm tired, I had a bad day at work; the person in front is driving too slowly, and so on. It's so insidious we hardly register it, this drip, drip, drip of negativity that feeds into everyday life. So many of us are guilty of it, yet we hardly notice. I vowed to try and stop complaining when I arrived home.

Over the next rise I spied a collection of shacks, one of which sold water. A man swung in a hammock and fifteen women and children sat torpidly under a metal awning, staring as I downed a whole bottle. Everyone cowered as another violent thunderclap ripped overhead.

'Where's the nearest hotel?' I asked, using Google translate. My phone was passed around the group, everyone squinting at the screen uncomprehendingly.

'Muong Sanxai,' the man in the hammock replied, seemingly the only one who could read. Muong Sanxai was about twenty miles away; I had a chance of making it before dark.

From here the road dropped sharply down to the Attapeu valley. For 1,000 metres I snaked interminably down, jolting over rocks and ploughing through deep sand, Panther's brakes squealing miserably. At the rusting hulk of a tank I stopped briefly to take pictures and clamber on the turret, but with time against me I had to press on.

My hands, neck and shoulders ached from the strain and at several points I let out yelps of frustration as I came upon another steep sandy downhill slope. The farther we went, the worse the brakes became. A hamster strapped to the wheels with paperclips would have been a more effective braking solution. Below me were deep valleys, tendrils of mist and pillars of approaching rain, but I was so focused on staying vertical I didn't have a chance to take it all in. It was not a pleasurable few hours.

At five o'clock, ten miles from Muong Sanxai, I dropped Panther again, precious petrol pouring out onto the sand as she fell. For the first time on my journey I lost my temper. I swore furiously into the empty air and aimed a vicious kick at Panther's seat. Hopping with pain and fury I apologised, dragged her up and stamped on the kick-start.

Nothing.

Silence.

Not even a pop.

More than ten tries later it was clear there was no convincing her. Panther was going nowhere. Since it was getting dark and there was no traffic, I was going to have to drag her off the road and find somewhere to sling my hammock. But with a wall of mountain on one side and a steep drop on the other, there was nowhere to go. I walked back to Panther determinedly.

'Right girl, you're *going* to start this time, OK!' I said out loud. I gave the kick-start an extra hard kick and she choked into life. We were damn well going to get to that town tonight, even if it wasn't until midnight.

More rocks, more sand, more vertiginous descents. I was so determined to get there I screamed at myself every time I faltered or threatened to go down again. I *wasn't* going to come off for a third time today.

At six o'clock the sun set behind pigeon-grey clouds and the thunderstorm broke. Blinded by the rain, I hunched over the handlebars and rode as fast as I could. Thunder crashed above me and fingers of lightning streaked across the darkness. I remembered a story Mick had told me about seven of his men getting struck by lightning and how storms like this could trigger UXO. My hands were sodden, my boots wet, my tyres skidded on wet rocks. Water dripped down my helmet and onto my face. I was dangerously low on petrol. *Please let me be close. Please let us get there soon. Please don't let me run out of petrol.*

Then, finally – lights in the darkness, the dusky outlines of houses, the flashing neon lights of a karaoke bar, the promise of shelter at last. Turning off the road I drove straight in to the middle of the open-sided bar, riding Panther across the wooden floor and stopping next to a table of men mid-ballad.

'Yeeeehah!' I cried, taking off my helmet and gloves and peeling my sodden self from the seat. The men stopped singing and looked at me with open mouths.

'*Hong ham* – hotel?' I asked a teenage boy behind the bar.

He shook his head and pointed to a concrete building opposite, then picked up an umbrella and motioned for me to follow him. I unstrapped my panniers and left Panther where she was.

The 'hotel' was damp and degenerate, a den of flickering lights and dripping walls. Through a half-open door I glimpsed two prostitutes sitting on a bed, gossiping as they put on their make-up. The boy opened the room at the end of the corridor, yelling at the girls as he did so, and I watched as the three of them changed the crumpled greying sheets. When he didn't know how much to charge me I gave him 40,000 kip and he left, closing the door behind him.

The fan clattered, the strip lights droned, the concrete floor hopped with tiny frogs. A glance under the bed revealed used condoms, broken beer bottles, old condom wrappers and cigarette butts. In the 'en-suite' a western-style loo was cracked and taped over, leaving a bucket, a cold tap and a hole in the floor. Thank goodness I didn't have diarrhoea.

But there was a bed, it was mainly dry and I was ecstatic to have made it here.

Today's ride had been my toughest yet. Ravenously hungry and in need of a drink, I changed and headed back to the bar where I was immediately pounced on by a small, suited and extremely drunk man. I recognised him as one of the two whose song I had interrupted. Like an over-amorous octopus he draped his arms around me and jabbered incomprehensibly, squeezing my waist and stroking my nose. Every time I extricated myself another pawing arm clutched at me. I showed him pictures of my sister's children, pretending they were mine but it did nothing to deter him. Instead he pointed to himself, held up five fingers and gave me his most virile smile.

By now the bar – a large wooden structure dominated by a cinema-sized karaoke screen – was filling up. Couples drank in shadowy corners and took it in turns to sing, their tuneless wailings blasting out of multiple stacks of speakers. Too tired to resist, I joined the Octopus, an older man and the two prostitutes at their table. The youngest of them, a stunning girl of about twenty, sipped her beer inscrutably as the other man leeringly inched a hand inside her denim hot pants. I hoped she was charging him lots of money.

When it came to our turn for karaoke the Octopus pressed the microphone into my hands, grinning idiotically. Why not?

I'll never see these people again. But alas, they had no English songs, not even 'Hey Jude', 'Bohemian Rhapsody' or anything by Abba. They were spared. Instead the elder of the two women took the microphone and closed her eyes to sing a mournful Lao ballad.

Emboldened by beer, soon everyone in the bar was taking it in turns to have their photo taken with me. They sidled up, passed their phones to each other and slipped their arms around my shoulders. The Octopus, who by now was almost sitting on my lap, took it one step further and lunged for a kiss. I ducked and said goodnight, scurrying through the rain and locking my door behind me.

Had I made it to Attapeu, I doubt my night would have been nearly so eventful.

In daylight I realised quite how close I had come to running out of petrol last night; a few miles more and I would have been pushing the bike through the rain. I filled up at a hut in the village, ate two bowls of *pho* for breakfast, took a few pictures of a surface-to-air missile still on its original launch beside the road, and was on my way.

From the brothel I headed due west across the Attapeu valley on a good tarmac road. For the first time in more than two weeks I was riding away from the Vietnamese border and the Truong Son. I buzzed across shimmering plains of cracked earth and yellowed paddies, thankful for the cooling effect of my still damp jacket. Across a wide, newly built bridge over the Sekong was the town of Attapeu. Street lights paraded down a neatly planted central reservation on the main drag and shaved, robed young monks cycled leisurely along an unbroken pavement. In the large *wat* compound were gilded stupas, a dozen golden Buddhas, delicious-smelling frangipani trees and washing lines draped in orange robes. Faded frescoes in the main *wat* depicted the heavens and hells of Theravada Buddhism: impala pulling Buddha's golden carriage, wolves ripping the bowels out of contorted figures, Buddha levitating over a crepuscular scene of hangings and torture, beatific saints and devil-faced gods.

It was only mid-morning, but after yesterday's ride I felt in need of an easy day. And it was definitely time for a treat. The hotel I chose was a one-hundred-room behemoth with a weedy tennis court and hovering staff; surprisingly luxurious, amazingly cheap and echoingly empty. Exhausted, I spent most of the day in my room, catching up with writing, sewing up my panniers and calling home. At supper in the massive dining room two Lao businessmen talked seriously, ignoring the pair of smartly dressed women they'd hired for the night sitting silently alongside them, eyes lowered, shifting their glasses uncomfortably, while a pair of waitresses lingered awkwardly with trays full of Heineken. At breakfast they had gone, and five uniformed staff stood stiffly as I took on the five-star forty-foot-long buffet singlehanded. Like a hungry hobbit I bobbed up and down, gorging on watermelon, sweet mango, fresh juices, sticky pastries, *pho,* omelette and toast. What a waste to prepare such a feast for a single hungry biker. How odd it hadn't occurred to them to cater for one, not a hundred.

With Panther washed and my panniers basted together, I set off west for Si Phan Don, a backpacker haunt on the Mekong. It was 130 miles away near the Cambodian border, but on flat tarmac I would be there in seven or eight hours. Straight across the plains I rode, past small *bans,* desiccated fields and muddy ponds boiling with water buffaloes. Stopping at one such watering hole to take photos, I scarpered when a grumpy albino bull with drooping horns eyed me crossly. Having so recently been in Africa I was still suspicious of their apparently placid nature. If their savannah cousins were so dangerously irascible, surely these ones were prone to the odd tantrum too.

A few miles to the north rose the sheer southern shoulder of the Bolaven Plateau, an extinct volcano that spreads across much of Champasak and Attapeu provinces. Up there were waterfalls, rivers and luxurious resorts, down here was flatness and wilting heat.

It's funny how we don't miss things until they're gone. A few days ago I'd have given one of my back teeth to be gliding along this smooth black surface. But today, as the Truong Son receded to shadows behind me, the prospect of a day on tarmac seemed too easy, dull even. I thought of the mountains we had battled over, the disappearing jungle, the breakdowns, my time with the Mistys and Mick and John; I didn't want my Laotian adventure to be over.

But Laos hadn't finished with me yet. Soon the tarmac disintegrated to suspension-shattering dust and potholes, swiftly followed by a river crossing. At least 60 metres wide, there was no visible way to cross. Behind me a group of white-shirted schoolchildren gathered under a tree to watch, hooting and cackling like vultures as I waded in up to my thighs. *Could they help me carry it across?* I asked them in sign language. In response, they guiltily pointed downriver and said *bak* – ferry. A mile south a sharp-faced boy rowed me over on a wooden pontoon, smirking as he tried to charge me $10.

On the far bank, beyond two huts selling petrol, snacks and water, three dirt tracks wiggled off confusingly in different directions. None of them looked like the main road west. On my one map of Laos the road from here to Highway 13 on the Mekong was marked as a thick orange line dotted with settlements. It was the country's most southerly east–west artery; it had to be in decent condition. But the 'road' I chose was a slender deeply rutted track made almost impassable by sharp slabs of black volcanic rock and fallen trees. Convinced I had taken a wrong turn I turned around and bumped back to the huts.

Two men and a woman were lounging at a table in the shade staring into space. Yes, they said, that was the right road; in three hours I would hit Highway 13. Not quite believing them, I bought 2 litres of rust-red petrol in old Pepsi bottles, two more litres of water, and tried again.

For an hour my wheels slid down ruts and the engine scraped over jagged basalt. The floral shirt I had put on to mark our survival of the Truong Son darkened with sweat and dirt. In a gloomy tunnel of trees two Vietnamese moped supermarkets came the other way and greeted me with a *xin chào*. I pictured them riding around the corner before hurriedly stopping to scribble 'pink moped seen heading into the jungle' on their secret notepads. On a beautiful stretch of earthy track through undisturbed jungle I stopped for water and a pee. Patches of sunlight trickled through the jade canopy, butterflies flopped and fluttered and a bird trilled in the trees. I stood, listening, feeling, imprinting the moment as a memory, aware that in a few weeks' time my adventure would be over and life would move on. I wanted to savour every second of it, to live in the now, to remember what it felt like to be alone in the jungle.

Three hours from the huts, I was nowhere near Highway 13. Instead I was puzzling how to navigate another seemingly impossible twenty-metre river crossing deep in the forest. Up and down the bank I rode, weaving through trees and bumping over roots, trying to find people or a way across. A lone woman with a bulbous goitre shrugged and carried on gathering wood. Two men fishing on the far bank did the same. There were people here, this was a 'main' road, there *had* to be a way across. Returning to the ford to mull the matter over, I heard the faint screams and laughter of children. Ducking under branches and scanning the ground for bombies, I walked through the trees to find them. The shrieks became closer then receded eerily, echoing through the forest.

'*Sabadi*!' I waved when I spied the gaggle of bodies splashing in the water. Twenty heads turned and squawked with excitement and a young woman scrubbing clothes on a rock looked up and smiled. I made motorbike motions with my hands and pointed up river. They understood. At the woman's command the herd of glistening, nut-brown imps stampeded out of the water and up the bank. They flocked around me as the leader, a well-muscled ruffian of about ten, held up five fingers with a vulpine smile. 50,000 kip – £4.20; it was a lot, but I was in no position to negotiate. We had a deal.

Lao children like these are a world away from our mollycoddled urban offspring. Smart as bobcats, by the time they're eight they can hunt, fish and look after each other, roaming the jungle in feral packs. This raggle-taggle bunch of

Mowglis may have only come up to my waist but they were tougher than most British adults would ever be. Small as they were, I had to trust them. I jokingly made strongman gestures with my arms, at which they giggled and bounded off through the trees, naked bottoms glinting in the sun. By the time I caught up with them they were swarming around Panther, the leader hacking at lengths of bamboo with a machete, marshalling his tiny troops. It was a scene straight out of *The Lord of the Flies*. Removing my luggage, I watched as they thrust two long poles through the spokes and hoisted my precious Panther over their heads.

The leader barked his orders and in they all dived, five or six children on either side. I stood on the bank with the smallest ones, clapping and whooping with encouragement. The bamboo buckled. Brown water lapped at the wheels, but slowly they wobbled across. Triumphant, they put Panther down on the far bank and hurtled back for their money. The leader took my fistful of notes and sat on a rock, divvying out the booty with the professionalism of an Irish bookie. When it had all been snatched away he looked at me with imploring eyes and said, 'dollar, dollar.' I knew then I wasn't the first foreign biker to come this way.

The track continued through sun-dappled jungle, across narrow rivers and up steep rocky banks, some so vertical it felt more like an exercise in rock-climbing than biking. The wheels jammed in crevasses. The engine thudded on rocks. And I yowled like a Soviet weightlifter as I heaved, lifted and pushed Panther up steep ladders of black rock.

'You *are* going to get up here, Panther,' I yelped through gritted teeth, as I forced her up a slope. The fire of determination had been lit again. Come blood, hell or high water I *was* going to get us to Highway 13.

At 4 p.m. we hit another wide river crossing where the water rushed over the black, slippery rocks of a shallow causeway. Not bothering to take off my sodden boots I steered Panther over the first rocks, only to be hollered at by a teenage boy on a moped behind me. Grabbing my top box he hauled me backwards out of the water and made it clear I should follow him, smiling kindly. Over the rocks we bumped, sliding, splashing, straining, thudding; aching and soaked to the thighs. On the other side I thanked him and he was off, racing ahead of me on a sandy track belted by brown fields.

At last I was out of the jungle.

But my hopes of reaching Si Phan Don that day were fading with the light. Looking for any nearby guest houses on the GPS, I saw – rather improbably – that there was an *auberge* less than 10 miles away.

It was an odd place that I found, on a corner in the middle of a dusty village. Rows of cobwebbed wooden bungalows stood padlocked and empty. Hammocks hung limply. In the deserted restaurant a wooden sign hung sideways off an old nail; the peeling paint read, 'Elephant rides, mopeds for hire, trekking in forest'. But there were no elephants, no mopeds and it felt like no one had stayed here for years.

In a hut at the entrance a gasping old woman lay on a bed at an open window, eyeing me as her stooping toothy husband walked out and addressed me in French.

'*Parlez-vous anglais?*' I asked back.

'A little,' he croaked, taking in the soaking, sweat-caked, begrimed, dusty creature before him.

I asked him for food. 'After you wash,' he replied pointedly, leading me down a dirt path to the first hut.

But by the time I'd hosed off and sat down for supper, I was too tired to eat. I forced a few mouthfuls of sticky rice and fried vegetables down, talking in snatches of pidgin French and English to the old man. He seemed evasive and a little careless with the truth. He said the elephants were in the jungle, he had once been a French teacher and yes, lots of foreign tourists stayed here. When I looked in the guestbook though, there were only a handful of entries – all in French – in the past year.

Between talking to me, the old man shuffled in and out of his house, moonlighting as the village doctor. A trickle of people came and went, smiling at me shyly, leaving with bandages and boxes of pills. Among them was a square-faced little boy who cried as he waited with his mother, then beamed when I handed him some bananas.

That night it felt hotter than the Danakil Depression. I tossed and turned, fanned myself with a map and poured bottles of cold water over my head and torso. But nothing alleviated the smothering heat. Amplified by the sultry darkness the sound of a nearby party drifted through my mesh window, and every twenty minutes or so a logging lorry howled past. Dog-tired as I was, I couldn't sleep.

After all the rigours of the day it was odd to think that only this morning I had woken up in my luxurious balconied room at the Attapeu Palace Hotel. It felt like weeks ago. How funny to think I'd woken up, put on my best shirt and promised Panther we'd have an easy day on tarmac. Instead I had spent ten hours crunching over rocks, wading through rivers and fighting through the dark jungle. Rather than drinking gin and tonic at Si Phan Don, here I was at a weird *auberge* in a village I didn't even know the name of. Life is so rarely what you expect it to be.

CHAPTER 15

MEKONG SUNSETS

It was an uneventful twenty miles west to the rarefied tarmac of Highway 13 the next day. All I remember is the dust, which erupted from the wheels of passing vehicles and billowed about me in an obliterating veil. By now the Titian scourge had sewn itself into every part of my being, permanently coating Panther and me in an orange carapace. My jacket was impregnated with tiny particles of orange, my gloves dyed ochre. Dust had permeated my goggles and turned the inside of my helmet a pale shade of saffron. My nose, pores, ears and eyelashes were clogged with the stuff. Panther's tyres were orange, her paintwork dulled, the black seat ingrained. After a month on the Trail, we had been reduced to dust.

Built by the French and stretching all the way from the northern border with China south to Cambodia, Highway 13 is Laos' main road. Seven years previously Jo and I had driven our tuk tuk along its northerly reaches, fearful of alleged Hmong guerrillas. This time it would be taking me south. Hitting the tarmac and turning left beside a sign reading 'Attapeu 116 km,'

I paused for a final look back towards the Truong Son, so aptly named the 'Long Mountains'. I bid goodbye to the boonies, the dirt tracks, the enfolding arms of the Laotian jungle, then twisted the throttle and struck south.

Wilting with heat and fatigue I buzzed along at 25 miles per hour, attempting to revitalise myself by singing a medley of Madonna's *Immaculate Collection*. The plains of Champasak province fanned out on either side of me, scalded to a featureless beige, thirsting for the rains. Traffic was light and I played tag with a frequently stopping yellow bus, bursting with people and luggage. Panther, I noticed with dismay, was once again rattling like a bronchitic tractor after yesterday's torment. She would probably make it the 50 miles to Si Phan Don, but after that she was going to need attention.

Si Phan Don – meaning 'Four Thousand Islands' – is a riverine archipelago that stipples the lowest reaches of the Mekong in Laos. A bucolic paradise of golden sandbars and palm-fringed islands, it is home to fishermen, wallowing water buffaloes and the critically endangered Irrawaddy dolphin. More recently, however, several of the larger islands have become colonised by an invasive foreign species. Resistant to dirt and local customs, the backpacker first arrived on the islands in the mid-nineties. Since then this intruder has spilled across Don Det and Don Khon, marking its territory with a trail of scabby bungalows and Nutella and banana pancakes. Less than two decades after the first backpackers 'discovered' Si Phan Don, it has become one of their favoured dry-season colonies.

Dreaming of gin, pancakes and a day in a hammock I rode Panther up a plank onto the small ferry to Don Det. No more than the usual wooden platform, there was just enough room for a German family to stand next to me, the first tourists I had seen since meeting Olivier and JJ in Nong.

'Vat is your bike called?' asked the father, a model Teuton with Pacific-blue eyes, white blond hair and a clipped Bavarian accent.

'You mean the make, or her name?' I replied, expecting an exacting Germanic response.

'No, her nickname, she must have one.'

He laughed when I told him.

We put-putted through the aquamarine waters of the Mekong, between tiny islets exploding with sugar palms and betel trees. Calm after her raging descent from the Tibetan Plateau, the world's twelfth longest river meandered about us, caressing the sides of the ferry. Already she had travelled through Tibet, China, Burma, Thailand and Laos, changing names three times as she plunged south. In Tibet she started her journey as *Dzachu* – River of Rocks; in China she dropped a torrid 5,000 metres to become *Lancang Jiang* – the Turbulent River; in Thailand and Laos she was *Mae Nam Khong* – Mother of the Waters. And before disgorging herself into the South China Sea she would have two more incarnations; as the Khmer *Tonle Tom* – Great One; and lastly, *Cuu Long* – Nine Dragons – in Vietnam. Now, at the end of the dry season she was as at her calmest, but in a few months the monsoons would churn the Mekong into an unrecognisable boiling brown cauldron.

Shortly, we rounded a sandbar and Don Det came into view. Bungalows and palms spilled from the edge of the island and a small beach was sprawled with young westerners in various states of repose. Dominating the scene was an ample bronzed bottom, nominally clad in a dental-floss style bikini; just the sort the local chief had requested people not to wear on his island. Around it, other girls cavorted in the shallows and noisy English people sat in groups puffing on spliffs. Among them a lone water buffalo enjoyed its morning ablutions, nobly ignoring the two French boys who laughingly tugged at its horns.

Nervous to be among this unfamiliar tribe, I rode Panther down the plank and across the beach, pausing to say goodbye to the Germans. A bearded topless male slobbed past me, shooting me a disapproving look. 'Hey, can you turn the engine off, it's disturbing the peace,' he drawled in an American accent.

What a self-righteous prick, I thought, acquiescing to his demand, then wishing immediately I hadn't and scowling at him as he walked away.

I rode slowly down the main strip of Don Det, aware of Panther's sickening noisy engine. Sunburnt travellers traipsed listlessly, drifting in and out of roughly built shops, cafés and Robinson Crusoe style bungalows. I smiled at them. Some smiled back. Most stared grumpily past me. Backpackers often look pissed off. I'd once been told by one that it was because they travelled for the memory, not for the experience. Tattoos and dreadlocks were the norm, skinny arms sported jangles of bangles. Clothes were old and faded – Thai fisherman's trousers bought in Bangkok's Khao San Road or Indian dresses bought in Delhi's Paharganj. A few months ago these sorry-looking individuals might have been smartly dressed city dwellers, but it didn't take long to cultivate the unkempt backpacker look, to morph into one of the Tribe. I'd done it myself, gone to Ko Pha Ngan aged eighteen and come back two months later with green hair, no shoes, a neon tongue stud and a rucksack full of ripped grubby clothes.

Wooden signs advertised the usual traveller essentials: boat trips, money exchange, laundry, bus tickets, Wi-Fi, tubing, trips to see waterfalls and dolphins, transfers to Siem Reap, Pakse, Vientiane and Luang Prabang. A few had dedicated signs shouting 'WE HAVE NUTELLA'. It was exactly the same scene you would find in traveller haunts in Goa, Bali, Manali and Ko Lanta; the same menus, the same décor, the same Bob Marley tunes, the same books, the same clothes; as if all of them had studied the same unwritten Traveller's Handbook. Among all of this the islanders continued to live; children walked to school, men fished off the side of wooden canoes, women washed clothes in the river, cows and dogs wandered down the dirt pathways.

When Panther had first broken down in Kaleum it had felt somehow exciting. Now it was just a bore. For the third time in two weeks I spent the best part of a day squatting beside a greasy sweating mechanic as oil and engine parts spilled on the floor. A pint-sized Lao, he was so lean I could see every muscle, rib and vertebra standing out on his shirtless back as he worked. Again the cam chain and cam sprockets had broken, damaging the valves and cylinder barrel. Again her engine had to be disembowelled and rebuilt. Again I handed over 300,000 kip and rode her away sounding fully restored. It was hard to fathom why the same thing kept happening over and over again. It could have been due to poor quality parts, or each mechanic setting the cam timing wrong. Or maybe it was simply that Panther couldn't cope with the Ho Chi Minh Trail. So much for a sybaritic day spent lazing in a hammock.

That evening I retreated to the quieter island of Don Khon and ordered the gin and tonic I had been longing for. Blissfully happy, I sat at a quiet riverside bar savouring each sip, watching the crimson sun slide languidly between the palms. Below me fishermen paddled home on their pirogues, through water that rippled and shimmered like a bale of tangerine silk. It was a magical scene.

For the entire two hours I sat there, a middle-aged French couple next to me typed wordlessly away on their matching Apple laptops, missing every moment of the most glorious Mekong sunset.

After the remoteness and solitude of the Trail, my brief stay on the islands seemed a hallucinatory interlude. Si Phan Don was the 'other' Laos; the 'secret gem of Southeast Asia' that featured in breathy, clichéd travel articles and top-end tourism brochures. It was the Laos that the vast majority of the country's 3.3 million tourists in 2012 would have fallen in love with; the Laos of gilded stupas, smiling monks, *bo pen yang* and Mekong boat trips. But where I had been there were almost no *falangs*, few signs of Buddhism and no gin or boutique spas. I'd spent nearly every night in a brothel; people had fled in fear because I was foreign; and every day I'd been faced with the greed and corruption of the Lao government. I read an article in a British broadsheet about Si Phan Don a few months later and hardly recognised the glossy polished Laos it spoke of. And for some reason it made me angry. I wanted people to know what was really happening in Laos; how whole villages had lost their homes so the tourists could play golf in Luang Prabang; how the nice garden furniture they had just brought at their local furniture store was made from wood illegally logged in Laos; how their gold wedding ring could have come from this plundered land; how people here are still being sent to re-education camps and being murdered for speaking out against the government.

Discombobulated by this other Laos I drifted around the islands the next day. At the tip of Don Khon a young man in a floppy straw hat approached me and asked if I wanted to see the dolphins.

'Yes, why not?' I said, handing over 60,000 kip. The two of us stepped into a motorised pirogue and spluttered off.

Like tiger spotting in Chitwan, I thought the boat trip would just be a pleasant thing to do; I never believed for a minute we might actually see any of the shy, incredibly rare Irrawaddy dolphins. Once plentiful, the dolphins were dynamited indiscriminately by the Khmer Rouge, who used their oil to power lamps and grease their weapons. Remaining populations provided live target practice for Vietnamese and Khmer soldiers between 1979 and 1995, and were decimated by gill-net fishing. But since 2006 the near-extinct animals have seen a reversal of their fortunes, with their numbers increasing incrementally each year. Still, with the WWF estimating a total of only eighty individuals inhabiting a 120-mile stretch of the Lao and Cambodian Mekong, they're not out of the red yet.

In a deep pool beside a stone pillar marking the border, the young man turned the engine off.

'There,' he whispered, Attenborough style, pointing ahead of the boat.

Twenty metres away three grey, round-nosed, stubby-finned dolphins arched through the water, silent except for the rasping of their blowholes. We drifted for half an hour, the dolphins swimming at a safe distance, water lapping at the edges of the boat. The man told me they were often here, but I still felt lucky to have seen them.

Later, I met Matt and Sile at my new guest house – Mr B's – on Don Det. Don Khon had been a bit on the quiet side, even for a thirty-something like me.

'Your bike's deadly,' admired Sile in her Dublin brogue.

In their early twenties, they had been teaching English in South Korea and were doing the traveller circuit around Southeast Asia. Last week they'd been in Angkor Wat and Phnom Penh, next week it was Vientiane and Luang Prabang.

Matt was a flashpacker. Altogether less grotty than their dishevelled relatives, flashpackers travel with iPhones, iPads and expensive DSLR cameras. They wash frequently and prefer accommodation that's a few notches above the cheapest, most cockroach-infested dive. And in Matt's case they go out for dinner each night dressed impeccably in a spotted shirt, chino shorts and espadrilles, a sartorial cut above the usual traveller riff-raff.

'One of the advantages of being gay,' laughed Matt, when I commented on how dapper he looked.

Over a bucket of mojito that night he commiserated that he was 'the only gay in the traveller village'.

'I haven't met one gay guy in all my travels, it's miserable,' he griped.

To prove his point he leant over the table and showed me the Grindr app on his iPad mini. 'Look, the nearest gay guy is two hundred and thirty-eight kilometres away in Siem Reap. And he's not even fit!' he moaned.

Squint-eyed from alcohol, we wandered back to Mr B's, past Mr M's, Mr Mo's and Mr Noi's. Nearby, one of the islanders was throwing an extravagant house-warming party, and a Lao popstress was strutting up and down a large stage in a gold dress, belting out hits.

'Don't go to that party,' warned an English girl walking by. 'They don't want *falangs* and it's full of drunk fuckers.'

When I pointed out it was their island she flounced off grumpily

My final night in Laos was spent mostly awake, my hut vibrating from the noise of the islanders' party.

I was woefully unprepared for Cambodia. Just as it dangled off the southern tip of Indochina, the bulbous toe to the slender boot of Laos, so it had fallen to the bottom of my 'to do' list before leaving England. Like a student who shuns a new or difficult subject in favour of more familiar topics, so I had pushed Cambodia aside, concentrating my research and preparations on the initial two countries of my trip. I could do research on the way, I promised myself on all those quiet evenings in Laos. But so enmeshed had I been in getting across the Truong Son, I'd barely given it a second thought.

Now, as I covered the last few miles of Laotian soil, I considered how unprepared I actually was. I had no map of the country, neither a paper one nor a digital version for my GPS; I had only just started my first book about Cambodia – *First They Killed my Father* – a distressing tale of a family torn apart by the Khmer Rouge; I didn't know a single word of Khmer – someone had told me what 'hello' was, but it had already slipped my mind; I had no currency, or any notion of how many riel there were to the pound or dollar; no idea what the border post was like; and was even unsure which side of the road to drive on. I had done some research on the Trail in Cambodia, but most of what I knew about the country I'd learnt from Mick in Dak Cheung: the landmines, the atrocities of the Khmer Rouge, years of civil war, skeletons filled with gold, mad old generals with bile-yellow eyes. But of the practicalities of travel there, I was largely ignorant.

None of this particularly bothered me though. I had obtained my visa in London, had dollars and sign language, and knew it was a straight 40 miles from the border to Stung Treng, a large town at the confluence of the Sekong and Mekong Rivers. There I assumed I could find a map, a cashpoint and somewhere to spend my first night. As for the border crossing, worrying about my lack of customs paperwork or bike insurance was futile at this stage. I would just have to smile and hope for the best.

Like the fraying edges of an old cloak, Laos petered out towards the border. There were no houses here, just bony earth and wilting scrub. A few hundred metres from a white archway marking the end of its territory, I stopped to look back at the country I'd had such a tumultuous relationship with over the past month. At times it had been my bitter foe, at others my dearest friend, our bond intensified by adversity. I wondered if I would ever come back and if I did, what I'd find there. In a year so much had changed, I hardly dared imagine what the future held for the place once known as 'the land of a million elephants'. With a heavy heart I said goodbye and rode towards the archway.

I found the Lao border guards lounging in a shack, smoking and picking their teeth as they stared at a booming television.

One of them stood up, mopped the sweat off his brow with the hem of his greying white vest and shooed me towards a small cabin.

'Passport and two dollar,' he said, sliding open the window and holding out a chubby hand.

'Two dollars? For what?'

'For stamp,' he said, without a hint of guilt.

Matt and Sile had told me about this, how their bus from Angkor Wat had been held up here while fifty backpackers fought pointlessly with the guards about the $2 scam. It was a tiny amount but, with all the busloads of travellers coming through here, one that added up to a healthy extra income. Not bothering to argue, I peeled the notes out of my wallet and handed them through the window.

'OK, you go,' he said, passing back my freshly stamped passport, with no mention of customs paperwork or insurance.

With a last lingering look back I rode Panther across no man's land, towards the garish orange buildings of the Cambodian border.

'You go customs,' said the guard there, handing me back my passport and slotting my three dollar notes into the top pocket of his green uniform. He pointed at a small glass cabin twenty metres up the road.

My chest tightened; customs would see the bike had never been legally exported out of Vietnam, or legally imported into Laos. At best it would be a fine, at worst I could be sent back to Laos. Crawling towards the cabin in first gear, I eyed the open road ahead, deliberating whether to just pull the throttle and burn it out of here. But with a top speed of 35 miles per hour, Panther wasn't the ideal getaway vehicle. Even a policeman running at top speed wouldn't be far behind me. At the last minute I stopped and, smiling and brushing the dust off my shirt, handed Panther's paperwork through the window. The lone officer shuffled the Vietnamese papers blankly, his heavy gold wristwatch glinting in the sun. Then without so much as a stamp, a question or an attempt at extortion, he waved me on and resumed fiddling with his iPhone.

And that was that, Panther and I were in Cambodia. Bamboozled at such a quick and easy border crossing I stopped around the corner beside a small spirit house. Six plastic figurines stared through a fug of incense, their little platform overflowing with cans, bottles, balls of rice, candles and dead flowers. Not wanting to repeat my spiritual faux pas near Dak Cheung, I offered a bottle of water and asked the spirits to look after us on the road ahead. Then with a kick, a click and a twist of the throttle we were off, into the oven of Cambodia.

Like a hound sniffing the air for a distinctive scent, I buzzed south down the empty Highway 7, hunting for anything that identified this as a new country. Not so long ago, before French diplomats waved their meddling pens over the borders of Indochina, this part of the country had been under Laotian rule, and the differences here remained blurred. The road, an extension of Highway 13 in Laos, was the same straight two-lane tarmac. The earth was just as parched, the eye of the sun as incendiary. The forest that flanked parts of the road was weedy and partially logged. The few houses I saw, set back from the road in cracked fields, were the same stilted wooden affairs favoured by the Laotians. Only the red and gold billboards advertising *Angkor*, *Cambodia* and *Anchor* beers, in the strange Khmer script, betrayed this as no longer Laos.

As I was overtaking two Honda mopeds wobbling under ten-foot-wide loads of hand-woven baskets, their drivers and I slowed down to say 'Hello!' and study each other. They seemed taller and darker than the average Lao with high, rounded cheekbones. Or was I imagining the difference in my search for a new national identity? If I had seen the same men in Laos, where there are large groups of the related Mon-Khmer peoples, would I have thought them any different? Sometimes differences are only apparent when you are told they exist.

One thing was certain, despite having 15.2 million people to Laos' 6.3 million and inhabiting a landmass roughly a third smaller, this new country so far felt just as empty as its northern neighbour. Apart from the two men on their mopeds I rode towards Stung Treng in almost total isolation.

Blame it on the heat or exhaustion, but my memories of Stung Treng are strangely undefined. There was a modern Chinese-built bridge over the Sekong, minutes before it merged with the mother waters of the Mekong; then a bustling town with hooting buses, more cars than I had seen in all of Laos and a market spilling with colour and rubbish. At the first guest house I spotted – an attractive white building on the riverfront – the receptionist spoke good English and they had Wi-Fi and banana pancakes, those staples of the backpacker existence. Outside two young Englishmen swapped travellers' tales over *Angkor* beers, smiling absent-mindedly as I trudged in, weighed down by my kit.

My currency issue was easily solved by withdrawing several hundred dollars' worth of riel from the glassy air-conditioned bank around the corner. Not that I would need it, the English-speaking young man behind the counter said, everyone accepted dollars here. At the guest house I purchased an English-Khmer dictionary, slotting it into my bumbag in place of the Lao phrasebook. And at a cluttered electronics store beside the market I bought a local 3G SIM card from a young Chinese man with fleshy pale double-jointed fingers and wisps of black hair sprouting between his knuckles. He spoke English in a high-pitched effeminate voice, leaning over a covered glass counter as he told me how his parents had come here from Sichuan in the eighties. I asked him how many Khmer-Chen – Chinese Khmers – there were in Cambodia today.

'One hundred and eighty-one thousand,' he replied with certainty.

There had been almost three times this amount before Pol Pot came to power in 1975; Pol Pot and several of his closest cronies were of Chinese descent themselves. By 1984 there were only 61,400 Khmer-Chen left.

He gave me back my phone and pulled back the blue cloth that had been covering the counter. Underneath were rows of new smartphones.

'Chinese phones,' he said, with a roguish grin, picking up a handset that looked identical to an iPhone 5. 'New iPhone 5, only $80, everything same, can't tell difference to look at, only software different.'

It was like buying a Ferrari for a tenth of the price, only to find it was made of cardboard and powered by a hairdryer.

That evening I watched a hazy sunset over the Mekong beside a bank carpeted in rubbish. Later at the guest house I drank *Angkor* beer with a bony boastful Swiss biker, a serious English IT engineer turned round-the-world cyclist, a silent Dutch girl and an English backpacker. The biker, who had arrived at dusk on a battered muddy Kawasaki, seemed in awe of his own endeavours and dominated the conversation. He was only twenty-five, he said, but had already biked from Alaska to Ushuaia on his own. Now he had hired his dirt bike in Phnom Penh and was spending a month touring Cambodia. His neck was wreathed with Oms, cowrie shells and Mayan symbols – badges of his travels.

'I've done so many cool things,' he bragged in an urgent, lisping voice. 'I don't know how I'm going to find a woman who can do all these amazing things with me.'

Even though we sat under a fan, sweat beaded on his nose as he spoke, pricking his skin like raindrops on a magnolia leaf. He was an altogether unappealing specimen.

'I hate all these backpackers with their iPads and their *Lonely Planets*,' he went on, ignoring the presence of the others.

Travel breeds a peculiar type of snobbery, one that has nothing to do with class or money. In his own eyes he was a fully-fledged member of the travel aristocracy; one of the elite who had thrown off the shackles of air-conditioned buses and group tours. To him, backpackers were a sub-species, a lowly breed of traveller to be mocked and derided. But as I listened to his odious boasts I realised I was in danger of becoming a travel snob too. Although I preferred not to talk about my past travels or tell people I was writing a book, I must admit I'd felt a certain smugness as I rode my own bike onto the beach at Don Det. And I'd scoffed at how backpackers travelled in Wi-Fi obsessed packs. But for many of them this was their first taste of travel, the first time they had been let loose in foreign climes. At least they were travelling, seeing the world. Who was I to criticise them?

Not wanting to hear any more from the sweaty Swiss man I bid everyone goodnight and walked up the tiled stairway, nostalgic for the brothels of Laos.

CHAPTER 16

TRAIL HUNTING WITH MR D

*'History has demonstrated that violence as well as
sensuous pleasure is intrinsic to the Indochinese and
to the Cambodians in particular.'*
Jon Swain, *River of Time*

While evidence of the Ho Chi Minh Trail in Vietnam and
Laos abounds, in Cambodia what was dubbed 'The Sihanouk
Trail' has largely vanished from existence and memory.
Before I left England I had searched for references to it in
books, asked Digby and Don Duvall what they knew of it,
written to various contacts in Phnom Penh and contacted
every single Cambodian and Southeast Asian expert at
London's School of Oriental and African Studies. But the
history books made scant reference to it, neither Digby nor
Don could tell me anything, and the email responses from
Phnom Penh and SOAS provided only clues. An American,
Marcus Rhinelander, who had walked the Trail in 2005,
said stories and substantiation had dried up once he reached

Cambodia. His main memories were of weeks walking through deep sand, cajoling a grumpy translator.

People knew it had existed; that the north-eastern wilds of Ratanakiri and Mondulkiri had once hidden a skein of trails, Viet Cong training camps and rest areas; that the porous Vietnamese border areas of Svay Rieng, Kratie and Kampong Cham had acted as NVA base areas; that supplies from China, the USSR and North Vietnam had poured in through the port of Sihanoukville; but beyond that, details were sketchy. Hampered by the Cambodians' age-old fear of being absorbed by their neighbour, the hold of the Vietnamese communists in the country was always much weaker than in Laos. Destroyed by the passage of time, civil war and the Khmer Rouge, the Sihanouk Trail had become a ghost.

In early 1970 Cambodia remained a green oasis of peace amid the turmoil of neighbouring wars. Visitors at the time recall its apparent serenity, its markets overflowing with local produce, the pristine jungle and well-tended rice paddies. There had been whispers of communist cells and revolts since 1930 but, apart from a few localised peasant uprisings, Cambodia was at peace. At the helm of this idyll was King Norodom Sihanouk. Charming yet mercurial, he was an eccentric combination of an oriental despot and an educated Frenchman. At the same time as entertaining foreign dignitaries with music and the finest French wines, he would be displaying the heads of rebelling peasants on spikes in the capital. He loved jazz, fast cars, film-making and women, and would exclaim *Oh là là!* in a shrill voice whenever he was excited. Nixon described him as, 'vain and flighty... prouder of his musical talents than his political leadership.'

But on the whole, his people loved him and he loved them. Not only had he won their independence from France in 1953 – Cambodia had been a French protectorate since 1864 – but he had managed to preserve the nation's freedom ever since. To his 'children' he was a scion of the god-kings of the mighty Khmer Empire; the builders of Angkor Wat who had once ruled over most of Siam and Indochina.

But Sihanouk was as slippery as a greased pole, a political chameleon who shifted sides whenever he felt his country's fragile neutrality was under threat. One minute he would be fawning over the Americans, the next he would be in cahoots with the Chinese. A 1959 Pentagon report had dismissed the Cambodians as, 'indifferent farmers, incapable traders, uninspired fishermen and unreliable labourers [who] cannot be counted on to act in any positive way for the benefit of US aims and policies.' Perhaps they might have stayed this way had Sihanouk not made one fatal decision. In 1966, in return for a thirty per cent share of the shipments, the king was persuaded by the Chinese to allow the North Vietnamese to traffic war material through Sihanoukville port. From here it was only a hundred miles to the border with South Vietnam. Over the next few years up to 85 per cent of the Viet Cong's heavy arms came through the port. Sihanouk's collusion with the Vietnamese communists would have cataclysmic consequences for both him and his country.

American intelligence knew that Hanoi was using Cambodia as a backdoor into South Vietnam. But it wasn't until Nixon came to power in January 1969 that they took decisive action. Over the next four years he and Dr Kissinger, his national security advisor, authorised a top secret bombing campaign against the country, dropping nearly three million tonnes of bombs and leaving half a million dead. Pilots were forbidden from telling their superiors, log books were falsified, records were burnt and Congress was kept in the dark. Nixon's intent was made clear in a recorded phone call to Kissinger in December 1970, 'I want everything that can fly to go in there and crank the hell out of them. There is no limitation on mileage and no limitation on budget. Is that clear?'

Amid all this, on 18 March 1970, the US instigated a bloodless coup against Sihanouk, replacing him with the right-wing General Lon Nol, thus ending two millennia of monarchy. Incensed, the deposed king threw in his lot with the communist Khmer Rouge rebels, plunging the country into a five-year civil war which cost Lon Nol's US backers $1 million a day.

The war and the bombing tore apart the old Cambodia, creating the chaos from which Pol Pot emerged to take power. Radicalised by the burning of their villages and the murder of their families and livestock, people fled into the arms of the Khmer Rouge. Before Sihanouk and the bombing had bolstered their cause, they had been a forest army of a few thousand poorly armed guerrillas. By 1973 Pol Pot's followers numbered 200,000 and the countryside was falling like dominoes to the reds. Two years later, on 17 April 1975, the Khmer Rouge army – fanatical deadly teenagers in black pyjamas – marched into Phnom Penh. Year 0, the start of four unimaginable years of genocide, had begun.

Driven by an extreme interpretation of Maoism, The Khmer Rouge – led by former teacher and Buddhist monk Pol Pot – sought to create a pure, agrarian society led by a classless peasantry. The rich, the intellectual and the educated were systematically eliminated. Phnom Penh became a wasteland, its two million inhabitants driven into the countryside and forced to work on collective farms. Marched at gunpoint in the scorching April heat, thousands died in the first few weeks. Lon Nol himself had fled to Hawaii, his suitcase stuffed with a million US dollars. But those of his regime who remained were rounded up and shot. Families, money, schools, learning, hospitals, past knowledge, modern medicine and music were all destroyed. The words for mother and father were replaced by 'comrade'. The national bank vault was blown up, the national library turned into a pigsty. Everyone was forced to wear the same black pyjamas, to work on the farms from 3 a.m. to 11 p.m., starved, beaten and murdered for the slightest intransigence. You were killed for being unproductive, for laughing, for stealing food, for being too pretty. It was, as journalist John Pilger has said, 'Auschwitz in Asia'.

Although five of his children were killed Sihanouk, incredibly, survived, kept under house arrest in Phnom Penh and occasionally dragged out on symbolic visits to collective farms. But by 1979 almost two million of his people – a quarter of the population – were dead.

It's possible that if their former king hadn't allowed the Vietnamese communists to use his port, none of this would have happened. Few people might know about it today, but the Sihanouk Trail was a hinge upon which subsequent Cambodian history turned.

If I wanted to find out more about the Sihanouk Trail, I would need a translator. With a translator I could go into villages and talk to the elders. Even though a quarter of Cambodians had died under the Khmer Rouge, there had to be *someone* who remembered *something*. The old Trail map I'd found and photographed in the museum at Ban Dong in Laos showed a red line flowing east from Stung Treng past the towns of Lumphat and Ban Lung. Near the border with South Vietnam it paused at a supply base marked as Bo Kham. It wasn't marked on Google maps and there was no mention of it on the Internet, but with a translator I might find out more. I felt like a pirate hunting for treasure, armed only with a faded map scrawled on a shred of muslin. In this case Bo Kham was the treasure; if I could find it, I felt sure I would discover something about the Trail.

Ban Lung, the capital of Ratanakiri province, was a hundred miles east of Stung Treng on a $73.3 million Chinese-funded road completed only four months previously. A nascent hub of adventure tourism, it had a handful of guest houses and trekking agencies. One, I read in the *Lonely Planet*, was run by a Swedish biker called Nisse. It seemed a good place to start.

It was a dull ride to Ban Lung. The forest here was long gone, replaced by miles of rubber plantations; dark corridors of trees laid out with robotic uniformity. First planted by the French, and now by the Cambodians and Vietnamese, each tree dripped sticky white latex into small collection bowls.

Rubber is a booming industry in Cambodia, as it is the world over. In the decade between 2001 and 2011 global rubber prices increased almost tenfold. The more our global population grows, the more people join the vehicle-owning middle classes in the developing world, the more our demand for rubber surges. I'm one of these people. I was riding a bike with rubber tyres and wearing boots with rubber soles. I had a camper van and two motorbikes at home and I had no idea where the rubber in their tyres was from. For all I knew it could have been the plantation I was now riding past. In 2010 alone 800,000 new cars hit the streets in Beijing. That's a heck of a lot of rubber tyres, and thousands more acres of land needing to be cleared for plantations. Like so much of Indochina, Cambodia's forests were being decimated by the demands of our rising global population.

I've said my piece about the devastating impact of logging, but in Cambodia the situation is just as dire. It's been estimated that between 2000 and 2005 alone, Cambodia lost a third of its tree cover. In 2007 the NGO Global Witness released a report which revealed how, 'A tiny elite is riding roughshod over the people and legal system to get its hands on the country's natural resource wealth.' A few months after the report was published Global Witness was kicked out of Cambodia. Since then several notable anti-logging campaigners have lost their lives. Chut Wutty, the director of the Cambodian Natural Resource Protection Group, was murdered in April 2012. Five months later a Cambodian journalist investigating illegal logging was found shot dead in the boot of his car. It's a depressingly similar situation to the one in Laos.

The edge of the road fluttered with plastic bags and discarded food wrappers, and a trickle of new Land Cruisers skimmed by. At Stung Treng at 8.30 a.m. the thermometer at the guesthouse had read 35 degrees in the shade. By midday it must have been over 50 degrees on the road and I was thankful for the aid of my engine. But with no jungle, no mountains, no sign of the Trail and no adversity to tackle, I felt strangely bored and disengaged. The monotony of the plantations didn't help, their dark lines making me think of the Khmer Rouge, as if nature itself was being turned into a giant work camp. For entertainment I slalomed between the white lines and tried to remember the lyrics of Michael Jackson songs, only stopping once, at a shack where a man hand-pumped petrol from a barrel shaded by a stained yellow parasol. Behind him his wife slept at a table, her head buried in her folded arms.

Ban Lung, known locally as *Dey Krakhorm* – red earth – after its rust-coloured soil, was bigger than I'd expected. It had roundabouts, a dual carriageway through the middle and a glass-fronted Honda showroom. On the far side of town, near a volcanic lake where local families picnicked and swam, was the biker's guest house, an orderly collection of Swedish-style chalets set among the palms and hibiscus. Its owner, Nisse, was a phlegmatic Swede with faded tattoos, short grey hair and a garage full of dirt bikes. He had been in Cambodia for fifteen years 'by accident' – gold mining, running a guest house and leading motorbike tours – but he knew nothing of the Trail, and couldn't recommend any translators. He did have an old map of the country though, which I photocopied and took with me. On it, written in tiny letters next to the Vietnamese border, was a place called Ba Kham. It was close enough to the location and spelling of the place called Bo Kham on my Trail map to warrant trying to find.

It was only a week until Cambodian New Year, a three-day celebration coinciding with *Songkran*, *Pi Mai* and *Thingyan* – the Thai, Lao and Burmese equivalents. Based on the Hindu solar festival it was an orgy of feasting, worship and carousing which spilled over into the weeks either side. Already all the trekking guides in town had packed up and gone home to their families. The only one who hadn't was Mr D, a chain-smoking thirty-two-year-old Khmer who had been guiding in Ratanakiri for ten years. Round-faced, flat-nosed and thick-lipped, he had a pubescent moustache and spoke English with a cockney accent. He knew nothing about the Trail, hadn't heard of Bo Kham and had the enthusiasm of a corpse. But he was available, he spoke good English and could ride a moped. We arranged to leave the following morning.

When Mr D arrived just after 8 a.m. I was kneeling on the gravel beside Panther, replacing her blackened spark plug.

'Where you get your bike from?' he asked, looking at Panther disdainfully.

He screwed up his face when I told him. 'Your friend in Hanoi no good – why he not get you better bike?'

Biting my tongue, I looked over Panther's seat at his hired 125-cc Honda Wave moped and asked if it was any good.

'Better than yours,' he said curtly, cupping his hands to light a cigarette.

If he carried on like this we were not going to enjoy a harmonious relationship. Panther may have let me down a few times but she was my Trail partner, and I was fiercely protective of her.

Armed with the old and new maps we set off east towards the Vietnamese border along the same unblemished tarmac of Highway 78. Mr D rode in front of me, slouching over the handlebars, flip flops hanging off his feet. Several times we overtook mopeds carrying wide trays of water snails, their drivers advertising the slimy snacks with the aid of crackly megaphones. Lightly cooked in chilli they were quite delicious, insisted Mr D. Judging by how people rushed out of their houses waving for the mopeds to stop, he wasn't the only one who thought so.

We were heading for the heartlands of Ratanakiri, Cambodia's remotest, least populous and most ethnically diverse region. Meaning 'mountain of gems' it was historically a land of forest-dwelling animists and jungles teeming with rare and undiscovered species; gaurs, tigers, sun bears, Asian elephants, giant Ibis and hundreds of types of tree. A 1997 survey of Virachey National Park, in the north-east corner of the province, counted 189 species of tree in one half-hectare of forest. Remote and far from central government, over the centuries it had shifted between Siamese, Lao – many of the place names in the province are of Lao origin – French and Cambodian rule and acted as a hideout for rebel groups. Pol Pot built his earliest bases of support here among the disenfranchised tribal minorities, and the North Vietnamese burrowed their supply lines through its leech-infested forests. Nowadays Ratanakiri was embroiled in a new war between conservation and rabid resource extraction. The front line of this was Virachey, rife with illegal logging, poaching and mining. Outside the park the war had already been lost; a decade earlier we would have been riding to Ba Kham along a dirt track through virgin forest, now the red earth was planted in a banausic grid of rubber and cashew plantations and not a patch of jungle remained.

A few miles before the Vietnamese border the road split, a dusty laterite track leading north to Ba Kham and Virachey. At my urging we stopped at a scrappy Vietnamese roadside café, where an old man was noisily sucking on a bowl of pork and rice. We asked him if he knew anything about the Trail. Without looking up he shook his head and spat a lump of gristle on the floor. No one else knew anything either, so we started up the bikes and turned north.

Minutes later I squealed Panther to a halt. Bomb craters! The red earth to the right of the track was pockmarked with those familiar holes, punched into the soil like the thumbprints of a destructive giant. Filled with shrubs and rubbish they were dotted around a simple wooden house, outside of which two lean teenage boys sawed at a truck engine.

'Look, bomb craters!' I said excitedly to Mr D. 'That's a sure-fire sign we're on the Trail. Let's go and ask those people if they know anything.'

As odd as it was to feel excited about such a symbol of death, it was thrilling to at last find visible evidence that I was back in Trail territory. With a sigh Mr D got off his bike and walked over to the boys, dragging his feet as he went. They didn't know anything they said, but their father might. He was currently relieving himself in the bushes but would be back soon.

We waited for ten minutes in the hot sun watching the boys work. Presently a small very dark man in a pair of grimy underpants appeared from behind some cashew trees. His thick black hair was matted with dust and dirt, his hands covered in engine oil.

'Yes, they are from American bombs,' he said, knotting his forehead as he looked between us.

He told us that the road we were on was indeed the Trail, but as he was only forty-six now he was too young to remember much. His sons continued to saw at the rusting metal, ignoring our conversation.

'We did find the crashed remains of a US helicopter over there about ten years ago,' he pointed to beyond the cashew trees, 'but we sold everything we found, there's nothing left now.'

'What about bombs? Has anyone near here found bombs or had any accidents?' I had to explain what I meant to Mr D, who in turn asked the man.

He shook his head. Strangely, no one I spoke to in Cambodia mentioned UXO or seemed to understand what I meant when I asked about it. MAG later told me that although the north-east of the country is packed with UXO from the war, the local people are relatively unaware of it. The country's problems have meant that clearance has been slower and more limited than in Laos and Vietnam. Language and literacy barriers in these remote areas have slowed the process yet more.

No more details were forthcoming so we shook hands and left them to it. It seemed odd that people could live among all these bomb craters yet have so little interest in why and how they came to be there.

A little farther on we stopped at an unmemorable dust bowl of a town for a lunch of fly-blown rice and bony fish soup. Above the din of a dubbed Thai film Mr D proceeded to tell me how awful his life was, hunching over his soup as he spat out bones and bitterness. His father had died of illness seven years previously; two of his siblings had also died; he never saw his mother or remaining brother; he hated the Cambodians – when his father had been ill and needed medicine, no one in the village had helped; his family had been too poor to send him to school so he had only been educated for three years; he hated his family for being so poor; he hated Cambodia but didn't have enough money to leave; he suffered from depression (no kidding); he didn't like his job; he didn't have a girlfriend and no one would want him anyway. As much as I felt sorry for him, I didn't want to spend the next few days drowning in his disenchantment. But every time I tried to take misery off the menu he firmly hauled it back. It wasn't the most joyful of luncheons.

More bomb craters signalled our arrival in Ba Kham, a rubbish-strewn village of about thirty stilted wooden huts on the banks of the wide fast-flowing Tonle San River. On the far bank the edges of Virachey National Park spilled into the clear water. It was an idyllic location, but one underpinned by a pervasive poverty. The packed earth was littered with human and animal detritus and pot-bellied children peered down from the dark windows of the huts. Beside an EU-funded well a patronising sign instructed the villagers how to be more hygienic, the sort of sign a teacher would draw for a class of five year olds. On the 'correct' side smiling, clothed people pumped water from an EU-branded well and washed their clothes in separate bowls. On the 'bad' side pigs, skinny buffaloes and villagers all drank, played, washed and defecated in the same puddle of water. The French colonials used to compare ethnic minorities to children; so apparently did the EU and the German NGO who designed this sign.

Weaving through the craters and huts we parked the bikes under a tree at the top of a riverbank worn smooth by the passage of feet. A thin grey-haired man came and squatted beside us, one eye twisted into a weeping, unseeing scar. Mr D explained what we were looking for. Did the Trail go through here? Did he remember the bombing, or seeing the Vietnamese around here? Would anyone in the village remember anything about that time? As we spoke children scrambled out of the water and crouched around us to listen.

'Oh, I don't know,' said the old man. 'I'm only fifty-six. I'm not old enough to remember all that. And I didn't live in this village then, I lived on the other side of the river in the jungle.' He pointed north over the Tonle San into the vastness of Virachey. If he was fifty-six he would have been a teenager at the height of the bombing. Surely he could remember something about the planes, the noise, the bombs dropping in the jungle.

'Ooooh, yes!' he whistled, and shook his head. 'I remember the planes.'

He then looked at me suspiciously with his one remaining eye. 'Why are you asking all these questions? It's making me nervous. Why don't you ask that old man down there, he might know something?'

He waved a gnarled hand towards the edge of the river, where a skeletal figure in a black trilby was slowly washing his pots and pans, then stood up and walked away.

The children formed a row beside us, chattering away as four women sat behind them and searched their hair for lice. Another small elderly man sat down and asked us what we wanted. This village was Jarai – an ethnic minority who mainly lived in Vietnam's Central Highlands, but with a small population in Ratanakiri – he told us, and he was the *mey poom*, or village chief. Twenty-seven families lived here, there was no school or temple and few people spoke Khmer. He didn't know how old he was, maybe about fifty-four. And no, he was too young to remember the war or the bombs.

'These people are so stupid, they're like children. They're so ignorant, they don't know anything. Their Khmer language is terrible; I'd get more sense out of a four-year-old Khmer child,' cursed Mr D as the chief wandered back to his hut.

To prove his point he asked the children how old they were, to which none of them knew the answer. His racism towards the minority Jarai was shocking, but is sadly shared by many Khmers. The animist Jarai have no written script of their own and illiteracy is high. Just as the Lao minorities are looked down upon by the lowland majority, so the Jarai are derided by the majority Khmers.

After half an hour the old man finished his washing and crept up the river bank, removing his trilby as he stopped and crouched in front of me. A startlingly unusual looking individual, he had pale freckled skin, hawkish bloodshot eyes and features too big for his cadaverous face; nothing like the other Jarai in the village. He smiled, revealing a mouth pullulating with gold bejewelled teeth; an arresting display of wealth in such poor surrounds. It instantly made me recall the old gangster in the Serbian film *Black Cat, White Cat*. Unblinkingly, he gave the same answer as the other two. 'Oh, I don't know. I can't remember, it was far too long ago. Anyway, I was living in the jungle on the other side of the river then.'

And with that he unfolded his emaciated legs and wandered off with his pots and pans. Disappointed, I walked down the bank and sat by the river, watching three young boys mend fishing nets. Shy at first, they beamed wonderful gap-toothed smiles when I took their photos, screaming in excitement when I showed them the screen.

It was obvious the people here were unwilling to remember the past, especially not for an outsider who appeared in their village unannounced and asked too many questions. The Jarai's contact with outsiders has rarely ended happily for them.

In the early sixties, when he began to wage his guerrilla war against Sihanouk's regime, Pol Pot's strongest base of support was among the 'noble savages' of Ratanakiri. To Pol Pot these minorities practised communism in its purest form. They were, he said, 'completely illiterate people who did not have even the slightest idea of cities, automobiles and parliament, but who dare to fight under the guidance of the Party.' By the late sixties whole villages in Ratanakiri were defecting to the Khmer Rouge, and many of Pol Pot's personal bodyguards and local leaders were picked from among the Jarai and other tribes. Later on, as Pol Pot ramped up the killings, they were purged, starved and murdered in the same way as other Cambodians, their bodies flung into mass graves in the forests of their ancestors. It was no surprise they were so suspicious of me; under the Khmer Rouge questions often preceded a fatal axe blow to the back of the head. Whatever the truth about the Trail here, I wasn't going to find out this time.

'I know someone in a village on the other side of the river in Virachey. Let's ride there and see if we can find out anything,' said Mr D in a rare display of willing.

We clattered over a wooden bridge into a desolate landscape of slash-and-burn, arriving as the light faded at the village of Ket, a disorderly settlement of inveterate filth. The single street was piled with plastic bags, bottles, crushed beer cans and rotting vegetable matter. Tiny piglets trotted through the rubbish, squealing and motherless. A naked boy, his face smeared in snot and red dirt, downed a sugar cane juice and threw the plastic glass on the ground. But even the rubbish was conquered by the dust, which smothered everything in a choking amber veil. People, animals, wooden shacks, tin roofs and the plastic Chinese-made toys hanging from the shop fronts; everything was coated in that ubiquitous red dust.

Mr D rode off to find the people he knew and I sat at a café, watching a handsome Khmer boy crushing sugar canes into sweet delicious juice. Next to me a young Vietnamese woman and three burly Khmer men were smoking and playing a raucous game of cards, gambling over a pile of notes. Every few minutes a moped would rattle by, little more than flakes of rust held together by bundles of exposed wires. Luxuries such as fairings, exhausts and proper seats had long gone and the young boys who rode them could hardly reach the pedals. In some ways Cambodia seemed so much more developed than Laos. But in villages like Ket it seemed worse off. The people here were likely among the quarter of the country's population who lived on less than a dollar a day.

Despite appearances Ket was a Jarai village, overtaken in recent years by lowland Khmers drawn by work on new rubber plantations. But the migrant workers had turned it into a colony of feckless squatters. The only Jarai I saw were a few women who padded past with baskets on their backs, fat black cheroots hanging out of their mouths.

As darkness fell Ket, a village with neither electricity nor sanitation, reverberated with the noise of diesel generators.

For some reason Mr D had fallen out with the family he knew, so we were relegated to spending the night in a grove of cashew trees behind their hut. In Laos a settlement of this size would have had a guest house of sorts, but the same wasn't true of Cambodia. Exciting as it was to finally be using my Snugpak 'Jungle Hammock Extreme,' the space doubled as a communal loo and rubbish tip and we shared it with a thundering generator. Beside us a poor Vietnamese family lived like refugees under a botched structure of wood and tarpaulin. Miserable, Mr D sat in his hammock drinking beer after beer, each one plunging him into a blacker mood.

'I don't know why I'm alive, there's nothing good about my life,' he whined, downing the last of his beers and zipping himself into his hammock. Following suit, I folded myself into my green cocoon and tried to block out the generator noise, barking dogs, diesel fumes and the stench of human shit.

Midway through a strange dream about waking up with crowds of children peering at me, I was shaken awake at 5.45 a.m. by Mr D.

'Get up, get up! It's starting to rain.'

He was just in time. Moments after I'd scrambled upright, unclipped my hammock from the trees, stamped into my boots and dashed for our neighbour's tarpaulin, the heavens opened. Drowsily, we crouched under the flimsy shelter with a breastfeeding young woman, watching the rain as it poured off the sides and dripped through numerous holes, dissolving the dust to an orange sludge. An hour later it abated, replaced by black swarms of flying ants and moths.

In popular imagination tribal chiefs are men resplendent in feathers, tigers' teeth and jewels, their skin emblazoned with tattoos. But like the man I had met in Ba Kham, Ket's Jarai chief, Jamien, was nothing like this. He was a small man in a faded yellow football shirt, with short greying hair combed into a side parting and rounded genial features. We found him sitting on the steps of a large longhouse at the Jarai's marginal settlement behind the mephitic main strip.

'I'm seventy,' he said, inviting us to a low table inside the longhouse to talk, 'so I remember that time very well.'

He pointed in the direction of the main drag. 'The Trail went right through here. First the Vietnamese soldiers used to carry the guns and ammunition on foot. Later they brought trucks with rice, medicine, clothes, ammunition and guns.'

'How did you feel about the Vietnamese being here, bringing the war to your home?' I asked, watching his expression as Mr D translated. Although the Cambodians and Vietnamese are age-old rivals perhaps the non-Khmer Jarai didn't share this enmity.

'At first we welcomed them because we had a common enemy – America. I helped them build a camp near here and guided the soldiers through the jungle. But sometimes they stole food from our fields and raped our women.'

At times, hindered by Mr D's sloppy translation, I struggled to understand what Jamien was saying. It was like trying to see your reflection in a muddy pond; there would be glimpses of clarity, but the overall effect was blurred. What was certain though was that the bombing sent the Jarai fleeing into the forest.

'Between 1966 and 1973 there was bombing every day. Even though we fled to the jungle, ten people from this village were killed. During the daytime we worked in the fields with leaves tied to our backs so the planes wouldn't see us. But it didn't always work, a bomb landed near me in a rice field one day and the shrapnel nearly took my leg off.' At this he pulled up his jeans to show us a badly scarred kneecap.

1966 sounded too early, but recently declassified records show that the bombing of Cambodia – albeit on a smaller scale – was started by Lyndon. B. Johnson as early as 1965. Jamien's memory could well have been correct.

We talked for the best part of an hour, the chief looking wistfully into the distance as he dredged up old memories. If only I could have seen into his mind's eye. Throughout it all Mr D wore the expression of a man condemned by boredom. He yawned, lit one cigarette after another and said, 'Oh not much, just more information' when I pressed him about what Jamien was saying.

Lastly I asked Jamien what he thought of all the deforestation.

His expression changed and he hung his head sadly. 'I'm very angry about our rainforest being cut down. There used to be so many wild animals – tigers, elephants, monkeys, wild pigs. Now there are only a few birds left, and our ancestors have gone. We tried to protest against it happening but we were powerless, no one would listen. Now it's gone forever.'

I said goodbye and walked away through the mud, saddened by the fate of the Jarai. I asked Mr D if he had found the conversation interesting. 'No, not really,' he replied. 'You ask too many questions.'

It was almost time for Mr D to go.

CHAPTER 17

THE LUMPHAT EPISODE

From Ket we slid south towards Lumphat, the old provincial capital of Ratanakiri, through sludgy sand and more rubber and cashew plantations. Squat cashew trees fanned over our heads, the dark groves sweet with the scent of rotting fruit missed by the recent harvest. The sand slowed our progress and at 4 p.m. we stopped at a roadside café for iced coffee. A night in a hammock hadn't done me any favours, and while Mr D sat and smoked I paced up and down, stretching my legs and holding my aching back. Four men sat cross-legged under a tree gambling over a game of cards, their arms inked with tattoos. Opposite, a chained monkey walked in maddened circles around a pole, its paws rubbing the dirt smooth.

Near Lumphat the sky began to boil with angry purple clouds which massed into pillars and drained the fading daylight, harbingers of an almighty storm. Upping the speed we raced the last few miles to town, reaching it as the first sploshes of rain thudded into the dirt and diving into the nearest shelter; an open-sided mechanic's shop scattered with tools, bits of moped and dripping containers of oil. A dark green hammock was slung between two beams. Seeing us, a young boy appeared from the shadows and Mr D spoke to him in rapid Khmer, their voices barely audible over the drumming of the deluge on the tin roof.

'There's no guest house in Lumphat,' said Mr D, 'but the boy says we can put our hammocks up and stay here if we want. His family has gone to another town for New Year, so he's on his own and would be glad of the company.'

Mr D disappeared into the darkness to wash at a well, but I was more worried about Panther than my filthy clothes and face. She was becoming increasingly temperamental and for the last two days had been stuttering like a badly-serviced Lada. Tomorrow morning I would be continuing without Mr D and couldn't risk her conking out on me. In the flickering beam of my head torch I knelt beside her, oiling and tightening the chain, cleaning the spark plug, tightening the brakes and changing her oil. Outside the road continued to swell with the falling rain.

After a bland supper of instant noodles and warm beer we were in our hammocks by 9 p.m., Mr D and the boy chatting in Khmer, me reading in the light of my head torch. It was well after midnight when the rain finally ceased.

Cloth-headed and stiff, I was woken at 6 a.m. by the boy playing tinny Cambodian pop on his new Samsung smartphone. He had barely put it down since we arrived, telling us his parents had saved up $800 to buy it for him. Rolling up our hammocks we filled the bikes with petrol, gave the boy a few dollars and rode though the puddles to find breakfast.

Nowadays Lumphat is a ruin of a place, a once thriving hub reduced to a scattering of huts and craters by Nixon's bombs. There's no electricity and one run-down café sells tea, coffee, water, Coca-Cola and instant noodles. That morning the café was full of men drinking tea, sucking noodle soup and flicking cigarette ash on the dirt floor. All of them were swivelled in the direction of a noisy television, which blasted out adverts for skin-whitening creams and shampoo. Outside a young Chinese road surveyor in orange overalls looked through the sights of a theodolite and scribbled on a clipboard. Ravenously hungry and half-asleep, I ordered two bowls of noodle soup and three coffees from the young waitress, fortifying myself for what lay ahead.

South of here lay the Tonle Srepok River and a single dirt road known as the Mondulkiri Death Highway. Really a skein of oxcart trails, the road ran 30 miles south to the town of Koh Nhek in Mondulkiri province. From there it continued another 60 miles to Sen Monorom, a popular trekking destination. The Chinese had just started work on upgrading it but for now it was a dirt track through uninhabited forest, notorious enough for the *Lonely Planet* to dedicate half a page to it. It warned that the road was impossible in wet season, and that in dry season it should only be attempted by 'hardcore bikers' with 'years of experience and an iron backside'.

I'd heard about the road, I'd read about it in the *Lonely Planet*, but never for a second did I consider not attempting it. The North Vietnamese *boi dois* had walked this same route, trudging the last few hundred miles towards Sen Monorom and Saigon. The only other way south was a 300-mile diversion back via Ban Lung and Stung Treng. Panther and

I had survived the Truong Son, surely there was nothing we couldn't tackle now.

After breakfast I paid Mr D – including a tip he didn't deserve – and without a thank you or goodbye he took the money and sped off back to Ban Lung. Never had I encountered such a bitterly negative individual. At first I'd felt sorry for him and listened to his outbursts. I'd tried to counsel him; yes, he had been dealt some bad cards, but the angrier he was the worse his life would be, the more his relationships with other humans would deteriorate. His bitterness was locking him in a vicious cycle – perhaps, I suggested, it would help to try and focus on the positive aspects of his life? But now I was tired of him, fed up with being doused in his ice-cold buckets of misery. Not only was he grumpy, racist, rude and idle, but his habits irritated me. I loathed the way he leant over his handlebars and squeezed his blackheads in the wing mirror every time we stopped, and how he hoiked in the dust after every cigarette. I was glad to see the back of him.

The Mondulkiri Death Highway beckoned. Under a pewter sky I stuffed 5 litres of water into my basket and panniers and left the safety of Lumphat. I was worried about the effect of the last few days' rain but Mr D had assured me the road would be OK, as had an arthritic old man in the café. According to them, I would be in Koh Nhek by lunchtime.

The wooden planks of the old bridge banged under my wheels as I rode out of town across the Tonle Srepok, next to the giant concrete pillars of its half-built replacement. Beyond, teams of steamrollers rumbled over the soggy earth, flattening a swathe of red through the trees. But within a few miles I'd left the rollers behind and was on a waterlogged track through a silent bleak landscape of partially logged forest. The early rains had churned the surface into a morass of lakes, ruts, ridges and bogs through which I splashed and heaved; gambling whether to gun it through the murky water, chance the glutinous mud or find a diversion through the remaining trees. Old tyre marks gave me clues but nothing was predictable. The lakes could be a few inches or a few feet deep. Certain patches of mud were more lethal than others and the trees hid sharp stumps, thorny undergrowth and the threat of UXO and landmines. And every few miles my way would be blocked by the concrete cylinders of a partially built drainage ditch, around which I would have to lift and push my reluctant steed.

I didn't always make the right decision. At one point Panther's back end sank up to my panniers in black mud and I had to struggle and pull and grunt to get her out, my legs swallowed by the sticky slime. Farther on a yellow digger lay abandoned in the mud.

But stubbornly I persisted. We were averaging little more than walking pace but if we kept buggering on, metre by metre, minute by minute, we would make it before nightfall. Even when the first human I saw – a young man on a moped with two dead cockerels strung over his handlebars – stopped and pointed to the mud, motioning that it came up to his handlebars and telling me not to go on, I ignored his advice and ploughed on anyway. *If you listened to everyone in life who told you not to go on you would never get anywhere,* I thought. He might well be right, but I had to see for myself.

By midday I had drunk 3 litres of my water and was a sweating muddy mess. Two things then occurred simultaneously;

Panther's engine emitted a terminal sounding grinding noise, and a pair of men appeared on the track in front of me. They were staggering and distressed, their long-sleeved shirts wet with perspiration.

'Our car is stuck in the mud,' said one of them in English, mopping his brow with a beige baseball cap. He was about forty, with a square face and a slightly undershot jaw. 'Don't go on, you'll never make it. There's no food, no people, no water, no phone reception. If you get stuck, you're in big trouble. We've been walking for two hours to find help.'

I gave them a litre of water and they carried on while I paused to consider my options. I was only about twenty miles from Koh Nhek, such a tantalisingly short distance. Going back would mean riding several hundred extra miles, all of it on boring tarmac. But I was down to 1 litre of water, had barely any food and feared Panther was about to throw the towel in once and for all. Ignoring one warning was forgivable, to ignore a second one would be foolish. Dejectedly, I turned around and rode slowly back in the direction of Lumphat.

I came upon the two men sitting under a tree a little farther on.

'Can he borrow your bike to go and get help?' said the one who spoke English, pointing at his companion. 'I'm the civil engineer in charge of building this road. He's my driver, he wants to ride to where the road workers are and ask them to bring a digger to tow us out.'

Instinctively I said yes, unloaded my luggage and handed the second man my keys, watching him slide off up the track. The engineer and I waited under the tree, a thin leafless specimen offering little respite from the sun. Trained in Australia, the man had a wife and two children who lived in Phnom Penh. But his work meant he barely saw them; last year he had spent twelve months in Malaysia; in a few months from now he would be starting a three-year contract on the highly controversial Xayaburi Dam in Laos. He sat cross-legged on the ground as he talked, picking at fallen leaves, emphasising his words with a jut of his chin or a tear of a leaf. I'd only just rid myself of one angry resentful man, and now here was another.

'I hate seeing so little of my family but the salaries are so low in Cambodia. I'm the chief civil engineer on this road, but I only get a thousand dollars a month, plus a car and driver. I tell my children to study hard, that I pay for their education with my *sweat* and my *blood*.'

He particularly didn't like the Chinese. Every time he said the word 'Chinese' he prefixed it with a vituperative 'fu-CKING,' spitting out the second syllable as if he had swallowed a wasp. The 'fu-CKING Chinese' had given Cambodia a $40 million loan to build the road. They knew Cambodia wouldn't be able to pay back the loan, so instead they would demand Cambodian land. They were too cunning he said, and the 'fu-CKING Chinese surveyors' never listened to him.

'When my driver comes back with the digger, follow us to our car. It's a Ford truck so we can put your bike on the back and I'll take you to Koh Nhek, where my office is. You won't get there any other way.'

An hour and a half later his driver returned on Panther, followed by a Caterpillar digger driven by one of the road workers. Both he and Panther were coated down one side in mud from a fall yet he handed her back to me without so much as a thank you. Poor old girl, she looked a sight; this was Cub abuse of the highest order.

'Follow us,' said the engineer, he and his driver jumping onto a small exterior platform of the digger.

Off they rumbled, ploughing through the mud with ease, the earth vibrating as it went. Panther's slime-caked tyres were no match for the digger's monstrous tracks; soon they were 500 metres ahead and rolling inexorably on.

Struggling through a sea of mud, Panther sunk again. This time no amount of pushing and pulling could shift her, the mire had her in its vice-like grip. I ran after the digger, waving frantically, yelling and slipping in the mud. But they couldn't hear me and never thought to turn around. The yellow beast trundled on and disappeared from view.

For the first time on my journey I felt a stab of panic. There was no other help for miles; I *had* to get to that digger. If I couldn't get the bike out myself and ride to them, I would have to catch them on foot. Leaving Panther impaled in the bog, I took my valuables and remaining water and set off at a brisk walk. It was dizzyingly hot, I didn't know how far it was and there was no guarantee the engineer would wait for me. My boots, weighed down by several extra kilos of mud, felt heavier with every step.

Don't panic. Just put one foot in front of the other and keep going, I told myself as I trudged through the sparse forest, pushing aside creeping feelings of hunger and dehydration. *One foot in front of the other. Left. Right. Left. Right.*

After an hour I rounded a corner and saw the digger towing a blue Ford pick-up out of a deep lake. I would never have made it across that with Panther.

'What happened to your bike?' asked the engineer irritably as I approached. The two men were thigh deep in water next to their disabled truck. It was obvious their moods had worsened.

I explained what had happened.

'OK, once we get the car out, the digger will go back with you, pull out your bike and then bring you back here,' he said grudgingly.

'Please wait for me. I really need your help. I'll ride back here as fast as I can.'

For what seemed like an age I perched on the edge of the digger as it rumbled back towards my stricken bike. When I'd been trying to keep up with it earlier it had been too fast, now it felt frustratingly slow. The engineer promised he and his driver would wait for me, but I suspected they wouldn't if I took too long. He was hungry, cross about the car and keen to get back to Koh Nhek before nightfall.

Half an hour later Panther came into view, still sticking out of the bog like a spoon in a yoghurt pot. The Caterpillar driver and I hauled her out and I motioned to him that we should hurry back to the waiting engineer. By now it was 5 p.m. and the sky was robing itself for another epic storm. He pointed at his watch, then at the sky, pursed his lips and shook his head. It was the end of his working day and no doubt he wanted to drive back to his base near Lumphat. Again I felt that wave of panic. If he didn't accompany me and I became stuck again before reaching the engineer's car, I would be stranded. Pulling the helpless female act I produced my Khmer dictionary and pointed to the word 'afraid' looking at him pleadingly. It didn't work. He shook his head again, climbed back into the digger and rumbled off north.

There wasn't a moment to waste. It was getting dark, the first rain was beginning to fall and I hadn't eaten since breakfast. Worst of all, I only had a quarter of a litre of water left. Panther and I *had* to make it to the car, a beacon of salvation in what was now a worrying situation. I sped through the mud, taking my weight off the seat and paddling the ground with my feet to force her through the worst bits. This wasn't the same determined engagement I'd felt on the hardest days in Laos, this was desperation. Panther was struggling, grinding, faltering and squealing. In my anxiety to get there I knew I was pushing her too hard, revving her engine too much to coerce her through the mud. I doubted she was going to make it much farther. If we could just reach the car everything would be fine.

But the engineer had gone.

To my utter, sickening disbelief I rounded the final corner and there was no car, just an empty swamp. They had damn well gone and left me. I could be angry about it later though, for now I just needed to get out of there. Somewhere between here and Lumphat lay the road worker's camp where the digger had come from: I hadn't noticed it on the way, but finding it was my best hope. What a mess today was turning out to be.

Without hesitation I swung Panther around and ground back along the darkening track. But a few minutes later she sunk again. This time, the mud was up to the top of her wheels and even the brute force of fear couldn't budge her. Suddenly the situation seemed critical. Without help it was impossible for me to haul her out. But I was alone in the jungle and very low on water. I had no choice but to leave her and walk for help. Unstrapping my panniers I waded out of the bog and carried them into the trees. Then, calmly and methodically I worked out what essentials I needed to walk out of there. First I wrapped my precious diaries, laptop and camera in a dry bag and put them in my small rucksack. With them I packed my hammock, last two rehydration salts, water purification tablets, Leatherman multi-tool, head torch and my emergency packet of Chia seeds, the only food I had with me. I kept my bumbag on, with other essentials such as money, passport, iPhone, GPS and lucky talismans. Everything else I zipped into the panniers and hid in the trees, marking the location on my GPS. Although the GPS didn't have a map of Cambodia on it, the extremely basic world map it came loaded with at least gave me the ability to mark the location as a waypoint which I could find my way back to. Having done this I took the keys out of the ignition, abandoned poor Panther and set out north.

Fuelled by fear and pounded by rain I squelched and slipped through the deserted forest. As twilight melted into darkness the air came alive with an eerie echoing orchestra of frogs; their croaks, trills and gribbits bouncing off the trees in stereo sound. A lone parrot flapped low over my head, its silhouette just visible in the twilight. I plodded through the rain, talking to myself to keep calm, acutely aware that situations like this could go very wrong very quickly. I was alone. I was a long way from help. I was weak and dizzy from hunger, physical exertion and dehydration. I only had a few sips of water left. I had been exposed to extreme heat all day and had lost a lot of liquid through sweat. I was beginning to feel disorientated; convinced I could hear the digger nearby. Sometimes it was ahead of me, sometimes behind, sometimes somewhere in the trees. But in reality it was nowhere.

For the first time in my life I felt that death was a possibility; a stupid, pointless, lonely death on the aptly named Mondulkiri Death Highway. I thought of a conversation I'd had with my four-year-old godson Hari on the way to Heathrow, during which he'd told me with absolute certainty that if I rode a motorbike on my own in another country I would die. Maybe he was going to be proven right. I cursed the engineer and his driver. I had lent them my bike. I had given them water. He had *promised* to wait – he knew how much I needed their help. Then I felt idiotic for putting all my faith in strangers, for being so naïve as to give away my water and lend them my bike. I cursed myself for being so stubborn and stupid, for ignoring the warnings, for being so obsessive about following the Trail. How stupid to think Panther and I could battle our way through anything. If I did die, it would be death by hubris; my own stupid fault.

The fear and anger would alternate with calm rationality.

'Look, there's no point being angry with the engineer. It's happened, deal with it,' I told myself. 'Left, right, left, right. One foot in front of the other. Just... keep... walking...'

For minutes on end my mind would clear of all thoughts except the basic desire to walk, to put one foot in front of the other until I reached someone or somewhere. I wasn't going to die. As long as I could keep on walking I would be fine.

This went on for several hours until in the darkness behind me I thought I heard an engine. It wasn't an aural delusion this time. A few hundred metres behind me a beam of light was weaving its way in my direction, accompanied by the buzz of a motorbike's engine. It stopped as it drew up beside me and the face of a thin young Khmer man blinked in the light of my head torch. The relief to see another human! What on earth was he doing out here in the dark, in his shorts and flip flops, miles from anywhere?

'Can you help me?' I said in English, with more than a hint of desperation.

'Yes. Me, Mr Chum. I help you. I help you,' he replied in robotic, faltering English, turning off his engine.

'Thank you! Thank you!' I said. Then, 'Water, water!' pointing to my empty water bottle.

'No water, no. Me live Lumphat, thirty kilometres away, water Lumphat. Me, Mr Chum. I help you. You stay me and my wife Lumphat, OK?'

He patted the seat of his Chinese 125-cc motorbike and motioned I get on behind him. Riding two-up in these conditions could easily mean another four hours to get to Lumphat. I needed to find water before then, but I had no choice. Against the odds I had come across another human, one who spoke fragmentary English and wanted to help me. I swung my leg over the seat and off we rode. I would think about how to get back to Panther tomorrow.

My new friend Mr Chum seemed oblivious to the rain, the mud, the distance we had to go or the fact he'd rescued a distressed foreigner in the wilderness. As we struggled through that accursed mud he chirruped away as if we were having a picnic on a sunny riverbank. In high-pitched pidgin English he asked me about my country, my husband, my children, Manchester United and Wayne Rooney – the mere mention of Potato Head's name making Mr Chum coo with delight – his words filtering back to me through the noise of the engine and the patter of rain. Even on the frequent occasions I'd have to slide off and struggle through the quagmire on foot, Mr Chum continued to fire questions at me from the bike I was staggering after. Silences would be filled with a 'Me, Mr Chum. I friend! I help you!' followed by a triumphant cackle. I wondered if this stranger with his stuttering English was a few buns short of a picnic. But so what if he was; he was my saviour and for that I was extremely grateful.

I must have been with Mr Chum for two hours when I saw the lights in the jungle.

'Mr Chum, we stop here please, water, water.'

In a clearing were rows of machinery, lights, a jerry-built shelter, voices and men lying in hammocks. Surprised faces looked up at me from games of cards as I stumbled into the light. It was the road workers' camp I had missed earlier.

'Hello, can you help me?' I asked, addressing no one in particular.

A kindly, gentle thirty-something called Bun gave me boiled water and a bowl of rice. I could stay the night he said in good English. Someone would help me get my bike in the morning. It meant leaving my friend Mr Chum, but it made more sense than carrying on with him to Lumphat.

'Thank you, Mr Chum. You saved me, thank you,' I said, enveloping him in a sweaty hug. He refused any money from me then pootled off into the darkness. I hope he realised how lucky I had been to find him.

Babbling with relief I sat under the shelter on an empty water container. Bun gave me water, a dry shirt and a clean *krama* – a traditional checked Cambodian scarf – to wear as a sarong. The foreman, a tall dark muscular Khmer with thick wavy hair and exceptionally white teeth, poured me shots of warming rice wine and honey. To think that only hours earlier I'd thought I could die, yet here I was with water, shelter and sustenance.

Around midnight, aching and exhausted, I clipped my hammock between two posts and fell asleep in a row of snoring men.

It was a cool damp night. The air buzzed with mosquitoes and I slept intermittently, curled into a ball like a pangolin in Bun's oversized shirt. At 5 a.m. a chicken flapped onto my head, jolting me awake and an hour later the first steamrollers grumbled out of the camp. Soon afterwards, Bun insisted on going with one of the other men to fetch my bike. I felt like a useless feeble female and hated that I was putting these kind men out.

'It's OK,' he said laughing, the two of them setting off squeezed onto a tatty Daelim moped.

There was a sombre mood at the camp that morning. The bad weather had stopped supplies getting through so there was no food and barely any water left. The men mooched around, smoking and getting dressed before climbing into their cabs. Meanwhile I waited anxiously, causing a cannonade of titters when I stood up and my sarong fell about my ankles. Two hours later Bun, still laughing, rode a stuttering Panther into the camp, followed by the other man on the Daelim. Not only had they managed to pull her out, but they had retrieved my panniers from the trees. Only my helmet was missing. I realised that in my panic last night I had left it hanging on my wing mirror, ripe for any opportunist who chanced upon it. There was nothing I could do now, it was gone and that was that. I was alive, and I had Panther. Everything else was inconsequential.

I'll never forget those road workers; poor men who worked for a pittance and lived in that makeshift jungle camp. They fed me, watered me, lent me clothes, rescued my bike and, before I left for Lumphat, gave me a litre of fuel, refusing my offers of money. Not for a moment had I felt remotely threatened, despite being outnumbered by men at about fifty to one. Now I was leaving, and I had nothing to give them except gratitude. Months later I am still kicking myself that I didn't take Bun and the foreman's address. I would have so liked to send them a thank you present when I reached home.

I wasn't out of the woods yet. Lumphat was still ten miles north and I had no helmet, only a few sips of water and had barely eaten for twenty four hours. Neither was Panther in any state for another endurance test. The poor girl had spent the night in a bog and I could feel a major revolt in the pipeline. She ground and rattled, stalling whenever we hit a difficult patch, my sweat dripping onto the handlebars as I kicked and kicked her to life.

'Come on Panther, come on Panther, we *have* to get there, *we have to get to Lumphat*, just get me to Lumphat,' I pleaded. 'I promise I'll put you on a truck and get you fixed and be nice to you, just get me to Lumphat.'

Slowly, surely, we nosed closer until, several hours later, I rounded a corner and saw the concrete pillars of the bridge ahead of me.

'We've made it Panther, we're safe,' I told her as we clattered back over the wooden planks. Up the final hill we sputtered, a sorry pair, beaten by the Mondulkiri Death Highway. When she stalled again outside the café I didn't try starting her again – she'd delivered me to safety, that was enough. Slumping in the same red plastic chair I'd sat in twenty-four hours previously, I ordered four bottles of water, two bowls of instant noodle soup and thanked my lucky talismans I'd made it.

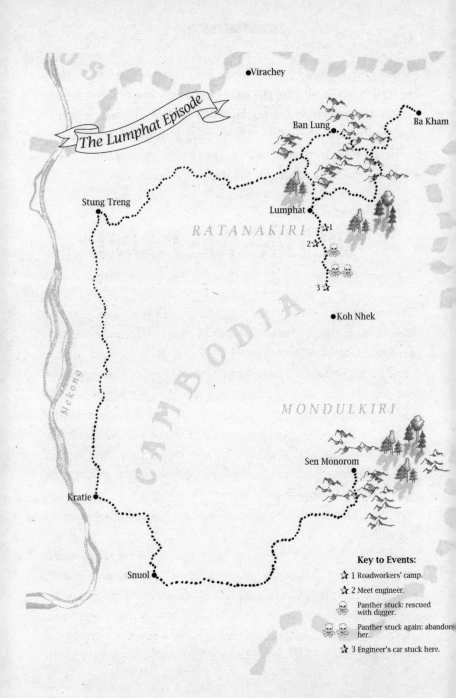

The Lumphat Episode

Virachey

Ba Kham

Ban Lung

Stung Treng

Lumphat

RATANAKIRI

☆ 1

2 ☆

3 ☆

Koh Nhek

Mekong

CAMBODIA

MONDULKIRI

Sen Monorom

Kratie

Snuol

Key to Events:

☆ 1 Roadworkers' camp.

☆ 2 Meet engineer.

Panther stuck: rescued with digger.

Panther stuck again: abandon her.

☆ 3 Engineer's car stuck here.

CHAPTER 18

THE LONG WAY ROUND

The recovery process was swift and painless. Panther was lashed to the back of a van and delivered to the best mechanic in Ban Lung. Lilliputian and fishbone thin, he rose to the challenge, pushing aside his other jobs to operate on the pitiful patient. All day and all night he worked: washing, stripping, cleaning, replacing and rebuilding. In town I bought a new helmet, a $22 white open-faced affair that made me look like Evel Knievel. It would shatter like an eggshell in the event of an accident, but it was the best Ban Lung had to offer. Back at Nisse's I rehabilitated myself with lashings of gin, chips and banana pancakes, an industrial wash and a long sleep in a real bed.

Early the following morning Panther and I were ready to hit the road again. There she was outside the mechanic's shack, sunshine glinting off her glossy pink flanks, her idling engine purring like a contented cat. The freshly-showered mechanic squatted beside her, a clean red sarong wrapped around his pint-sized waist. Through Nisse's Cambodian stepson, who had come to help me translate, he explained that the whole bike had been taken apart, washed and rebuilt. She'd had a new piston and valves, a new cam chain – the fourth one – a new clutch, a new crank shaft, a new gasket set and an oil change. Since the new piston needed to be kept cool for the first hundred miles, he had rigged Panther to a homemade drip. A 10-litre water container had been strapped between the seat and the handlebars, from which a tube dripped onto a damp cloth wrapped around the cylinder barrel. It made her look like she was fresh out of intensive care. Not since the first day I rode her in Hanoi had she sounded so purringly perfect. What a difference a day can make.

Blue sky, scudding cotton wool clouds, hot wind, scorching sun and the smooth quiet buzz of Panther's drip-cooled engine. It was a beautiful day to be riding a Cub in Cambodia. But as I rode west towards the Mekong town of Kratie on that same dull Highway 78 my mind interrogated the events of the past few days. Should I have turned back when the first man warned me about the mud? Was I too hasty in giving the engineer and his driver water and lending them Panther? If I'd left the two men under the tree, ridden on to Lumphat and sent help back to them I would have probably been OK. Was I right to leave Panther and walk for help or should I have stayed and waited for someone to pass? Did I panic unnecessarily? Round and round the questions tumbled, exploring, questioning, doubting, blaming. The engineer had shafted me. That was for sure. If I had a crash between now and Saigon and died of head injuries, it would all be that bastard's fault.

No.

Stop.

Dwelling on the engineer or my missing helmet was futile. Anger wasn't going to get me to Koh Nhek or get my helmet back. Maybe the helmet thief needed it more than me. Maybe one day it would save him in an accident. What had happened had happened. It was all part of the adventure. I must accept it and ride on.

New Year – *Chaul Chnam Thmey* – was two days away and Cambodia was on the move. Shoulders and faces were pressed against the windows of overfilled cars and boots were stacked with boxes of fruit. Careering minibuses lurched past with furniture, mopeds, grinning young men and bunches of gasping chickens lashed and clinging to the back, each one bursting with more than double its usual capacity. Not since Vietnam had I watched my wing mirror so carefully.

Near Stung Treng I turned south past repetitive political billboards exhorting people to vote in the upcoming elections. Mostly they featured the smug bespectacled faces of Hun Sen, Chea Sim and Heng Samrin, the elderly leaders of the ruling Cambodian People's Party. A former Khmer Rouge cadre, the one-eyed Hun Sen – he lost his eye in the battle for Phnom Penh in 1975 – has been in power since 1985 and is one of the longest-serving prime ministers in the world, an elected dictator in a fragile multi-party democracy.

Far less ubiquitous were billboards for the Cambodian Human Rights Party, FUNCINPEC – Cambodia's royalist party – and Sam Rainsy's Cambodian Rescue Party. At the time of writing, three weeks after the July 2013 election, Hun Sen's narrow victory over Sam Rainsy is still mired in allegations of rigging and corruption. External committees have been called in to investigate the results and tanks have been deployed on the outskirts of Phnom Penh. Cambodia might have democratic elections, but whether they are fair is another matter.

Ten o'clock, midday, two o'clock, four o' clock. I counted down the hours and the miles, stopping only to buy petrol and sweet fragrant mangoes dripping with golden juice. I fidgeted in my seat, swung my legs and leant over Panther to check her drip was still in place, trying to ignore the fact that the new helmet dug into my forehead and throttled me with the chinstrap. Just north of Kratie the road merged with the eastern bank of the Mekong. All at once I was in the melee of a thriving riverside community, an effusion of colour and life entirely different to the gloomy plantations and wizened fields that had brought me here. Silted houses hunkered beneath an avenue of palms and roadside stalls overflowed with trays of dried fish, mounds of fresh coconuts and crates of beer. Everyone was in party mood. Men were putting up colourful awnings, garrulous groups were drinking outside their houses and skipping children waved and yelled 'Hello!' and 'Goodbye!' as I rode by. Slowed to a crawl, I wove between wobbling bicycles, plodding oxcarts and doe-eyed water buffaloes, pausing to watch the sun slide between the drooping palms.

At the end of this was Kratie, a faded colonial town favoured by the French, whose unkempt villas still loitered on leafy side streets. Missed by the US bombardment, Kratie had the air of an ageing duchess; one who had seen better days but still retained elements of her youthful elegance. Flocks of sparrows twittered in French-planted boulevards and jaunty ponies pulled carts past two-storey shophouses, their shuttered windows and crumbling cupolas rotting with damp and neglect. Along the riverfront little stalls were hung with bundles of the local specialties: *krolan* – bamboo tubes filled with sticky rice, coconut milk and beans, and *nehm* – tasty little banana leaf parcels of herbed, spiced fish. Families took the air here at dusk, strolling under the fluttering red and blue Cambodian flags and leaning over the low river wall to admire the sun setting over the golden spit of the island of Koh Trong.

Parking Panther on this promenade, I lit a cigarette and dangled my legs over the wall, watching as the last sliver of sun stained the river blood red. Like the Mekong herself I too was nearing the end of my journey. Saigon was only 150 miles from here, the same distance I had covered today from Ban Lung. I could be there in a few days if I wanted. An idea which had started as a trickle in my imagination over a year ago was nearing its completion. I was happy, thrilled by the adventure, delighted to be sitting here watching another Mekong sunset. But I was tired, a cumulative tiredness that clung to me with increasing persistence. Five weeks of hard riding, extreme heat, poor diet and lack of sleep were chipping away at my energy levels. Driven by my mission, I'd had little downtime. When I wasn't riding I was writing, researching, downloading and sorting photographs, charging equipment, tinkering with Panther, hanging around mechanics, typing the odd blog. It was a rip-roaring adventure, but it was no holiday. I would pause for a day here and get some rest before girding my loins for the final push to Saigon.

It was fortunate I wasn't looking for any Trail romance in Kratie. I took off my jeans that evening to find my legs inflamed into a mass of angry red lumps, like those of a syphilitic sailor's. They had been a bit irritating all day, but now – oh, the itchiness! All I wanted to do was scratch and tear at my skin. But the more I itched, the angrier and redder the lumps became. I guessed it was caused by some poisonous plant my legs had caught on during the Lumphat Episode, but when I opened my panniers a colony of furious red ants flooded across the white tiled floor. It was days before the lumps disappeared, and nothing would rid me of the maddening itch.

The countdown to New Year was even more feverish the next day as people hawked, shopped, chopped, gutted and gossiped in the market amidst buckets of squirming fish, baskets of sumptuous fruit and boxes of cakes and gaudy golden decorations. It had the frantic air of Christmas Eve, of the knowledge that tomorrow everything would be closed. Sitting on a stool beside a mountain of spiky red rambutan, I watched the women as they rushed about their errands and dashed into hairdressers' for that last-minute coiffure. Most of all I looked at their pyjamas, for not since Hanoi had I seen such a splendid array. There were Pingu pyjamas, Mickey Mouse pyjamas, Hello Kitty pyjamas, Angry Birds pyjamas, pyjamas with pandas and teddy bears and flowers and cute little puppies. Fat women rode mopeds in pyjamas. Old women grilled fish in pyjamas. Age or occupation didn't seem of consequence; nearly all the women in Kratie wore pyjamas. I liked them so much I ventured into the innards of the market and spent $9 on a psychedelic orange floral pair for myself. Maybe I could get the pyjama trend to catch on in England.

Among the frenzy of preparation was the odd po-faced *barang* – the word for foreigner is almost identical in Lao, Thai, Khmer, Arabic, Persian, Hindi and Ethiopian, all stemming from the crusading Franks, the first foreigners in the Middle

East. They were here for the sand of Koh Trong and a sight of the Irrawaddy dolphins and Mekong mud turtles. They mooched through the market and sat in sulky tattooed groups drinking beer, thumbing iPhones and talking about which bus they were going to get to Si Phan Don. I was happier sitting alone, watching people, reading and writing my diary. But as I sipped my first gin and tonic at a riverside bar that evening, a gangly young man with a crooked smile loped over and asked to join me.

'Sure,' I replied, remembering the 'Yes' rule and putting down my book. It was the same depressing one about the Khmer Rouge and just a moment ago I'd been crying over it, looking every bit the miserable po-faced *barang* myself.

Bartak was Polish and laughed at everything. He had been to Thailand and was on his way to Laos, but didn't want to go to Vietnam where he'd been told 'everyone gets ripped off'. He even laughed when he told me he was lonely travelling solo, and missed having someone to share his experiences with.

'Don't you get lonely?' he asked me. 'I mean, what did you do on all those nights in Laos when there was no one to talk to?'

I considered his question, thinking about those nights in Ta Oi, Kaleum and Attapeu; those long days of riding. I'd felt alone at times, yes, but never lonely. Not once. When I wasn't occupied with Panther or fiddling with equipment I'd spent contented evenings just sitting, watching, thinking, writing. I had revelled in the simple art of observation, undistracted by companionship or television. Consumed by the purpose of my journey, I hadn't had time to feel lonely. Backpacking can be a purposeless occupation; drifting between towns, islands, hostels and air-conditioned buses, only talking to people if you have the courage. I may have been alone in the jungle, but I always had the Trail.

I'd wanted to go to Phnom Penh, but New Year had put the kibosh on my plans – the city would be a ghost town for the next week and the few people I'd planned on meeting there were all away on holiday. It would have to wait for another visit. And it wasn't part of the Trail anyway. And as much as I would have liked to sit out the holiday period in Kratie, my fast-approaching flight to England didn't allow for this either. Instead I would go to Snuol – an apparent dive of a town forty miles south-east of Kratie – spend the night there and cross back into Vietnam the next day. The Hindu solar calendar meant nothing to the Sino-influenced Vietnamese; they had celebrated *Tet* two months previously, on the same day as Chinese New Year. Over the border, it would be business as usual.

Buoyed by the blue sky and holiday atmosphere, I turned my back on the Mekong and rode out of Kratie the following morning. Away from the river the road ran through flat dry sparsely populated farmland and straggly banana plantations. Panther was still on a drip so I dawdled along, listening out for any irregularities in the buzz and whirr of her engine, promising her it was going to be an easy day. Smiling families overtook me, their mopeds buried under two parents, up to four children, bunches of lilies and carnations and boxes of mangoes, custard apples, bananas, lychees, rambutan and dragon fruit. As well as these, a steady stream of Land Cruisers and cars pelted by. In Vietnam and Laos people generally graduated from bicycle to moped to Land Cruiser. In Cambodia the middle classes liked to own cars. But not just any old car; in my ten days in the country the only make of car I saw was a Toyota Camry. I never did find out why, but the Camry has more of a monopoly on Cambodia than even the Lada on Russia.

At noon I stopped for a gourmet roadside picnic, sheltering from the sun under a clutch of banana palms. First on the menu were *nehm* and *krolan*, bought from an elderly Khmer-Chen lady on the riverfront in Kratie. Unwrapping the little green parcels of *nehm* felt like Christmas. First I undid the ribbon, next I unfolded the banana and mint leaves, and finally I reached the succulent little morsels of raw fish spiced with chilli, ginger and lemongrass. The *krolan* was sweet and sticky, eaten like a rice lollipop straight out of the bamboo. Pudding was fresh-off-the-tree mangoes, given to me by the owner of my guest house in Kratie. Of all the roadside snacks I'd had this was definitely the tastiest, and I savoured every bite and burst of flavour.

Farther on I turned into the decorous pink and gold carved stone gates of a pagoda and parked among tall slender coconut palms. Ninety-five per cent of Khmers are Theravada Buddhist and at New Year people flock to their local temples to give alms to the poor, food to the monks and offerings to Buddha. I'm not a Buddhist but after my recent near miss on the Mondulkiri Death Highway I wanted to say a little thank you to Buddha too. An area the size of several football pitches was scattered with pagodas, stupas and icons of Buddha, among which coconut palms and mango trees whispered in the breeze. One of the pagodas was newly built and had candyfloss-pink walls, swept concrete steps and dragons rearing off glittering golden roofs. Others had broken balustrades and faded orange paint, the dirt around them thick with litter. If it wasn't for the carved '1995' on their roofs you would have thought they had stood for a century or more. But everything here was modern, rebuilt since the time of the Khmer Rouge, who murdered the monks and destroyed over 3,000 monasteries. It wasn't until 1991 that Theravada Buddhism was officially reinstated as the national religion and the rebuilding of *wats* began.

As I walked up the steps of the nearest, shabbiest temple a woman with a radiant gap-toothed smile materialised, genie-like, and beckoned me to follow her. I did as she said, kneeling before a gilded Buddha and slipping 1000 riel – about 15 pence – under his fat golden toes, thanking him and the universe for looking after me so far. Down the steps we tripped, my self-appointed guide jabbering away in Khmer as we knelt, thanked, lit incense and stuffed notes under the feet of a dozen beatific Buddhas. Every time I lifted my camera to take a photo she dashed into the frame, pulling her long black hair behind her ears and smoothing down her stained orange T-shirt as she grinned into the lens. Afterwards, she took my hand and led me under the mango trees to her house, a simple stilted dwelling behind the temple complex. A brood of people lounged in the shade beneath, stirring as we appeared: babies, children, parents, aunts, uncles, grandparents, great-grandparents.

'*Soursdey Chnam Thmey*!' I said, 'Happy New Year!' – the only Khmer I had managed to learn.

A shrunken, shrivelled crone shuffled over to inspect me.

'*Soursdey Chnam Thmey*!' I said, bowing my head and putting my hands together in greeting.

Her wrinkled face creased into a myopic toothless smile as she returned the greeting, before creeping back into the shade. For half an hour we sat under the house communicating in sign language and the few words I was able to look up quickly in my dictionary. The children, adorable little things with huge brown eyes, dimpled cheeks and missing teeth, giggled excitedly and tumbled over each other to have their photos taken. All over Southeast Asia families lived like this, with three or four generations under one roof. I'd seen it every day. But now, among these gambolling children, I felt a fleeting pang of sadness for my own family. My parents were divorced and I lived on the other side of England from them and my sister, only seeing them about six times a year, if that. My father, in his early seventies, lived alone. These people were poor and no doubt had their problems and familial squabbles, but they had each other and a sense of community and mutual help which so many of us in the West have lost.

I wasn't able to dwell too long on this however, for my guide, deciding it was time for the next part of the tour, tugged at my arm and off we trotted. At another temple she gave me biscuits and a bottle of water. Then, as quickly as she had appeared, she was waving goodbye and hurrying back towards her house. What a delightful, unexpected interlude.

It is the habit of the traveller to try and simplify and categorise nations, to sum them up in a few neat homogenising adjectives: the Italians are flamboyant, the Russians surly, the French amorous, the Lao lackadaisical. Yet after just over a week in Cambodia I was struggling to define the country and its people. I could now see that the Khmers looked very different from the smaller, paler Lao and the Sino-influenced

Vietnamese. Taller and darker, their looks were the result of the Indianisation of the country that had occurred from the first century AD. Traders from the Bay of Bengal brought with them people, ideas and technologies, shaping Cambodia's history and identity for a thousand years. The Khmer script is derived from Sanskrit, Hinduism flourished until the twelfth century and Angkor Wat was consecrated to the Hindu deity, Vishnu. You could have swapped some of the Khmer men I saw with an Indian *chai wallah* and never known the difference.

But beyond this shallow visual level it was hard to get a handle on the beautiful but damaged country. I couldn't stop thinking about the Khmer Rouge. I looked at old people and questioned how they had survived, at people my age and wondered what had become of their parents. When I saw an old man in gold-rimmed spectacles it brought to mind the murdered intelligentsia; how in 1980 only one lawyer was found to have escaped the purges. I was haunted by the idea of second-generation PTSD and how seventy per cent of the population was still under thirty. In my imagination the legacy of the Khmer Rouge was everywhere, but nearly all the Cambodians I had met seemed so at odds with their recent history of violence and suffering. They were optimistic about the future rather than bitter about the past. According to the UN Cambodia is still worse off than Timor-Leste and Iraq, and thousands have lost their homes and land under the corruption and land-grabs of Hun Sen's government. But, with the exception of a few, I found them to be a warm proud charming people, neither as curious as the Vietnamese nor as shy as the Lao. How Pol Pot could have come to power here and almost obliterate a nation was quite beyond me.

On 30 April 1970 Snuol was a small plantation town of two thousand people. A week later it had been razed to the ground, the first victim of a joint US and ARVN invasion of the Cambodian border areas, aimed at destroying NVA bases and the fabled Viet Cong headquarters – COSVN. Nearby, infantry from the 1st Air Cavalry found 'the city' – a huge NVA base area of bunkers, storage sheds, hospitals, truck repair facilities, mess halls, ammunition dumps, a pig farm and a swimming pool. I had read an account of this online and emailed the author, a former 1st Cavalry Lieutenant, to try and find out more. When we spoke on the phone a few weeks later he told me they caught the communists by surprise. 'A lot of the equipment and ammo was just out in the open, they never thought we'd come over the border. Our operation was so successful I don't think the VC fired another rocket for six months.' The Viet Cong headquarters, though, was never found.

Despite the tactical successes, the campaign caused a storm on the Home Front. The war in Vietnam was unpopular enough, but news that US ground forces had invaded neutral Cambodia sparked nationwide anti-war riots. Within a week a third of US colleges had gone on strike, seven students had been shot dead by the National Guard and 100,000 people had marched on Washington D.C. Over the following twelve months, millions more took part in angry protests all over the country. An entire army company was on almost permanent deployment at the White House and machine guns were dug in on the presidential lawn. Gonzo journalist Hunter S. Thompson summed up how many Americans felt about Nixon when he described him as 'dark, venal and incurably violent'.

Nowadays Snuol seemed a dilapidated grotty town with little to recommend it. If it wasn't New Year I might have been able to find someone who spoke English who could tell me what had happened in May 1970, but my timing was impeccably awful and I rode along the main street past shuttered shops and an empty market. Staying here held little attraction. *Maybe, just maybe*, I thought, *I could get as far as Sen Monorom today* – the Mondulkiri town I had been trying to reach before I became so hideously stuck in the mud. It was 80 miles east of Snuol along a new Chinese road that hugged the Vietnamese border. I was wary of pushing Panther, but Sen Monorom was a definite link to the Trail, somewhere the tired *boi dois* had marched through as they neared the end of their journey. I would have driven three hundred extra miles to reach it, but maybe I'd find someone or something that could add to the fragmented puzzle of the Sihanouk Trail. And even if I didn't, psychologically and geographically it would mean almost closing the gap on my defeat. The scent had gone cold since Lumphat, the thrill of the chase dwindling. As pleasant as it was to be riding through Cambodia, without the Trail it felt like the soul was missing from my journey.

Pulling Panther over to the side of the road I tossed a coin, a ten-pence piece I found lurking in my wallet. Heads I'd go to Sen Monorom. Tails I'd stay in Snuol.

Heads it was.

It was 2.30 p.m. and I had 80 miles to cover before nightfall. Giving Panther a quick check over – oil, petrol, drip, tyres – I pulled the throttle and off we jumped. We sped east along the unblemished black tarmac, through a trickle of Muslim villages where minarets rose up between the wooden houses and the women's heads were swathed in headscarves. These were the Cham people, the last remnants of the Kingdom of Cham which had once ruled over most of Vietnam and who still spoke the Austro-Polynesian language of their Indonesian ancestors.

At the epic speed of 30 miles per hour I flew past the sign for Mondulkiri province, cheering at having finally made it. On a North Vietnamese military map I saw later in Saigon, this road was marked as a vein of the Trail, but there was nothing to suggest that now. In spite of Nixon's 'softening up' of the area there wasn't a single visible bomb crater.

The road began to wind and climb and for the first time in Cambodia I was riding through frothy verdant jungle in the shadow of soaring silver trunks. Mondulkiri – meaning 'meeting of the hills' – is Cambodia's largest province and for now remains cloaked in virgin forest. Less populous and even more remote than its northern neighbour, Ratanakiri, eighty per cent of the population are the minority Bunong people. The rest are Khmer, Cham and Chinese. Elated to be among this effusion of nature once again I stopped to take it all in, watching a pair of dark green parrots as they flew over a fan of palms. Even if I found nothing of the Trail in Sen Monorom it would be worth it just for this.

Climbing farther, to 750 metres above sea level, the trees gave way to fabulous undulating grassland splashed with copses of pine and dark pockets of jungle. The different topography up here has led to Mondulkiri rather optimistically being referred to as 'the Switzerland of Cambodia'. Red tracks snaked over distant emerald hills and the sky was so vast it seemed to scoop up the edges of the earth. Exhilarated by the ride and the beauty I dived up and over the hills, zipping up my jacket as the sun lowered and the altitude rose, families picnicking at roadside shrines shrieking and waving as I rode by. As the sun set I drove over a crest to see Sen Monorom, Mondulkiri's only town, sprinkled over a cluster of hills.

With everywhere either closed or full for New Year, it was after dark by the time I found a room in a small family-run guest house down a dirt track on the edge of town, hidden among avocado trees. They were closed, a young man told me, full of visiting family, but there was one spare room I could have for the night. They brought me *Anchor* beer and fish caught that day in the nearby river and asked me questions about where I had been. 'Oh, so brave!' said the owner's pretty daughter. But they knew nothing of the Trail.

When I woke up in the morning all the family, except the young man, had gone to the pagoda. He'd been up since before dawn, he said, making offerings and lighting incense at their New Year's altar. Every family built one of these in their home on *Moha Sangkran* – the first day of the celebrations – decorating them with exotic fruits, candles, cans of orange juice and Coca-Cola, sprays of flowers and icons of Buddha. Theirs had the addition of a bowl plump with shiny avocadoes, picked from the trees around the guest house.

At the pagoda the psychedelically painted wooden walls reverberated with the sonorous chants of several hundred worshippers. They knelt in rows in their finery, their hands clasped together, a reverent throng of silk and lace and freshly washed hair. I crept in and sat at the back to watch the proceedings, the family in front of me nudging each other and smiling at the appearance of a *barang*. At the front twenty young monks sat cross-legged on a low platform. They looked serious and slightly embarrassed, their platform overflowing with an ever-multiplying quantity of edible offerings. A single decrepit old bonze sat separately, his toothless gums chewing through the first of fifty plates of rice before him. Beside him a clutch of shaven-headed female mendicants, their cheeks hollow from age and poverty, had riel pressed into their hands by the wealthier congregants.

Afterwards, as I wandered around the hilltop compound, I saw a scowling dirty urchin hurling stones against a wall. Cambodian New Year, like Christmas, can't be a happy time for everyone.

From the pagoda I rode up to a look-out point on a hilltop north of the town. Known as *Samot Cheur* – Ocean of Trees – the ridge looked north over the emerald forests of Mondulkiri. I hadn't found any concrete clues to the Trail in Sen Monorom, but from here I could imagine Koh Nhek in the far distance and mentally make the journey. Parking Panther on the summit I turned off the engine, took off my helmet and drank in the vista below me. For as far as I could see the hills were robed in a lustrous rippling green, interrupted only by the glint of sun on distant Bunong roofs. Flotillas of cumulus clouds sailed across an azure sky, their shadows forming dark pools on the surface of the sylvan ocean. There was the sound of piping birds, a hooting gibbon and the low constant hum of bees. But otherwise there was silence. It was one of those rare magnificent views, the memory and majesty of which will always stay with me.

For an hour I sat there, watching the clouds drift across that monumental landscape. I thought of what had happened to me in the mud of that dark forest, and of the *boi dois* who had trudged through those trees with their guns and backpacks, so nearly in South Vietnam. It was hard to envisage this peaceful landscape blighted by Nixon's bombs.

Inevitably my mind turned to the end of my journey, to riding into Saigon and parking in front of the gates of the Reunification Palace. North Vietnamese tanks had burst through these gates on 30 April 1975, thus 'liberating' the South and proclaiming a unified independent Vietnam. There was nowhere more fitting I could think to end.

I realised, sitting there, that there was one thing I had to do before I reached Saigon. I had to sleep alone in the jungle. It had been what I'd feared the most before leaving England. I knew I would kick myself if I didn't do it, even feeling that I had failed a part of my mission. There was no jungle left over the border in Vietnam. If I was going to do it, it would have to be tonight.

The decision made, I took a last look over *Samot Cheur* and rode back down the hill into town. It was mid-afternoon already; the sooner I left and found a place to camp the better.

An hour later I was riding south again, my basket stuffed with water, bananas and a fruit I didn't know the name of. Since nearly all the shops were closed it was the best I could find. It wasn't exactly gourmet, but it would be enough to survive the night.

After ten miles I spotted a little track which dived off the road, snaking east over a cluster of partially forested hills. *Why am I torturing myself like this?* I wondered as I rode along the dusty track, Panther's tyres once again staining red, scanning the hills for a hidden spot where I could sling my hammock.

It needed to be near enough to the road to get Panther there, but far enough away that no one could see me. For all my fears about snakes, spiders, UXO and landmines, in reality people were my biggest risk. After half an hour of searching I settled on a hillside a hundred metres off the track, bumping through short grass and young pines until I was over the brow of the hill and sure I was out of sight.

'Never ever ride off the track in Cambodia,' Mick had said, but here I was doing just that. Mondulkiri hadn't been a heavily mined province, and it was extremely unlikely that these young pines would have been planted in a minefield. But still, his words rang in my head.

It was dusk by the time I parked Panther under a pine tree and turned the engine off. In this sea of green she stood out like a sunburnt Scot, so I pulled a few fallen branches over her sides then turned to admire the view. By chance I'd chosen an excellent spot; a gentle grassy hillside sloping down to a copse of jungle, beyond which lay a panorama of rolling hills. As far as I could see, potted capsules of forest exploded out of the hills, incongruous with their Arcadian surrounds. Up here flourished a cool highland air, a twittering skylark, a hovering kestrel, the arboreal familiarity of a Scottish hillside. I could almost imagine I was in Glencoe. But down there, only a few hundred metres away, was the dark exotic forest, howling with monkeys and slithering with snakes. As lovely as it was, I was glad to be up on my hillside perch.

Anxious at the prospect of a night out alone I tied my hammock between a pair of small pines, fumbling with the ropes and talking to myself like a child.

'Don't worry, you've been quite brave so far; you've nearly got to Saigon; there are no tigers here; you haven't seen any snakes or spiders; there's really nothing to be afraid of; you'll be fine.'

Afterwards, standing by my hammock I watched the evening light filter through the trees and soak the clouds orange, listening as the darkness pressed the 'on' button and the jungle below exploded into life. Up here was just the hum of bees and the ring of cicadas. Down there a screaming sawmill was launching into its twilight shift and a thousand shrill fire alarms were being set off. The difference was astounding, a powerful reminder of why it's so important to preserve the forests and their incredible biodiversity.

In my haste to leave Sen Monorom and find somewhere to camp I had done abysmally with my shopping. The bananas were unripe, an avocado I'd been given at last night's guest house tasted like soap and the weird fruit was, well, weird. I had also failed to buy any alcohol, a major error when faced with a potentially terrifying night alone in the wilds of Cambodia. What I would do for a beer, or a whisky, or some of my long finished gin, or just anything alcoholic. I might even have considered drinking lighter fuel if I'd had it. Instead I put on my pyjamas – so bright they were almost visible from the International Space Station – did a creature check with my head torch, and zipped myself into my hammock.

Safe in my suspended sanctuary I watched the new night unfold. A crescent moon rose over the hills and lay on its back among a million glittering eyes. Insects bashed into my hammock, their wings whirring like chopper blades. A light breeze rustled the trees. On the far horizon banks of cloud drifted across the sky switching off the stars as they went. In their wake came a spectacular lightning show, which lit up the clouds and the distant hills, coming closer every minute. I had no tarpaulin and the thin branches of the pines would offer no shelter against the storm. The best I could do was shove my panniers into a dry bag and put on my waterproof trousers, fleece and motorbike jacket. If it rained, I would just have to crouch under a tree until it passed.

The approaching storm brought with it gusts of cold damp air and I pleaded with it not to venture this far. When a shooting star streaked across the sky above me, suspended in the atmosphere for what felt like a minute, I closed my eyes and wished for it not to rain, then fell into a broken sleep.

My wish must have worked, for although it was shiveringly cold, the storm never came to my hillside. At dawn I was woken by warm golden shards of light filtering through the pines and lay in my hammock, smiling, overjoyed to have escaped the rain and death by terror. Gone was the harsh screeching cacophony of twilight. In its place was an angelic trilling choir of birds, gently rousing the hills from their slumber. All except one, that is, who every thirty seconds let out a hoarse thuggish shriek; a brawling drunk in the chancel. I imagined the other birds drawing up petitions and forming pressure groups to get rid of their unsavoury neighbour, such a blight was he on their aural landscape.

Savouring the view a little more I then packed up and rode down the track, happy and extremely hungry.

CHAPTER 19

A SAIGON CONCLUSION

'Nothing is more precious than independence and liberty.'
Ho Chi Minh, former President of North Vietnam

Cambodia was sleeping off a collective hangover and the road back to Snuol was gloriously empty. At a roadside shack a bleary-eyed young boy sold me 3 litres of fuel in Pepsi bottles, but shook his head when I asked about food. In the first village I came to, a family was eating bowls of rice outside their café. No, they were closed, they said, waving me away like an unwanted beggar. The same happened across the road, although this time at least they sold me an iced coffee. Bored, a passing policeman wandered over and sat down to interrogate me in bad English. Why was I travelling alone? Did I like Cambodia? Where was I going? Where was my husband? Why didn't I have children? Weak with hunger, I wasn't in the mood for such an inquisition.

'You must be very unhappy to want to ride all over the place on your own like this,' he said.

He looked personally aggrieved when I told him I wasn't visiting Angkor Wat. So much so I wondered if it was an arrestable offence. Cambodians are immensely proud of the Angkor temple complex near Siem Reap, the symbol and soul of their nation. The largest religious edifice on the planet, its magnificence is a reminder of their former glories. Tellingly, it was one of the few cultural artefacts not destroyed by Pol Pot, who sought to stand on the shoulders of the Khmer kings and emulate the might of their empire. 'If we can build Angkor Wat, we can do anything,' he bragged in a moment of hubris.

It wasn't until near Snuol that I finally found a dark dirty roadside café willing to sell me some food. Ravenous, I inhaled two fried-egg baguettes and three strong black coffees. Just beyond I came to a left turn signed 'Vietnam'. The 3G map on my phone, which had rarely worked since Stung Treng, told me this was an extension of Vietnam's Highway 13 – not the same Highway 13 as I had ridden on in Laos, but the same road on which the US and ARVN troops and tanks had advanced on 30 April 1970. Over the border were the towns of Loc Ninh and An Loc, both significant battlegrounds in the last years of the War. I knew nothing about the border post itself, but it seemed a good place to cross.

Like the very south of Laos, so this hem of Cambodia was an abandoned dusty wilderness. Its only prominent feature was a colossal golden casino, the words 'Gold City' emblazoned across its windowless façade. Banned from gambling in their own country, thousands of Vietnamese come to Cambodia every day, many of them running up crippling debts. 'Gold City' is just one of the dozens of casinos along the border between the two countries.

I took off my helmet and stood outside the wooden hut that was Cambodian passport control. In front of me a gaunt Vietnamese man pushed a bundle of passports through the window; another busload of Vietnamese here to lose their money in Cambodian slot machines. When he was done, a smiley guard came out to look at Panther, holding out his hand for my passport.

'*Soursdey Chnam Thmey*!' I said, saying the phrase for the last time.

'Where you going?' he said in English, looking at my Vietnamese visa.

Resisting the temptation to say 'the moon' I smiled and said, 'Vietnam.'

'Where you from?' he asked, still holding my British passport.

'England,' I replied, wondering what other insightful questions he had up his sleeve.

There were no 'stamp' fees or questions about paperwork. Without further ado he smiled, wished me a good trip and lifted the barrier. I had felt sentimental about leaving Laos, but I hadn't bonded so deeply with Cambodia. My visit had been too fleeting, my impression tainted perhaps by the Lumphat Episode. In Laos I had been immersed in the Trail every day, but in Cambodia the scent had remained frustratingly cold. As I rode across no man's land I didn't look back. Instead I looked forward to Vietnam.

On the Vietnamese side a guard was asleep in a large empty room, his faint snores audible through the glass window. My boots squeaked on the spotless white tiles as I walked towards him. He woke up, stamped my passport and promptly went back to sleep again. In three border crossings only one person had asked to see Panther's paperwork and so far not one person had asked to see my driving licence.

Outside three young guards – the only other people around – were admiring Panther.

'Hanoi!' they said, pointing quizzically to the plates. 'You moto Hanoi?'

I nodded. 'Hanoi, Laos, Cambodia, Ho Chi Minh.'

They gave me a thumbs up and cheerily waved me through.

There was no town to greet me on the other side of the border, just a crooked line of shacks: *pho* stalls, a petrol station, little shops selling cold drinks and signs in a script I could read. It was unmistakably Vietnam. Stopping at the nearest café I ordered *pho* and two coffees, the two women laughing at my vegetarianism. I laughed with them, happy to be back.

In between slurps of *pho* I reorganised myself for the final leg: money, phrasebook, SIM card, maps. Oh, yes – maps. The torn-out pages Digby had given me had been of the north of the country. The only map I had of the south was a fifty-pence French tourist one I'd bought on the street in Hanoi. Marked with pretty symbols to denote places of interest, it was going to be of little use in getting me to Saigon. Instead I would have to rely on pointing, sign language and the intermittent 3G signal on my phone. How I had remembered to pack emergency gin but not proper maps I'm still not quite sure.

Leaving the café I rode south along the potholed tarmac of Highway 13, through old French rubber plantations wilting in the April heat. I had become so used to the emptiness of the roads in Laos and Cambodia, of hardly having to use my wing mirror, but now, just as in the north, there were people everywhere. Mopeds shot out from behind trees when I least expected it. People wandered into the road without thinking to look. Russian-made Kamaz trucks came bolting up behind me, forcing me onto the verge. Barely a minute went by when I wasn't beeping or swerving. Back in the salmon run of Vietnamese roads I had to be hyper aware; if I had a crash in this tinpot helmet, I'd be toast.

At Loc Ninh I stopped at the first hotel I saw, a white concrete building on a hill behind the busy main street. It had musty corridors, an empty swimming pool and the word 'Karaoke' written in neon lights across the top. There were no other guests and I sat outside and wrote my diary, a cheeky teenage boy bringing me beer and food under a lamp flickering with moths. He sat with me, playing with his iPhone and flicking through my phrasebook, giggling when he came to the page with pick-up phrases like 'Kiss me,' 'Let's go to bed' and 'Easy, tiger.'

Come nine o'clock I was fast asleep.

By the summer of 1971 America's exit from the mess of Indochina was inevitable. Both at home and on the battlefield the writing was on the wall. The increasingly disillusioned grunts were near mutinous; drug use was rife, orders were being refused and rising numbers of unpopular officers were being 'fragged' – killed by their own men. The anti-war sentiment at home was now so widespread that continuing involvement in Southeast Asia was impossible. Nixon's lies and bellicosity had driven the US closer to civil war than at any other time since 1861.

As America's position weakened, so North Vietnam's grew. By now the Truong Son army numbered 100,000; soldiers, engineers and 'heroic' volunteers – many of them female – who filled bomb craters, built new roads, constructed underwater pontoons, cleared landslides, repaired trucks, shot down enemy planes, drove, dug, walked, pushed, carried and died. And by 1971 a thousand trucks were going south on the Trail every day, one witness comparing it to the 'Long Island Expressway – at rush hour'.

America might have spent billions of dollars on the biggest air war in history, but they were fighting a ruthless implacable enemy, willing to sustain huge losses in order to win. Just as the French had criticised Giap after Dien Bien Phu, so Westmoreland stated, 'Any American commander who took the same vast losses as General Giap would not have lasted three weeks.' In their determination to succeed, the communists would have fought to the last man.

The following spring Hanoi launched a massive unexpected offensive on South Vietnam, advancing south over the seventeenth parallel and east from Laos and Cambodia. One of the major battles took place in Loc Ninh which, after several weeks of heavy fighting, fell to the Viet Cong in April 1972. A museum in the town told the story of those bloody few weeks.

Eight months later, in January 1973, North Vietnam and the USA signed the Paris Peace Accords. By May America had withdrawn its remaining troops and airpower from Vietnam and Laos. For his part in the deal Dr Kissinger, the architect of so much destruction, was awarded the 1973 Nobel Peace Prize. America, said Nixon, had achieved 'peace with honour'. In fact it was a cowardly ignoble exodus on the part of the US negotiators, so keen to save their own political bacon that they hung their South Vietnamese and Lao allies out to dry. Lao

Prime Minister Souvanna Phouma was told that if he didn't sign the agreement there would be no more US aid. He signed and the aid stopped anyway. At noon on 22 February 1973, as the ceasefire came into play, the last US planes in Laos were ordered to pull out mid-battle, leaving their Royalist Lao and Hmong allies to certain deaths. Without the backing of the US it was only a matter of time before South Vietnam was overrun too.

Dong Sy, the commander of the Trail, didn't waste a moment. He mobilised a 50,000-strong workforce to build a single tarmac highway down the whole length of Vietnam. There would be no more scurrying about in the jungle dodging bombs, this super Trail would carry two thousand trucks a day to the South. It would eliminate the ARVN 'puppet' troops, facilitate the final advance on Saigon and be the key to fulfilling Ho's dream of a unified Vietnam. It was a Herculean task. Bridges were built, land cleared of UXO, mines detonated and forests cleared. By early 1975, sixteen years after Vo Bam's pioneers had walked south, a journey that had taken six months now took ten days.

My tiredness was becoming incurable. On several occasions in the past few days I had been overcome with fatigue while riding, pulling off the road to catnap under a tree. Coffee was ceasing to have any effect, however much I drank. In Cambodia the previous day I'd noted how the sight of stilted houses and water buffaloes no longer excited me. Six weeks ago it had been new and exotic, now it had become a quotidian reality. I berated myself; I had to hold on to every minute of this adventure, take it all in, keep my vigour and enthusiasm until the very last metre. But I could feel my brain had dulled.

With tiredness came irritability. At the Loc Ninh museum – a fusty set-up in an old French plantation owner's house – I was annoyed that all the explanations were in Vietnamese and the guide spoke terrible English. When we came to an old Trail map which seemed to show the locations of the elusive southern headquarters, I asked her where they were. She looked at me with an infuriatingly blank uncomprehending smile. Kowtowing to the Asian habit of saving face, I smiled back. Throwing my toys out of the pram wouldn't do either of us any good. Anyway it wasn't her fault, why should the poor woman speak good English? I was just being tired and unreasonable.

Saigon was only 80 miles south of Loc Ninh. I could be there today if I wanted. I could spend a few days by a pool or even go to the beach. It was a tempting image. But the Trail had become an addiction. Now that I'd set eyes on the accursed map I wanted to find those headquarters, to chase the Trail for a few days more. I'd read an online account of a US 1st Cavalry veteran who had visited COSVN – the Central Office for South Vietnam – a decade ago. He had described it as being north-west of the town of Tay Ninh, right on the Cambodian border. The account was outdated and the descriptions vague. I didn't know exactly where it was, what was there, or if I would be able to visit. But COSVN had been the nerve centre of the southern terminuses of the Trail, the headquarters of the Viet Cong. Like a dog with a bone, I couldn't give up yet. I would go to Tay Ninh – 80 miles west of here – and see what I could find. From there I would ride to Cu Chi, the famous Viet

Cong tunnel network where John had insisted I fire an M60, then on to Saigon.

South of the museum the road was under construction. Pulling my Buff up around my face I jolted over ruts and rubble, weaving in and out of diggers and rollers. Red dust sprayed from the bald tyres of thunderous trucks, their beeps sending mopeds swerving out of the way. At the next town I turned west, stopping for a coffee injection in a smart little roadside café. Café culture was big in southern Vietnam, much more so than in the colder north. Men played *co tuong* at the white tables, others swung in a row of hammocks. They looked up when I walked in, several of them leaving their games of chess to peer over my shoulder at my phone and ply me with questions. Was I alone? Where was I from? Where was my husband? Did I have children? Where was my bike? Why was I drinking three coffees?

From here the road ran due west through dozens of miles of rubber plantations. For the first time since Ba Kham I saw bomb craters among the trees, part of Nixon's efforts at wiping out COSVN. Not only had these plantations been the scene of numerous battles between the Viet Cong, US and South Vietnamese, they had earlier been the crucible of Vietnam's first ever communist uprising. Sick of the abuses of their French overlords, in February 1930 five thousand workers at Michelin's nearby Phú Riềng Rubber Plantation had risen up against their masters. It took eight hundred soldiers to quell the rebellion, the leader of which was imprisoned for five years. It was easy to imagine darting soldiers and whispered discontent in those dark oppressive miles of trees.

The area was still sensitive; a series of signs reading 'Restricted Area,' 'Frontier Area' and 'No Photography' indicated how close I was to Cambodia. I knew the border dipped down here in a bulge known as the Fish Hook, but I hadn't realised I was so close. Digby had warned me to be careful in this locale. Friends of his had been shot at by border police while riding along a road north of where I was. A few hours later I turned south into a flat landscape of fruit orchards and paddies, the villages merging in a continuous necklace of settlement. Happy to be away from the border I thrummed along in a hooting river of traffic, unsure when one town began and another ended.

I noticed, as I rode, how different the south of Vietnam was to the distant north. A thousand miles lies between Hanoi and Saigon, the same distance that separates London and Warsaw or London and Madrid. The world can change a lot in a thousand miles: climate, language, beliefs, ideologies, history, physiognomy. The north had been misty and full of the *nhà quê* – rural poor – wandering along the roadsides in their pith helmets and *non las*. The south felt wealthier, glossier, burnished by sunshine, its people more likely to be found drinking coffee, lying in hammocks and playing *co tuong* than breaking their backs in the paddies. Gone were the stilted houses, here the dwellings were neat concrete boxes painted in whites and blues and yellows. Even for an outsider the differences were easy to see. The two worlds might have been united under a single government in 1975, but fundamental differences still remained. Ask the southerners today what they think of the northerners and they would say they speak differently, are too serious, too keen on eating dog, and as cold as their climate.

The northerner would tell you the southerner speaks oddly and is too fond of capitalism. Differences like this exist in most countries, but in Vietnam it seemed to run deeper. Governments are easier to change than hearts and minds.

There was one other noticeable difference. Every day in the south I saw at least two people with missing limbs. I couldn't recall seeing even one in the north. It is one of the great ironies of the War that in their efforts to wipe out the Viet Cong, the US dropped almost four million tonnes of bombs on their ally South Vietnam; more than in any other theatre of the conflict. It's no surprise that the strength of the Viet Cong grew as the War dragged on.

I never did make it to COSVN. I spent a day traipsing between travel agencies in Tay Ninh trying to make it happen, but the obstacles were too numerous. It was in a very sensitive border area 50 miles north of the town. I couldn't take the bike up there; I would need a special permit; the permit usually took a few days, but if I paid the local police chief double he could probably speed it up; I would need a translator, but all the good English speakers had gone to work in Saigon. With time and a fistful of dollars it was possible, but I was running low on both. A few days later, in Saigon, I made contact with the American veteran, Dave Gallo, whose online account I had read.

'It's not worth the visit,' he told me over the phone from Dalat, where he now lived. 'It isn't the real deal anyway. The communists would never have been so stupid as to build a single static command post; they moved it all the time.'

With the COSVN mission aborted I left Tay Ninh the following morning and rode towards Cu Chi. Dangling above Saigon, Cu Chi had been a hotly contested communist stronghold in both the French and American wars. To survive the locals had dug themselves in; living, fighting and dying in a network of tunnels that was said to stretch as far as the Cambodian border. Icons of Vietnamese perseverance, the tunnels were an ideal final stop on my journey.

Tay Ninh lay on the northern edge of the Mekong Delta, the agricultural powerhouse of the nation. Fingering across the southern tip of Vietnam the Delta's fertile floodplains covered an area the size of Switzerland, a mirror-flat patchwork of vibrant greens and shimmering water.

One of the few wrinkles in this otherwise unbroken horizon was *Núi Bà Đen* – Black Virgin Mountain – an extinct volcano jutting discordantly from the plains. The French and Viet Minh had fought for control over it, so had the Americans and Viet Cong. In the end the Viet Cong had won, crawling up the slopes and overrunning the barbed-wire eyrie on the summit, killing twenty-three US marines. The mountain was now a sprawling religious complex, its slopes barnacled with red-roofed temples, souvenir shops and tacky restaurants. Genuflecting worshippers muttered prayers to fat golden Buddhas and fearsome Khmer goddesses. As I was whisked up its sides in a brand new Austrian-built chairlift, I imagined hard-faced soldiers scrambling up the scree, steeling themselves for attack. The vista from the top was spectacular, a great green quilt dotted with villages and sugar palms, so flat you could see the curvature of the earth. With views almost as far as Saigon, it was no wonder armies had been so keen to control it.

From the mountain I rode south-west towards Cu Chi through lush green paddies and orchards dripping with custard apples and mangoes. White clouds drifted above, their reflections mirrored in the watery backdrop. With the end now so close, the torpor of the last few days lifted. Instead I felt like a coiled spring, my emotions see-sawing between heart-bursting happiness and chattering anxiety. I could feel my shoulders tensing, my hands gripping the handlebars so hard my knuckles hurt. My thoughts kept leapfrogging to the end, to riding up to the gates of the Reunification Palace, to thanking Uncle Ho back in Hanoi. Then I would drag myself back to the present, repeating the mantra 'Here and Now, Here and Now' out loud to focus my mind.

I wasn't finished yet. I had to remain in the present, drink it all in, concentrate on the road. Anything could happen between now and the Palace.

My anxiety gave rise to indignation as to Vietnamese driving habits. I may have been used to them by now, but I was far from understanding the illogic of it. How could people turn onto a busy road with neither a glance to the left nor the right? How could people never ever look in their mirrors and think it was fine to swerve all over the road while texting, smoking or holding their baby? Why did young girls cycle the wrong way down the road in the middle of the counterflood of traffic? Several times the same people I had cursed then slowed down to wave, smile and ask me questions. People paid so little attention to other road users they might as well drive blindfolded. Their traffic sense defied every iota of human survival instinct.

I arrived at Cu Chi just in time to get the last tour around the tunnels. Parking Panther in the empty coach park, I bought a ticket and was ushered into an empty Nissen hut to watch a film. Made by 'Liberation Films Studio' in 1967, it told the story of how the heroic peasants of Cu Chi had defeated the villainous American enemy and their 'puppet' allies. Happy people toiled in the orchards and beautiful smiling girls bristled with weapons, 'a rifle in one hand, a plough in the other.' The 'killer Americans,' the robotic female voiceover intoned, had fired into 'chickens, ducks, pots and pans.' They had fought the communists with tanks, B-52s and napalm. Alsatians had been trained to sniff out the concealed entrances to the underground labyrinth. Battalions of tunnel rats – engineers chosen for their small stature – had crawled through the tunnels to lay mines. But armed with a 'love of their comrades and a hatred of US bombs and bullets,' the peasant heroes had fought back. Cu Chi was the gateway to Saigon, they weren't going to let it fall.

As the film came to its final triumphant end I was scooped up by a khaki-clad guide – a humourless thirty-six year old with withering halitosis. He hurried along the well-worn walkway, pointing out the mock-up field hospitals, staring mannequins and booby traps. I could tell he wanted to go home, that he'd had enough of answering inane questions for the day.

'This psychological warfare,' he explained, showing me a spiked bamboo mantrap. 'One GI fall down, others have to pull him out. It so horrible they all want to go home.'

By now it was getting dark and the twilight was speckled with mosquitoes.

'Is there malaria here?' I asked him.

'Only if you're weak,' he replied, looking me up and down pointedly. By now I'd lost quite a few kilos and my dirty jeans were hanging off me. I probably looked ripe for a bout of illness.

Following him through dark claustrophobic lengths of tunnel, my shoulders brushed against the packed-earth edges. They had been cleaned up for the tourists – emptied of snakes and spiders, scorpions and centipedes – but they were still horrible. I couldn't wait to reach the exit. It was anathema to me how people had survived for years in that dank crawling darkness. Thousands had died here too, buried in grids of identical white graves in a cemetery I had ridden past on the way. I knew it was a communist cemetery; those of the ARVN soldiers had been bulldozed by the victors after the war

'Both my parents and grandparents fight here. My grandfather die by American bomb,' said my guide, leading me back out into the twilight.

'How did they endure it?' I asked. He stopped, turned around and looked me in the eye. 'We were fighting for our country. If you love your country, you can do anything. The American GIs were fighting for nothing; they were fighting a pointless war.'

If he was asked to take up arms for his country tomorrow, I doubted there would be a second's hesitation.

'And American never knew who was enemy,' he went on. 'The people here just simple peasants not VC soldiers, but they fight. America didn't know who normal villager and who VC.' It was exactly this reason why massacres like My Lai had occurred. To the young GIs everyone was a potential enemy; South Vietnamese villages hiding real and imagined Viet Cong, caches of weapons and secret tunnel networks. The men who worked innocently in the paddies by day could be lobbing mortars into their bases by night. Such uncertainty bred paranoia and with it, violence.

'How do you feel about Americans now?'

His reply sounded like a well-rehearsed answer to a question he'd been asked hundreds of times. It was hard to tell if he was being sincere or not. 'If you forget one enemy you will have one more good friend. It's bad to hate.'

When the tour was finished I did what John had urged me to do in Dak Cheung; I went to the state-owned firing range next to the tunnels, bought $20 worth of bullets and selected an M60 from the arsenal of weapons on offer. At this time of the day it was empty, but they must have been making a few thousand dollars per day from trigger-happy tourists eager for a taste of Nam. I had never fired a gun before. It felt awkward and cumbersome as I leant over the shoulder shock and closed one eye. Another guide, a man old and small enough to have fought in the tunnels, tapped my shoulder and pointed at the target, a square of cardboard fifty metres away. I pulled the trigger, swearing in shock as bullets sprayed everywhere but the target. The guide chuckled. It must be a man thing, I concluded. That wasn't better than a nice cup of Earl Grey, let alone sex.

No one stayed at Cu Chi. They came by bus from Saigon and were back in time for tea. But there was one hotel, hidden in a dark grove of palms a few hundred metres from the tunnel entrance. Seemingly not used to either foreigners or guests, the dozing receptionist looked startled to see me and couldn't understand what I wanted. It was only after several minutes of semaphoring that he smiled in comprehension and led me to a simple clean room, memorable only for the fact that it was my last night on the road. They had no water or food so I started up Panther and rode down the road in the dark, searching for somewhere to eat. My Last Supper was a bowl of instant noodles I bought at a roadside shack, so spicy my lips burnt for an hour afterwards.

The hotel turned out to be adjacent to an overnight truck park. All night engines roared, male voices shouted and footsteps hurried up and down the tiled stairs. I lay awake, my mind a collage of faces and scenes. I thought of Digby, Cuong, George and Roger and our near miss with the cluster bomb. That was only five weeks ago but it felt like a year. I pictured Mick and John, the Lumphat road workers, the mechanic in Kaleum, all the people who had helped me along the way. I thought of those days in Laos when I'd fought to get Panther through the mud, sand and mountains. At the time I had cursed those execrable roads, but twenty years from now I knew those to be the days I would remember. I thought about Cu Chi and how, beyond the mannequins and propaganda, it epitomised why America could never have won. United by a mission to unify their motherland, the Vietnamese communists would have fought to the last man.

More than anything else my mind dwelt on how futile the War had been. More than six million men, women and children from Vietnam, Laos, Cambodia, America, Thailand, Australia, South Korea, New Zealand and the Philippines died. Tens of thousands have died since from UXO and the after-effects of Agent Orange. And for what purpose? The Reds won anyway. The outcome would have been the same if America had never fired a single shot.

Rising at 6 a.m, I dressed in my floral shirt and favourite underwear, pressing my nose to the bathroom mirror to slick on black eyeliner. Not that anyone would notice my efforts, but I felt I should dress for the occasion. Stuffing my belongings into my panniers for the last time, I noted how scuffed and red they looked after two thousand miles of riding. The dust that had been such a scourge was now a badge of the Trail, sewn into my kit and clothes for years to come. Pulling out my talismans, I ran my fingers over the smooth metal of the Buddha and the curves of the lapis, silently asking them to see me to the end of today without incident.

Panther had spent her last night in a shed next to the hotel, in the company of several other mopeds and a resident old couple.

'Hanoi?' said the man, as he watched me check her over in the morning, tuning her for the home run.

'Hanoi, Lao, Cambodia, Saigon!' I replied, hardly believing it myself.

His face creased into a smile and he shook his head, gabbling something to his supine wife. She rose from their mattress to watch, and the two of them waved goodbye as I cranked the kick-start and rode away through the palms.

On the final 30 miles into the heart of the metropolis there was no countryside anymore, just a seamless stream of little concrete houses and bending palms funnelling me south. Today was 20 April, ten days before 'Liberation Day,' the anniversary of Saigon's capitulation and the end of the War. Already commemorative flags lined the roadside, red and gold silk fluttering between the trees. Riding in the midst of them I thought about those last days of the War in Vietnam, how almost thirty-eight years ago to the day communist tanks were streaming down this very road. All the key southern cities had already fallen to Hanoi; only Saigon was left. In the end the tanks rolled into the city almost unopposed, along streets strewn with the abandoned uniforms of the deserting ARVN. The last Americans had fled in helicopters and most foreign correspondents had been evacuated. Among the very few who remained were the English writer and poet James Fenton and the soon-to-be-fired *Rolling Stone* journalist Hunter S. Thompson, who had flown in with $30,000 in cash strapped to his body. Both survived to tell the tale.

Today was a public holiday and the roads were even more chaotic than usual. Teenage girls in white *ao dais* pedalled in giggling groups, wobbling past wooden carts pulled by handsome conker-brown oxen. Swarms of mopeds buzzed by carrying families, trussed up pigs and cages of cowering dogs. Through the middle lurched overcrowded buses and hooting Kamaz trucks, neither of which slowed for anything or anyone. Typically, the day I needed it most, the 3G signal on my phone had gone kaput. All I had now was a compass and the knowledge that Saigon was to the south. I knew the Palace was in the centre near the west banks of the Saigon River, but I had no idea how to get there. It was like driving into London for the first time and trying to find Trafalgar Square. The victorious NVA troops had been in the same predicament. Like me, they had never been to Saigon. But getting lost trying to find the Palace and hoist their flag wasn't a fitting conclusion to Ho's dream. To avoid the embarrassment they had pulled passing Saigonese on to their tanks to show them the way. Winging it like this would add to the adventure, I told myself, keeping it exciting to the very end. Fate and pointing would get me there.

Gradually the buildings became taller, the palms disappeared and the traffic swelled to a raging torrent. I was in the northern suburbs of Saigon. Half beset by nerves, half bursting with anticipation, I followed the traffic south, beeping and babbling anxiously.

Outside the focus of my intent, the city remained a blur. There were high grey buildings, crowded pavements and old women selling lottery tickets at the traffic lights. There was stifling heat and a lingering smell of sewage. There were dark-skinned vagrants pedalling slowly on the inside lane, their bicycles festooned with sacks of tin cans and plastic bottles which they would sell for a few dong. And everywhere there was traffic, mopeds, engine noise, and masked faces under multi-coloured helmets.

Navigating a large roundabout I narrowly missed a sticky end. Walls of metal closed in on me, and I let out an involuntary scream as a lorry whined and shunted to a halt inches from my back wheel. Out of the corner of my eye I glimpsed a line of faces looking down at me through the dirty windows of a green bus. Pulling Panther to the pavement I stopped for ten minutes, my body shaking with adrenaline. What a shame it would be to get squashed so very close to the end.

Soon afterwards I stopped at a fork in the road and asked a young woman for directions.

'You go left and then straight on for nine kilometres. Once you get to the New World Hotel, ask someone how to get to the Palace,' she replied in perfect English. So many more people in the south spoke English, a legacy of their American alliance.

Thanking her, I kicked Panther into life. But the kick-start only spluttered and popped. The engine remained silent. I realised what had happened at once. In my anxiety to find my way and reach the Palace in one piece I'd entirely forgotten about petrol. Now, 5 miles before the end, I had run out of fuel. What an idiot! As luck would have it, there was a petrol station less than 400 metres up the road. I wheeled Panther there along the pavement, laughing at my ineptitude.

Now it was truly the final furlong. We inched towards the finish line, pulled along in ten lanes of traffic, a tiny particle in the city's endless two-wheeled cavalcade. Half an hour later the New World Hotel rose up on my left. I must be close. Outside it, the traffic lights turned red and I stopped in the front row amid a battalion of revving mopeds.

'Does anyone speak English?' I asked, addressing my neighbours.

'I do!' replied a teenage boy, leaning over the handlebars of his moped a few rows away.

'Brilliant! Do you know where the Reunification Palace is, please?'

'Yes. I'm going that way, follow me.' What a stroke of luck.

The lights turned green and a hundred tiny engines thrummed into life, leaping forward; the charge of the Honda brigade. The boy ducked and dived through the streets, past grand French buildings and down leafy boulevards. Every time I thought I'd lost him I caught sight of his brown helmet, bobbing like a cork on the sea of traffic. Then, there they were, the grey iron gates of the Reunification Palace, the same ones the NVA tanks had surged through on 30 April 1975. There was the fountain and the ugly white modernist Palace, rebuilt after two renegade South Vietnamese pilots bombed it in 1962. Lines of Vietnamese flags fluttered against the cloudless azure sky. Coaches spilled tour groups onto the pavement in front.

The boy said goodbye and I waved as he vanished into the traffic.

This was it. I rode Panther slowly towards the gates, savouring the last 100 metres of our journey, stopping only when I felt the front wheel bump against the gates and knew I couldn't go an inch further.

'We've made it, Panther,' I said out loud, leaning over the handlebars. 'We've bloody made it.'

A group of Japanese tourists stopped photographing the Palace and looked at me.

I didn't want to get off my beloved Pink Panther. I couldn't believe we'd actually done it. For ten minutes I just sat there, staring at the white façade, smiling, savouring the moment. Six weeks, three countries, 2,000 miles, four engine rebuilds and one hell of an adventure later, my Ho Chi Mission was finally over.

AFTER

Saigon felt like Hanoi's younger, brasher, more cosmopolitan sibling. The streets were wider, the buildings taller, the rats bolder, the nightlife seedier, the skyline drawn with cranes and shiny new high-rises. There were no nightclubs in Hanoi, but in Saigon I danced until dawn, downing tequila shots with a group of bawdy Russian businessmen and staggering home in the half-light. In Hanoi the tourists wandered hand in hand around the Old Quarter or were pedalled through the narrow streets in *cyclos*. In Saigon they poured out of tour buses in slack-jawed melees, a homogenous mass of name badges, white socks, sandals and zip-off trousers. They yapped and snapped and pushed and shoved then filed back onto their buses to tick the next place off their printed list.

Consequently, Saigon's hawkers were more cunning and persistent than their northern counterparts; sharp cries of 'Hallo! Hallo! Madam! Madam!' followed me wherever I went. Occasionally I gave in, buying a coconut for a dollar, taking a ride on a moped taxi or buying some lurid fake Calvin Klein underwear. Meanwhile Panther rested in the lobby of my riverside hotel. Now that our duty was done, I didn't dare get on her again. My luck had held this long, I didn't want to chance pushing it any further.

I wanted to find out more about what had happened here after Liberation Day. Saigon, the 'Paris of the Orient' was a decadent sensuous city, corrupted by the ways of the West, its ways abhorrent to the straight-laced North. Outside the communist resistance, there were many southerners who feared the consequences of their defeat. In Cambodia the communist take-over had been so murderous. How would Hanoi's victory compare? Many didn't wait to find out. Tens of thousands fought their way onto the last American helicopters in the final week of April 1975. And in the years to come an estimated two million more would flee overseas. They were ARVN soldiers, religious leaders, former politicians of the dissolved southern regime, mothers with blonde-haired children, prostitutes, anyone who had worked with or been a friend to the Americans. Many of these escaped crammed into unsuitable boats, only to drown, starve or be raped and murdered by unscrupulous Thai pirates. According to the United Nations around 400,000 of these 'boat people' died at sea. The lucky ones made it to Thai refugee camps, or to new lives in the West.

Others couldn't bear to leave their country, or didn't have the means to go. One such man was a former United Press International photographer called Mr Cuong. He had spent the War embedded with US and ARVN soldiers and his images remain among the most iconic of the conflict. He was on the roof of the US embassy as the last helicopter left at 7.53 a.m. on 30 April. He was there as the new flag was hoisted above the Palace only hours later. He'd had every opportunity to leave, but instead he stayed to face an uncertain future.

I had heard about Mr Cuong the previous year, and tracked him down when I reached Saigon. He lived in District 1, in a jewel of a building crushed between two gargantuan modern hotels.

'Come in!' he smiled, flinging open the door and leading me up a narrow staircase. He was a small round-faced man with perfectly dyed black hair and a spotless white Adidas football shirt. He must have been over sixty, but he looked a decade younger.

We perched at a little wooden table amid his distractingly impressive collection of antiques.

'Fourteenth century, Ming dynasty,' he said pointing to a blue and white vase. 'Nineteenth century, probably Khmer,' he nodded towards a beautifully painted silk Buddhist *thangka*. And so on.

His teenage son brought us a pot of bitter green tea, before going back to playing a computer game in the next-door room. I asked Mr Cuong about the War, about his photographs and about what had happened afterwards.

'I have two hundred relatives in America – nearly all my family went, but I wanted to stay here. I didn't want to leave Vietnam. The government was suspicious of me though, they thought I was a spy. So in 1984 they arrested me and sent me to a re-education camp. I spent the next seven years in twenty-eight different camps. I had no contact with my family and they had no idea if I was dead or alive.' He talked quietly, engagingly. He must have told this story countless times but he relayed it with great sadness, his eyes welling as he spoke.

'It was so hard in the camps – we had to work very long hours and there was barely enough food or medicine.' At this he stopped. 'Sorry, I can't tell you any more. It's too dangerous. The only people who will tell you the truth about the camps are the people who went overseas afterwards. For those of us still here, it's too difficult.'

In light of the ongoing political situation I asked him if he had ever consider leaving Vietnam. 'No, I love my country. When I die, I'll leave my antiques collection to the state. I'm Vietnamese, I'll never leave.'

No one knows how many southerners like Mr Cuong were sent to these re-education camps. But what is certain is that the North, so admirably persistent in their pursuit of victory, were equally ruthless in their rooting out of potential enemies. Estimates vary from one million to 2.5 million. With Stalinist brutality people were tortured, beaten, starved and forced to sign confessions of imaginary political crimes. Well over 100,000 died of torture, starvation and overwork, although again no one could tell you the exact number. Tens of thousands more were executed. ARVN cemeteries were bulldozed. Just as General Giap had said the life of 'tens of thousands' meant little, so Ho's successors were willing to sacrifice however many it took to create their socialist dream.

The story was the same in Laos where the communists, heavily backed by the Soviets and North Vietnamese, officially took power on 2 December 1975. They abolished six hundred years of monarchy overnight, establishing in its place the Lao People's Democratic Republic. Just as Somsack's parents had waded across the Mekong in the dead of night, so an estimated ninety per cent of the educated classes escaped overseas. Of those who stayed, around 40,000 were sent to re-education camps and a further 30,000 were jailed as political prisoners.

The Hmong bore the brunt of the communists' revenge and are still fighting for justice today. And the re-education camps are still open as I write. Recently I heard about a high-ranking politician in the Lao National Assembly being threatened with a stint in a camp for being too 'moderate' and having 'too many foreign friends.'

As the new rulers meted out punishment, the West turned its back on Indochina. Between 1968 and 1973 the US had given $74.4 million per year in 'aid' to their Royalist Laotian allies, spent a million dollars a day supporting Lon Nol, and splurged $165 billion on the war in Vietnam. But now they gave nothing. For the next two decades Vietnam was a dirty word, a reminder of a cringing expensive defeat. In 1979 the newly elected British Prime Minister Margaret Thatcher turned down a United Nations request to take in 10,000 Vietnamese boat people. And in the eighties the UN and World Health Organisation refused aid to Cambodia, whose people were dying of starvation and disease. It was the Vietnamese who had finally ousted the Khmer Rouge and set up an interim government in the shattered country; now Cambodia was in the wrong camp. Astonishingly, in the early eighties Thatcher sent teams of SAS soldiers to Cambodia to train a resurgent Khmer Rouge. That the West was willing to back Pol Pot over Vietnam was testament to the vengefulness that arose from defeat.

It is only in the last fifteen years that Vietnam has staggered back to its feet. Cambodia and Laos are still getting there. The War may have ended in 1975, but the effects are still being felt today.

After three days in Saigon I flew to Hanoi. Panther was already on her way, rumbling up the coast in a freight car on the

Reunification Railway. As my taxi drew up outside the same hotel in Nguyen Van To I remembered how much I loved the city, with its flower sellers, crooked crumbling buildings and intoxicating pull of the past. If Saigon was a steamy illicit encounter in a dark alleyway, Hanoi was the lover you would always want to come back to.

My two days in the capital were a time of goodbyes. By chance Roger van Dyken was also in town for a day so I met up with him and Cuong for lunch. Both of them greeted me with a 'You're alive!' as if they really hadn't expected me to be.

'Now young lady, I have a bone to pick with you. You never replied to the email I sent you,' said Roger over the din of the packed *pho* restaurant we were sitting in. 'I've been so worried.'

I had replied though, and showed him the proof on my phone. Over the next few weeks I would find out that a lot of the emails I'd sent during my time in Laos and Vietnam had gone awry. It could have been coincidence, but it felt like more than that.

'I come to Vietnam every year,' said Roger, 'and every time the same thing happens; after about ten days my emails start disappearing. I've always felt I'm being watched. This is still a communist country after all.'

Cuong couldn't understand why I'd had so many problems with the bike. He suspected it stemmed from a blocked oil filter, which – with all the hard riding – had caused overheating in the engine. It didn't matter anyway, it would have been less of an adventure without a few mechanical hiccups.

That night I met up with George Burchett and his wife Ilza at Colonel Quy's. The famous Vietnamese actor was at the next-door table again having his nightly bottle of champagne with two friends. George, Ilza and I drank gin and tonics and smoked by the twinkling waters of West Lake, and I showed George a photograph of his father that I'd found in a pamphlet at Cu Chi. The misspelt caption read, 'Burchette an Australian journalist came to Cu Chi liberation zone in 1963.' So much had happened since they'd wished me luck at this same spot nearly two months previously. George had called me brave then, but I still didn't feel it. Although the only time I'd felt afraid had been in the mud near Lumphat, I was still scared of spiders, ghosts and being eaten by a tiger. There was nothing brave about that.

There was no Digby this time. He was in Saigon, on his way to Singapore with his fiancée to buy an engagement ring; I had said goodbye to him a few days earlier. He'd been so instrumental to my journey; had I never met him I doubt I would be writing this now. I hoped it wouldn't be too many years before I saw him again.

There was one other person I had to see before I left Hanoi, and that was Uncle Ho.

On my last morning I rose early and joined the end of the half-mile-long queue. We shuffled past the goose-stepping guards with their pressed white uniforms, gold epaulettes and their stern patriotic stares. Soon we were in the dark interior, snaking up the stone stairs, filing into Vietnam's Holy of Holies, eyes adjusting to the dim tungsten light. Ho lay in a glass box, a frail old man in a starched grey suit. His skin was sallow and shiny, his hair wispy and grey, his slender hands folded over his chest. I noticed his long feminine fingernails and wondered if they still had to be cut once a year. *How different would the last fifty years have been without Ho?* I thought, as we walked past. He hadn't been the only young Vietnamese man fired with revolutionary Marxist ideals. Without him there may have been another leader, but it's unlikely they would have been as uniquely visionary and charismatic as Ho, or that thousands would be filtering through their mausoleum all these years later. With a last look at his thin jaundiced face I was ushered out, the family in front of me bursting into reverent song as we left.

My final goodbye was to the Pink Panther, my friend – and occasional foe – over the Truong Son. I couldn't take her with me. She was staying here in Hanoi, a new addition to Explore Indochina's two-wheeled collection.

'Oh my God! This bike so uncomfortable!' said one of Cuong's employees as he greeted me outside their motorcycle hire shop in the Old Quarter. 'I pick up from train station today and ride it here. I can't believe you ride it three thousand kilometres.'

I sat on Panther for the last time then bid her a sad goodbye, leaving her parked beside her new companion, Richard Hammond's pink Minsk from *Top Gear*. One day I shall go back and ride her again but until then, she's in good hands.

As night fell I stepped into a taxi and drove towards the airport. I had felt oddly numb about finishing until now, swept up in the excitement of Saigon. But as I sat in the back seat and watched Hanoi dissolve into its suburbs, the finality hit me like a juggernaut. As much as I wanted to go home – to see Marley, my family and friends – the thing that had occupied my mind for the last year was over. Tomorrow I'd be at home in Somerset. There would be no more of the thrill and uncertainty of the Trail, no more clamouring streets of

Hanoi, no more Panther. There would just be me and a laptop and a book to write.

I considered if the experience had changed me, if I was returning to England a different person. Fundamentally I didn't think it had. Bar a few kilos less, a new scar on my left shin, a much-improved knowledge of mechanics and a vault of extra memories, I was still me. I hadn't undergone a spiritual transformation or 'discovered' myself in some ecstatic epiphany. But I had learnt a few things on the Trail; insights that could only have come from travelling alone. In times of adversity, when the mire and the mountains had conspired to beat me, I had faced myself and passed the test. I hadn't cried or given up; I'd stuck my chin out and kept on going, mile by muddy mile. For someone as self-critical as me, this felt like a significant achievement. I hesitate to use the word proud, as it reeks of vanity and arrogance, but I did allow myself to feel a smidgeon of pride. Whatever the future held, I would always have the knowledge that I'd cajoled an ailing twenty-five-year-old Cub over the Truong Son. If I could do that, I hoped I could overcome a lot of life's difficulties.

I would miss the Trail. Following it had been thrilling, engrossing, sickening, enlightening, poignant and ceaselessly compelling. It was symbolic of both the immense resilience and the unfathomable cruelty of which we humans are capable. I had never tired of it. Even after six months of writing and intensive research, my obsession remains. I feel as if I have only scratched the tip of the iceberg and would love to return before it's too late. In six months, a year, two years' time, much of the Trail I rode will be unrecognisable. Kaleum will be underwater, the Mondulkiri Death Highway will be an asphalt highway and thousands more acres of virgin forest will have disappeared. Every month a little more of the old Trail will be lost forever. I feel fortunate to have seen what I did.

The taxi pulled up outside Noi Bai and I dragged my heavy bag into the departures hall. It was time to go home, something millions of people involved in the War never had the chance to do.

GLOSSARY OF TERMS

559 battalion: Also known as Group 559. The North Vietnamese battalion in command of the Trail, established in May 1959.

AC-130: Also known as the 'blind bat'. A US bomber used against the Ho Chi Minh Trail. The planes were fitted with infra-red sensors and were able to detect trucks moving down the Trail at night.

Agent Orange: A chemical defoliant widely used by the US in the War. Dropped from low-flying C-123s, the chemical denuded vast areas of jungle and poisoned water supplies.

ăn chay: Vietnamese for 'vegetarian'

ao dai: The traditional dress of Vietnamese women; a tight-fitting long silk tunic worn over silk trousers. They are designed to show a tiny, tantalising bit of skin where the slit of the tunic meets the top of the trousers.

ARVN: Army of the Republic of Vietnam (South Vietnam). The army was created and funded by the US. By 1973 it had the fourth largest air force in the world and was one of the best-equipped armies on the planet.

B-52: The Boeing B-52 Stratofortess was the principal bomber used by the USAF in the Second Indochina War.

bak: Lao for 'ferry'

ban: Lao for 'village'

bánh mì: Vietnamese for 'bread'

barang: Khmer for 'foreigner'

baw mi: Lao for 'don't have'

Binh Tram: Vietnamese name for supply bases on the Ho Chi Minh Trail

Blu 26: a type of anti-personnel cluster bomb

boi doi: North Vietnamese soldiers

bombie: The nickname for anti-personnel cluster bombs and one of the most widely used bombs in the conflict. Hundreds of tennis ball-sized bomblets were dropped inside a single casing. Once dropped, the casings opened up, scattering the bomblets over a wide area. Up to thirty per cent didn't explode, still remaining live in the ground today.

C-123: Military transport planes used by the US for spraying Agent Orange.

cao neo: Lao for 'sticky rice'

cắt tóc': Vietnamese for 'hairdresser'

COSVN: the Central Office for South Vietnam – the headquarters of the Viet Cong

co tuong: a game played in Vietnam, Chinese chess

đi B: To 'go South,' a phrase used by North Vietnamese soldiers who went south on the Trail.

đi đi: Vietnamese for 'go away'

DMZ: The Demilitarised Zone – the dividing line between North and South Vietnam.

dong: Vietnamese currency – at the time of writing there were 30,000 dong to £1.

EOD: Explosive Ordnance Disposal

F-4: The two-seat Douglas F-4 Phantom was a long range supersonic jet used by the US as a fighter-bomber. They were used by the US until 1996.

F-100: Another supersonic jet used by the US as a fighter-bomber and FAC.

FACs: Forward Air Controllers. These were slower, low-flying planes that would direct the bombers onto their targets, often by dropping marking rockets such as 'Willy Pete' – white phosphorus.

falang: Lao for 'foreigner'

Handicap International: a Belgian NGO specialising in UXO clearance

Hmong: The ethnic minority who dwell in southern China, northern Thailand and Laos. The Hmong, led by General Van Pao, fought with the CIA in Laos' secret war. An estimated 100,000 of them lost their lives. Those who weren't given residency in the USA, or didn't escape to refugee camps in Thailand, are still suffering at the hands of Laos' communist government today.

Kamaz: Russian-made trucks, ubiquitous all over the former Soviet Union and Vietnam

khawp jai: Lao for 'thank you'

Khmer: The dominant ethnic group in Cambodia. They make up around ninety per cent of the country's 15.2 million people.

Khmer-Chen: Cambodians of Chinese descent or mixed Khmer-Chinese heritage

kip: Lao currency – at the time of writing there were 12,000 kip to £1.

krama: A traditional Khmer checked scarf which can be worn on the head, or as a sarong or skirt.

laterite: A soil type rich in iron and aluminium, formed in hot and wet tropical areas. Nearly all laterite soils are rusty-red because of iron oxides. Much of the Trail was carved through laterite soil. Its high metal content can confuse metal detectors.

MACV: Military Assistance Command, Vietnam. In operation from February 1962 until March 1973, MACV was the body in charge of coordinating the US war effort in Vietnam. Its most famous boss was General William C. Westmoreland.

MAG: Mines Advisory Group, a British-based NGO who work to clear landmines and UXO in former conflict zones. For more information see www.maginternational.org.

Many-banded Krait: One of the most venomous snakes in the world, inhabiting parts of Asia.

MIA: Missing in Action

MiG: A Russian-made fighter plane used by the North Vietnamese during the War.

Misty Squadron: An elite volunteer squadron of US FACs tasked with helping to knock out the Ho Chi Minh Trail.

muang: Lao for 'town'

nam: Lao for 'water'

NGO: Non-Governmental Organisation

NLF: National Liberation Front, also known as the Viet Cong or the National Liberation Front for South Vietnam. This was a communist political organisation and army that fought the US and South Vietnam.

nhà quê: Vietnamese for 'rural poor'

non la: A traditional Vietnamese conical hat made out of woven palm leaves. Sometimes worn in Laos and Cambodia too.

NVA: North Vietnamese Army – also known as the PAVN (People's Army of Vietnam) or VPA (Vietnam People's Army). In this book the term NVA is used.

pa: Lao for 'machete'

Pathet Lao: The Lao communist party, who came to power in December 1975. The Pathet Lao were very closely tied to the North Vietnamese communists.

Pai sai?: Lao for 'Where are you going?'

phi: Lao for 'spirit'

pho: Vietnamese for 'noodle soup'

poo-so: Lao for 'girl'

riel: Cambodian currency – at the time of writing there were 6,650 riel to £1.

RLG: Royal Lao Government

sabadi: Lao for 'hello'

SAM: surface-to-air missile – used against US airpower along the Ho Chi Minh Trail

seventeenth parallel: The dividing line between North and South Vietnam, established by the Geneva Peace Accords in 1954. The line mainly followed the Ben Hai River.

sin: A traditional woven skirt worn in Laos

USAF: United States Air Force

UXO: unexploded ordnance

Viet Cong: The phrase Viet Cong comes from *Việt Nam Cộng-sản*, meaning Vietnamese communist (See also NLF)

Viet Kieu: Vietnamese living overseas

Viet Minh: Also known as the 'League for the Independence of Vietnam' – a communist organisation founded by Ho Chi Minh in 1941.

wat: Buddhist temple (this word is used in both Lao and Khmer) *wai*: Greeting traditionally used in Thailand, Laos and other parts of Southeast Asia. Both hands are put together in a prayer-like position and the head bowed slightly.

xin chào: Vietnamese for 'hello'

xin lỗi: Vietnamese for 'sorry'

TIMELINE OF THE SECOND INDOCHINA WAR

1840s to 1890s: Indochina falls under French rule.

1940–1945: Vietnam is under both French colonial rule and Japanese occupation. Ho and his Viet Minh organisation ally with the USA in their fight against the Japanese occupation. A fifth of Vietnamese die from famine.

Summer of 1945: The Allies hand Laos, Vietnam and Cambodia back to the French at the Potsdam Conference. Ho ignores this and declares himself President of an independent Vietnam.

1946: France and Vietnam begin the First Indochina War.

1946–1954: The First Indochina War. By the end the USA, although not directly involved, is funding eighty per cent of France's war effort versus the Viet Minh. The war costs 400,000 lives.

1953: 40,000 Viet Minh, led by General Vo Nguyen Giap, invade northern Laos. The Laotian Civil War begins between the North Vietnamese backed Pathet Lao and the US-supported Royal Lao Government.

1954: The French suffer a resounding defeat at Dien Bien Phu and as a result lose all their colonies in Indochina. The Geneva Accords takes place. Vietnam is divided into North and South at the seventeenth parallel with plans for reunification elections by July 1956. The Catholic Ngo Dinh Diem becomes the US-backed ruler of South Vietnam. Ho Chi Minh is internationally recognised as President of North Vietnam.

1959: General Vo Bam leads the first journey from North to South Vietnam on what will become known as the Ho Chi Minh Trail. Resolution 15 is passed, which states that the North will aid communist insurgents in the South in their struggle for independence and unity.

1961: John F. Kennedy becomes US President and sends 1,364 American military advisors to South Vietnam. The Laotian communists agree to allow the Ho Chi Minh Trail to pass through their territory.

1962: The Trail expands over the Truong Son Mountains into Laos.

1963: JFK is assassinated in Dallas. South Vietnamese leader Ngo Dinh Diem is assassinated in a US-backed coup. By now there are 16,000 US advisors in South Vietnam. Vice President Lyndon B. Johnson takes the helm at the White House.

1964: The Gulf of Tonkin incident occurs, followed by the passing of the Gulf of Tonkin Resolution. Long Tieng, the CIA airbase in northern Laos, is by now one of the busiest airports in the world, although it does not officially exist. Neutralist Lao Prime Minister Prince Souvanna Phouma gives permission for American 'armed reconnaissance' missions over Laos.

1965: The bombing of North Vietnam begins. In March the first US Marines land at Da Nang. By August there are 125,000 American troops in Vietnam. At this point the Trail is still limited to foot, bicycle and elephant traffic.

1966: Motorised transport begins to use the Trail in the dry season (October to April/May). 400,000 US troops are in Vietnam, although the vast majority of these are 'REMFs – Rear Echelon Mother Fuckers – pen-pushers who work in air-conditioned offices in Saigon. Dong Sy Nguyen becomes commander of the Trường Son Strategic Supply Route.

1967: 500,000 American troops are now in Vietnam. Among them is young intelligence officer Roger van Dyken.

1968: The Tet Offensive. The My Lai Massacre. In the spring America and North Vietnam begin talks in Paris. George Buchkowski arrives in Vietnam for his year-long tour.

1969: Richard Nixon takes over as President of the USA. Nixon has a very different approach to war than the more moderate Johnson. By April the death toll of US troops in Vietnam is so far 33,000. Nixon and Kissinger start the secret bombing of Cambodia. Huge anti-war marches takes place in Washington in November. Ho Chi Minh dies.

1970: Nixon announces the withdrawal of 150,000 US troops from Vietnam over the next year. Joint US and ARVN ground invasion of the Cambodian border regions. The invasion leads to massive protests. Seven students are shot dead by the National Guard. King Norodom Sihanouk is deposed by the right-wing General Lon Nol in a US-backed coup. Sihanouk throws in his lot with the Khmer Rouge. The Cambodian civil war begins.

1971: Lam Son 719 – joint US and ARVN ground-air invasion of southern Laos. Secret bombings of Cambodia continue. Khmer Rouge grows. As of February, approximately 325,000 American troops remain in Vietnam. 45,000 American soldiers have so far died in the conflict.

1972: Secret bombings of Cambodia continue. Hanoi launches the Easter Offensive. Nixon and Kissinger advance peace talks with North Vietnam. Anti-war movement in the US swells. Just before Christmas, the USA begins to bomb North Vietnam again in order to force their hand at the negotiating table.

1973: In January the USA and North Vietnam sign the Paris Peace Accords. In February the US withdraw all airpower from Laos, mid-battle. US pilots, many of them reluctant to leave those they have fought alongside for years, are told they will be court-martialled if they refuse to pull out. By May all ground troops and air power in Vietnam have been withdrawn. Kissinger wins the Nobel Peace Prize. 58,000 US soldiers have died, another 300,000 are wounded. The war is estimated to have cost the USA $165 billion. Six million Indochinese have died. Nixon bombs Cambodia until August that year. By now Lon Nol's cause is lost and the Khmer Rouge look set to overrun the country.

1974: War continues between North and South Vietnam. The Ho Chi Minh Trail is hugely expanded and improved on the Vietnamese side. Trucks can now make the journey south in ten days, whereas in the early days of the Trail it took foot soldiers six months. By the end of the war a million *boi dois* have gone South down the Trail and 33,000 have died on the Trail alone.

1975: 17 April, Phnom Penh falls to the Khmer Rouge. 30 April, the Fall of Saigon and the end of the war in Vietnam. Later in the year there is a full communist takeover in Laos and on 2 December the Lao monarchy is abolished. A mass exodus of non-communists begins from South Vietnam and Laos. All western aid to Indochina ceases.

1975–1979: Cambodia is ruled by the Khmer Rouge. Cross-border conflict between Vietnam and the Khmer Rouge. Khmer Rouge soldiers regularly cross into Vietnam's Mekong Delta region and massacre people. The on-going conflict results in the 1979 Vietnamese occupation of Cambodia and the removal of the Khmer Rouge from power.

1979–1989: Vietnamese troops occupy Cambodia and establish an interim government to rule the country.

1979: Sino-Vietnamese war. Chinese troops invade northern Vietnam in retaliation for Vietnam's invasion of their ally, Cambodia.

1980s: In Cambodia guerrilla factions of the Khmer Rouge continue to terrorise the populace. Thousands die from famine and disease, but the UN and World Health Organisation refuse the country aid.

1989: Vietnam withdraws from Cambodia, ending nearly half a century of war in Indochina. Laos opens its doors to tourists.

1995: The Clinton administration resumes relations with Vietnam.

1998: Pol Pot, the leader of the Khmer Rouge, dies.

2012: King Norodom Sihanouk dies aged 89. Cambodia goes into deep mourning for the man who had survived so much.

2013: Ants and the Pink Panther hit the Trail.

2013: General Vo Nguyen Giap, architect of the French and American defeats in Vietnam, dies in Hanoi aged 102.

ACKNOWLEDGEMENTS

No solo journey is truly done alone and there are a huge number of people who helped make the Ho Chi mission happen. Heartfelt thanks and deep gratitude goes out to you all. Firstly, without the passion, knowledge and generosity of Digby Greenhalgh this idea might never have left the starting the blocks. I was extremely fortunate to meet him, and to find that he was prepared to share his years of research and findings with me. Not only that, but Cuong and his company, Explore Indochina, sponsored me the Pink Panther – going to great efforts to find and pimp the bike and paint her shocking pink. Cuong and your mechanical wizards, thank you for finding Panther, for making her the best C90 on the planet and for nothing ever being too much effort. It's no surprise that Explore Indochina is such a brilliant company. Thanks also to Glenn Phillips for helping me with the odd bit of info and Vietnamese to English translation – and for finally introducing me to *Bia Hoi*! Don Duvall, thanks for your good company on the recce with Digby and I, for your marvellous map and for sharing some of your expertise. Another Trail junkie who was generous with their knowledge was Marcus Rhinelander

– I'm looking forward to reading your book when it comes out Marcus... I must mention also Virginia Morris, the other significant Trail-head.

Huge thanks to all the team at Summersdale: Jennifer Barclay, my editor, who had faith in me and commissioned this book before I'd even left England or written the first word, and for being such a thorough and insightful editor; Rebecca Legros, my copy-editor, for her sharp eyes and excellent fine-tuning; and Stephen Brownlee for his patience and good humour throughout. Much gratitude goes to: Bee Hayes, of As the Crows Fly, the extremely talented artist who did the beautiful maps in this book, and Emma Daniel, who did the fab illustration of the Honda Cub; Ingrid Turner at MAG, who was endlessly helpful, efficient and enthusiastic from the first moment I contacted MAG; also to her colleagues in Vietnam, Cambodia, Laos and the USA who gave me advice and fact-checked my final manuscript.

I was hugely fortunate to spend time on the Trail with some wonderful individuals who added greatly to my experience: George Buchkowski and Roger van Dyken, thank you for your company, your stories and your affection and I hope that one day you do find that Kid; to Mick and John Hayes, AKA the bomb brothers, for taking me into the bosom of the PCL family for those few brilliant days – you, Tim and Somsack were a much needed boost on my journey and I can't wait to see you again in NZ or Laos; to Mad and Bun, the Lumphat roadworkers, who will very likely never read this, but whom I shall never forget, and of course to my bonkers saviour Mr Chum; and to all the other Vietnamese, Laotians and Cambodians who helped me fix Panther, showed me the way, laughed with me and generally showed me kindness and humanity; George and Ilza Burchett; Ben and Bich at the Phong Nha Farmstay; Vath in Vilabuly and Roly at Handicap International in Sepon. Thanks to the Environmental Investigation Agency for their information on illegal logging in Southeast Asia; and a very special thank you to one particular Laotian expert who gave me vital information and contacts and who fact-checked parts of my final manuscript, but whom for political reasons cannot be named. You know who you are and I owe you a large drink or three! Thanks to my family, Noel, Fiona and Zara Bolingbroke-Kent, for their support and advice, apologies for any sleepless nights my wanderings may cause; and to all my lovely friends who sponsored MAG, whether it be £5 or £200, you know who you are - thanks for helping me raise over £2000 for MAG's excellent work in Vietnam, Laos and Cambodia. Particularly thanks to Scarlett who was a source of constant support and who went out of her way to find me some playmates in Saigon, so I didn't have to drink gin on my own at the end. Cate Hoekstra you were such a great companion at the end, thanks for taking me out clubbing, nearly finishing me off with tequila and generally being kind and lovely. Ewen Thomson, I probably wouldn't be writing this if you hadn't had the foresight to switch me off the Siberia shoot and pack me off to Laos with Digby, thank you. And Tim, Ben and Olly – what a time we all had on that crazy shoot....

Thanks to all my generous sponsors: Explore Indochina; Jason Beauchemin at Weise motorcycle clothing in Bristol for providing me with an Air Spin jacket, Dakar off road gloves and that superb helmet – all of it was fantastic quality and survived the test of the Trail; Julia and Jenny from The Adventurists

Visa Machine, who kindly provided my visas for Cambodia and Vietnam; Tom Morgan from The Adventurists; Caroline Bowler from Stanfords in Bristol; Mark Hill for the Boxer Gin (next time I'm taking a sidecar full of the stuff); Graham at Puncturesafe and Snugpak for their excellent Jungle Hammock Extreme.

Big thanks to Dervla Murphy, Lois Pryce, Jason Lewis, Ted Simon, Charlie Carroll and Kit Gillet.

And last, but absolutely not least, Marley – for tolerating my obsessions and my absences, and for his love and unwavering support. How lucky I am to not only be with someone who puts up with me and shares my passion for travel, but who is an excellent writer and has proofread every single page of this book. He was the first person to read my drafts and the last person to read my final edits, when I'd read it so many times the words had ceased to make sense. Thank you a million times over and I promise not to mention the word 'Vietnam' for the next five years.

BIBLIOGRAPHY

Baker, Mark *Nam: The Vietnam War in the Words of the Men and Women Who Fought There* (1981, Abacus, London)

Burchett, Wilfred G. *Vietnam: Inside Story of the Guerilla War* (1965, International Publishers, New York)

Cambodia's Family Trees: Illegal Logging and the Stripping of Public Assets by Cambodia's Elite (2007, Global Witness, London)

Country for Sale: How Cambodia's Elite has Captured the Country's Extractive Industries (2009, Global Witness, London)

Crossroads: The Illicit Timber Trade Between Laos and Vietnam (2011, Environmental Investigation Agency, London)

Dong Loc Past and Now (2008, Vietnam Press and Communication Development, Hanoi)

Fenton, James *The Fall of Saigon* (1985, Granta, Cambridge)

Haynes Service and Repair Manual: C50, C70 & C90, 1967 to 2003 (2006, Haynes Publishing, USA)

Hunt, Christopher *Sparring with Charlie: Motorbiking Down the Ho Chi Minh Trail* (1996, Anchor Books, New York)

Karber, Phil *The Indochina Chronicles: Travels in Laos, Cambodia and Vietnam* (2005, Marshall Cavendish, Singapore)

Khoi, Hoang *The Ho Chi Minh Trail* (2001, The Gioi Publishers, Hanoi)

Kiernan, Ben *How Pol Pot Came to Power, Second Edition: Colonialism, Nationalism, and Communism in Cambodia, 1930–1975* (2004, Yale University Press, New Haven and London)

Lewis, Norman *A Dragon Apparent: Travels in Cambodia, Laos and Vietnam* (2003, Eland, London (First published in 1951))

Mason, Robert *Chickenhawk* (1984, Corgi, London)

Morris, Virginia *The Road to Freedom: A History of the Ho Chi Minh Trail* (2006, Orchid Press)

Murphy, Dervla *One Foot in Laos* (1999, John Murray, London)

Newman, Rick and Shepperd, Don *Bury Us Upside Down: The Misty Pilots and the Secret Battle for the Ho Chi Minh Trail* (2007, Ballantine Books, New York)

Nguyen, Dong Sy *The Trans-Truong Son Route* (2005, The Gioi publishers, Hanoi)

Ninh, Bao *The Sorrow of War* (1998, Vintage, London)

Phong, Dang *Thang-Long Hanoi: The Story of a Single Street* (2010, Knowledge Publishing House, Hanoi)

Prados, John *Blood Road: The Ho Chi Minh Trail and the Vietnam War* (1998, John Wiley & Sons, New York)

Robbins, Christopher *The Ravens: The True Story of a Secret War in Laos* (2012, Apostrophe Books, Kindle edition)

Rubber Barons: How Vietnamese Companies and International Financiers are Driving a Land Grabbing Crisis in Cambodia and Laos (2013, Global Witness, London)

Shawcross, William S. *Sideshow: Kissinger, Nixon and the destruction of Cambodia* (1979, Simon & Schuster, New York)

Smith, Neil *The Vietnam War: History in an Hour* (2012, HarperPress, London)

Swain, Jon *River of Time* (1996, Vintage, London)

Tram, Dang Thuy *Last Night I Dreamed of Peace: The Diary of Dang Thuy Tram* (2007, Three Rivers Press, New York, translated by Andrew X. Pham)

Ung, Loung *First They Killed my Father: A Daughter of Cambodia Remembers* (2001, Mainstream Publishing, New York)

GUIDE BOOKS, PHRASEBOOKS AND DICTIONARIES

Lao 2008, Lonely Planet, UK and USA

Practical Cambodian Dictionary 1995, Tuttle, Singapore

Vietnam, Cambodia, Laos and Northern Thailand 2012, Lonely Planet

Vietnamese 2010, Lonely Planet, UK and USA

Have you enjoyed this book?

If so, why not write a review on your favourite website?

If you're interested in finding out more about our books, find us on Facebook at **Summersdale Publishers** and follow us on Twitter at **@Summersdale**.

Thanks very much for buying this Summersdale book.

www.summersdale.com